HG6024.A3 T75 2012
The number that killed us :a
 story of modern banking, flawed
mathemati
33663004781098

D1196848

DATE DUE

BRODART, CO.

Cat. No. 23-221

Praise for
The Number That Killed Us

"Finally, here is a book that puts value-at-risk, VaR, at the center of the financial crisis, where it belongs. Pablo Triana deftly traces the history of VaR, from what seemed like a good idea at Bankers Trust to a cancer that has infected the markets for more than two decades. In the late 1980s, when financial innovation began to explode, VaR-type models appeared to be a reasonable way of capturing mounting new risks with a single numerical measure. But, as Triana's in-depth research shows, regulators foolishly hard-wired VaR into the rules governing risk, and disaster soon followed. Even after numerous VaR-related crises—the Asian currency devaluation, the fall of Long-Term Capital Management, and the recent subprime and CDO fiascos—VaR remains a maddeningly central player, even as it promises to continue distorting risk and wreaking financial havoc. This book is a cautionary tale."

—Frank Partnoy, University of San Diego School of Law

The Number That Killed Us

A Story of Modern Banking, Flawed Mathematics, and a Big Financial Crisis

Pablo Triana

WILEY

John Wiley & Sons, Inc.

Copyright © 2012 by Pablo Triana. All rights reserved.

Published by John Wiley & Sons, Inc., Hoboken, New Jersey.
Published simultaneously in Canada.

No part of this publication may be reproduced, stored in a retrieval system, or transmitted
in any form or by any means, electronic, mechanical, photocopying, recording, scanning,
or otherwise, except as permitted under Section 107 or 108 of the 1976 United
States Copyright Act, without either the prior written permission of the Publisher,
or authorization through payment of the appropriate per-copy fee to the Copyright
Clearance Center, Inc., 222 Rosewood Drive, Danvers, MA 01923, (978) 750–8400,
fax (978) 646–8600, or on the Web at www.copyright.com. Requests to the Publisher for
permission should be addressed to the Permissions Department, John Wiley & Sons, Inc.,
111 River Street, Hoboken, NJ 07030, (201) 748–6011, fax (201) 748–6008, or online at
www.wiley.com/go/permissions.

Limit of Liability/Disclaimer of Warranty: While the publisher and author have used
their best efforts in preparing this book, they make no representations or warranties
with respect to the accuracy or completeness of the contents of this book and specifically
disclaim any implied warranties of merchantability or fitness for a particular purpose. No
warranty may be created or extended by sales representatives or written sales materials.
The advice and strategies contained herein may not be suitable for your situation. You
should consult with a professional where appropriate. Neither the publisher nor author
shall be liable for any loss of profit or any other commercial damages, including but not
limited to special, incidental, consequential, or other damages.

For general information on our other products and services or for technical support, please
contact our Customer Care Department within the United States at (800) 762–2974,
outside the United States at (317) 572–3993 or fax (317) 572–4002.

Wiley also publishes its books in a variety of electronic formats. Some content that appears
in print may not be available in electronic books. For more information about Wiley
products, visit our web site at www.wiley.com.

Library of Congress Cataloging-in-Publication Data:

Triana, Pablo.
    The number that killed us : a story of modern banking, flawed mathematics, and a
big financial crisis / Pablo Triana.
      p.   cm.
    Includes index.
    ISBN 978-0-470-52973-7 (hardback); 978-1-118-17154-7 (ebk);
978-1-118-17153-0 (ebk); 978-1-118-17155-4 (ebk)
      1. Financial futures.   2. Global Financial Crisis, 2008–2009.   3. Risk management.
I. Title.
HG6024.A3T75 2012
332.64'52—dc23

2011029937

Printed in the United States of America

10 9 8 7 6 5 4 3 2 1

ACC LIBRARY SERVICES AUSTIN, TX

To those interested in the safety of the markets,
the economy, and society.

Contents

VaR is an essential component of sound risk management systems.

— *Professor Philippe Jorion, April 1997*

I believe that VaR is the alibi that bankers will give shareholders (and the bailing-out taxpayer) to show documented due diligence, and will express that their blow-up came from truly unforesee-able circumstances and events with low probability not from taking large risks that they didn't understand. I maintain that VaR encourages untrained people to take misdirected risks with shareholders', and ultimately the taxpayers', money."

— *Trader and Best-Selling Author Nassim Taleb, April 1997*

A mega–financial cataclysm and a mega–public bailout later . . .

The risk-taking model that emboldened Wall Street to trade with impunity is broken and everyone is coming to the reali-zation that no algorithm can substitute for old-fashioned due diligence. VaR failed to detect the scope of the market's col-lapse. The past months have exposed the flaws of a financial measure based on historical prices.

— *Financial Reporter Christine Harper, January 2008*

It is clear in retrospect that the VaR measures of risk were faulty. When the crisis broke VaR proved highly misleading.

— *Financial Regulator Lord Turner, February 2009*

Introduction

When a Tie Is More Than Just a Tie

On September 10, 2009, former trader and best-selling author Nassim Taleb did something that he very seldom does: He wore a tie. By so graphically breaking with tradition (Taleb has publicly expressed his distaste for the blood-constraining artifacts, as well as for those who tend to don them), the Lebanese-American let the world know that that was a very special day for him, so special that it amply justified the sacrifice of temporarily betraying a sacred personal predisposition.

So what prompted the author of *The Black Swan** to uncharacteristically don such an alien piece of clothing? Well, he had been invited to a very solemn venue by very distinguished hosts, with such occasion quite likely demanding certain formalism in the way of attire. And

---

*Random House, 2007

that was an invitation that Taleb had every intention of accepting. In fact, he had been waiting and expecting for more than a decade; there was no way he was going to miss it. The raison d'être of the event for which his company was now being required had been close to Taleb's heart for most of his professional and intellectual life. It represented a central theme in his actions and ideas, close to an obsession, akin to an identity definer. He had through the years amply warned as to the havoc that might be wreaked should others massively act in a manner counter to his convictions. Such concerns typically went unheeded (to the detriment, it turned out, of society), but now he was being offered a pulpit that seemed irresistibly magnificent, impossibly far-reaching. This time, it seemed, the world would have no option but to attentively listen.

As Taleb entered the Rayburn Building of the U.S. House of Representatives in the Capitol Hill neighborhood of Washington DC that September morning, he must have felt anticipation and, especially, vindication. As he approached the sober room where several men and women awaited the start of the House Committee on Science and Technology's hearing on the responsibility of mathematical model Value at Risk (VaR) for the terrible economic and financial crisis that had caused so much misery since the previous couple of years, Taleb probably reflected proudly on all those times when, indefatigably, and in the face of harsh opposition, he alerted us of the lethal threat to the system posed by the widespread use of VaR in financeland. Now that the damage wrought by VaR was so inescapably obvious that lawmakers from the most powerful nation on the planet had been motivated into investigating the device, Taleb no longer seemed like a lone wolf howling in the markets wild, but rather appeared as imperially prescient.

■ ■ ■

What is so wrong about VaR, and why was Taleb so concerned about its impact? Most importantly, why should VaR be held responsible for the historic 2007–2008 credit crisis? VaR is a number that purports to estimate future losses deriving from a portfolio of trading assets, with a degree of statistical confidence, and presents two major problems: (1) it is doomed to being a very wrong estimate, due to its analytical foundations and the realities of real-life markets; and (2) in spite of such (well-known) deficiencies, it has for the past two decades become a ubiquitously influential force in the financial world, capable of directing decision making inside the most important banks. In other words, by letting trading activity be guided by VaR, we have essentially exposed our economic fate to a deeply flawed mechanism. Such flawedness, as was the case not only in this crisis but also before, can yield untold malaise.

The main issue with VaR is that it can easily and severely underestimate market risk. Given the model's powerful presence in financeland, that underestimation translates into recklessly huge and recklessly leveraged risk-taking on the part of banks. A particularly big problem is that VaR can translate not just into huge risk-taking and leverage for regular assets, but also for very toxic assets. As a tool that ignores the fundamental characteristics of assets, VaR can easily label the obviously risky as non-risky. VaR can mask risk so well that an entire financial system can be inundated with the worst kinds of exposures and still consider itself comfortably safe, assuaged by the rosy comforting dictates from the glorified analytical radar. VaR makes accumulating lots of toxic trading assets extremely feasible. VaR, in sum, enables danger.

VaR is an untrustworthy and dangerous measure of future market risk for one main reason: It is calculated by looking at the past. The upcoming risk of a financial asset (a stock, a bond, a derivative) is essentially assumed to mirror its behavior over the historical time period arbitrarily selected for the calculation (one year, five years, etc.). If such past happened to be placid (no big setbacks, no undue turbulence) then VaR would conclude that we should rest easy, safe in the statistical knowledge that no nasty surprises await. For instance, in the months prior to the kick-starting of the crisis in mid-2007, the VaR of the big Wall Street firms was relatively quite low, reflecting the fact that the immediate past had been dominated by uninterrupted good times and negligible volatility, particularly when it came to the convoluted mortgage-related securities that investment banks had been enthusiastically accumulating on their balance sheets. A one-day 95 percent VaR of $50 million was typical, and typically modest in its estimation of losses: At that level, a firm would be expected to lose no more than $50 million from its trading positions 95 percent of the time (in other words, it would be expected to lose more than $50 million only 12 days out of a year's 250 trading days). When you consider that those Wall Street entities owned trading assets worth several hundred billion dollars and that the eventual setbacks amounted to several dozen billion dollars, we can appreciate that VaR's predictions were excruciatingly off-base. The soulless data rearview mirror may have detected no risk, but certainly that did not mean that the system was not flooded with the worst kind of risk, ready to explode at any time. In finance, the past is simply not prologue, but someone forgot to tell VaR about it.

The fact that the mathematical engineering behind VaR tends to assume that markets follow a Normal probability distribution (thus assuming extreme moves to have negligible chance of happening, something obviously quite contrary to empirical evidence) can also contribute to the model churning unrealistically low numbers as big losses are ruled out, as can do VaR's reliance on the statistical concept of correlation, which calculates the future expected co-movement of different asset classes, based on how such codependence worked out in the past. If several assets in the portfolio happened to be uncorrelated or, better yet, "negatively correlated" in the past, VaR will take for granted that those exposures should cancel each other out, yielding lower overall portfolio risk estimates. However, as any seasoned trader would tell you, just because several assets were negatively correlated we can't infer that they won't move in tandem (positively correlated, implying that chances are that they can all tumble concurrently, thus painting a much worse overall risk picture) next month. Market history is flooded with cases when assets that were supposed to move independent of each other all tanked at the same time. Correlation in finance simply can't be captured mathematically.

And let's not forget that VaR measures risk only up to a degree of statistical confidence (typically 95 percent or 99 percent), thus leaving out the so-called "tail events," or those market episodes that have a lower chance of taking place. Big losses may lurk in those extremes, but that's beyond VaR's territory, so the model won't register such possibilities. Yet another rationale for taking VaR's results with a pinch of salt. If the very worst loss that took place in the relevant historical sample was, say, $500 million, then VaR won't be as high as $500 million because the model's statistical reach doesn't cover 100 percent of past bad scenarios, just 95 percent or 99 percent (if the 99th worst result in that sample happened to be, say, $34 million then that would be the 99 percent VaR, obviously well below the worst-case $500 million). The most unlikely scenarios are not captured by the model, and the most unlikely scenarios may be the ones we should worry most about. So even if the engineering behind the model was right (that is, even if VaR was an accurate forecast of what could be lost with 95 percent or 99 percent probability), VaR would still not be an entirely reliable measure of market risk given how it neglects the 5 percent or 1 percent probability events that can be so monstrously impacting in financial markets. Even if, a very big if, we could count on VaR up to the 95 percent or 99 percent confidence level, VaR still won't capture the unpredictable high-impact events that can quickly devastate many a trading portfolio.

As the alert reader may have by now noticed, the main problem with VaR is not so much that, as a tool that borrows from the past and from deficient and untrustworthy analytical foundations (while neglecting any fundamental commonsensical analysis of an asset's riskiness), its forecasts won't be accurate, but that it can be quite easy to arrive at a low VaR, and thus to allow for the accumulation of too much risk (it is obviously easier, and cheaper capital-wise, to get approval for a $1 billion trade when your VaR says that the max that can be lost from the punt is, say, $10 million as opposed to, say, $200 million; big positions that may not have been put on otherwise are put on because their VaR happens to be low). You just need a portfolio of assets that happened to have recently enjoyed benevolent calm and/or little correlation with each other. If you manage to compose such a grouping, the model will yell to the world that you run a sound, riskless operation. That's exactly what was taking in place on Wall Street all those years prior to late 2007. According to VaR, the situation could not have been rosier and less worrisome, risk-wise.

VaR's problem is one of original sin: trying to measure financial risk with precision may be utterly hopeless. Market prices change for one reason and one reason only: unpredictable, undecipherable, chaotic human action. Who knows who will buy and who will sell and when and how intensely? Can we numerically capture those wild spirits? Seems hard. A $50 million one-day VaR on a portfolio made up of, say, equities, currencies, and commodities is believable only if the human action behind price changes in those asset families ends up yielding a maximum daily loss of $50 million 95 percent or 99 percent of the time. Will that invariably happen? Can we guarantee it ex-ante? Even if the model is analytically very sophisticated, it seems tough to believe that it can divine upcoming market developments.

So VaR's "predictions" are bound to be wrong. But there are wrongs and there are wrongs. You can miss true risk on the upside (VaR overestimates risk) or on the downside (VaR underestimates risk). The latter scenario is naturally more worrisome, not only because its effects would be more harmful, leading to an excessive build-up of exposures on the back of such permissive loss estimates. But, again, the model's natural tendency may be in that direction. By itself, VaR will have large odds of delivering unrealistically modest numbers, as past data can't capture the next big never-before-seen crisis around the corner and as the Normality assumption rules out extremes. But there's another factor at play, further steering VaR towards lowly figures: Many financial operators have strong incentives to keep VaR as subdued as possible. Traders who want to trade in bigger sizes and who want to accumulate tons of high-risk assets, and bankers looking for enhanced leverage will fight to come up with the low VaRs that make those things possible. Since financial regulators have left them in control to calculate their own VaRs, the task is doable. VaR systems can be gamed until you arrive at your desired figure. Traders who want to trade more in an apparently "risk-lite" manner and bankers who want the greater returns on equity that leverage provides have vested personal interests (in the form of bonuses) in churning out a very subdued risk estimate. Databases will be played around with, volatility and correlation calculations will be tweaked, portfolio compositions will be altered, all with the goal of delivering the lowest VaR feasible. VaR will tend to be low, and thus risk will tend to be underrepresented, because that is its structural nature and because that's what makes a lot of influential people very happy. VaR will tend to paint a very optimistic picture, deceivingly so.

Such misplaced generosity would not be a big concern if VaR did not play a relevant role in the markets. But, rather unfortunately, the tool could not have played a more decisive part. Simply put, VaR may have been the single most influential metric in the history of finance. No other single number ever impacted, shaped, and disturbed market (and thus economic) activity as profoundly as VaR. VaR's perilously inexact estimations of risk mattered because the model mattered so much.

■ ■ ■

Invented by Wall Street in the late 1980s, VaR quickly became the accepted de rigueur market risk measurement tool inside dealing floors around the globe. Trading decisions and traders compensation began to depend on what VaR said; if the number churned by the model was deemed unacceptably large, a trader would be asked to cut down their positions, if the number was deemed comfortably tame the trader would be assigned more capital. If you made good money while enjoying a lowish VaR, you would be considered a hero by your bosses, someone capable of bringing in big bucks with seemingly minimal risk. Clearly, traders had every incentive to own portfolios endowed with low VaRs, and thus began a long-honored tradition to try to game the system into delivering subdued mathematical risk estimates. The pernicious effects of such gaming may have come fully home to roost during the credit crisis, two decades after the quantitative prodigal son was first allowed to infiltrate us.

Even more important than becoming the in-house method for calculating and managing risk (and for informing the rest of the world as to a firm's riskiness; VaR is regularly and very prominently displayed on banks regulatory filings and annual reports), VaR was adopted by policy makers as the tool to be used for the crucial purpose of determining the mandatory capital charges that financial institutions should face for their trading activities. Trading, you see, is not free. A while back, international regulators decided to impose a capital levy on market punting: for every trading position that a bank took on, a certain amount of capital had to be set aside to act as protective cushion for possible future setbacks. Naturally, the size of said capital requirement can play a huge role in the amount (and type) of trading assets that a bank would hold. If the charges are too exacting, accumulating tons of assets will be excruciatingly capital-intensive (i.e., excruciatingly expensive). You may want to build a $1 billion position, but if the capital charge is $200 million, you may consider the affair too capital-costly and forgo the trade; perhaps you don't have the $200 million to begin with. On the other hand, were the charge to be $10 million then you would surely forge ahead and build the (now very economical) position.

In essence, the size of the requirements will determine how much trading-related leverage a bank can enjoy. If the capital charge is modest, then traders need only to put up a small upfront deposit to own a whole lot of assets, being allowed to finance their portfolio mostly via borrowing. That is, by crowning VaR as the king of capital requirements, regulators essentially left the determination of banks leverage in the hands of a mathematical construct of dubious reliability. As the history of economic meltdowns clearly shows, few things can be as impacting as the amount of gearing and risk undertaken by financial institutions. If banks take on too much leverage and too much risk, they can easily go down, sinking the rest of the economy in the process. By endowing VaR with such powers, politicians made it a number that could, in fact, shape the world.

And, as we said earlier, because VaR can tend to be (or can be made to be) quite small, it follows that the reign of VaR is likely to deliver dangerously substantial leverage. Not only that. VaR can deliver the worst kind of leverage. VaR does not fundamentally discriminate between different types of asset families, treating, say, Treasury Bonds the same as, say, subprime CDOs (the convoluted residential mortgage-related securities at the heart of the 2007–2008 meltdown; essentially, re-securitizations of subprime mortgages) when it comes to measuring their future risk. All that matters is the recent behavior of the given asset, not its obvious intrinsic characteristics. The fact that Treasuries are per definition less adventuresome and more robust than CDOs would not matter one iota to VaR. VaR doesn't know that Treasuries are issued and backed by the U.S. government while complex mortgage derivatives are stuffed with toxic NINJA loans. VaR doesn't read the newspapers, or watch television. It doesn't know that the U.S. government is by its very nature a less risky debtor than an unemployed mortgage borrower. To VaR, Treasuries and CDOs are the same thing: just blips of historical data on a screen. If the CDO data (for, say, the last two years) happens to be less volatile than the Treasuries data, the model will say with a straight face that CDOs are less risky than Treasuries.

This is not theory, this can actually happen. Even the most lethal of asset families can spend a relatively long period setback-free, showing nothing but continuous gains in value as a bubble is built and sustained (in fact, it could be argued that the most toxic assets will, before their inevitable collapse, only show a rosy past devoid of setbacks, and their VaRs would in essence *always* be low; VaR may thus *always* vastly underestimate the most toxic risks). That's exactly what happened with subprime CDOs until the middle of 2007, and that is why according to VaR those Wall Street firms holding those assets were not facing much trouble and thus should not be demanded to post too much protective capital. Anybody with half a brain who chooses to use it understands that subprime CDOs are far from risk-lite. Unluckily for us, VaR was not endowed with a brain. The result: VaR permitted investment banks to accumulate untold amounts of very illiquid, very lethal assets in an extremely highly leveraged fashion (i.e., on the cheap, capital-wise). Just before the crisis, the typical VaR-dictated trading-related leverage around Wall Street and the City of London was 100 to 1 (even 1,000 to 1). That is, banks were forced to post only \$1 in capital for every \$100 (or \$1,000) of assets that they wanted to own. That's a lot of leverage. The most insignificant drop in value of your portfolio can wipe you out, fast. Given that the portfolio that was being financed with so little equity and so much debt was (thanks to VaR's blindness as to the true nature of an asset) inundated with poisonous stuff, it is easy to understand why the meltdown, when it inevitably came, was so shocking and so sudden. When asset prices began to dive following disruptions in the U.S. mortgage market in mid-2007, the huge and toxic trading positions that banks had built on the back of very modest VaR numbers began to bleed very large losses, quickly eating away the very small capital bases sanctioned by those very modest VaR numbers, and making the banking industry insolvent over night.

Too much risk-taking had been financed with too much debt. Courtesy of VaR. The model had been hiding tons of risk all along, under the statistical disguise. Subprime bonds and subprime CDOs (accumulated across banks by the hundreds of billions of dollars) are assets that can, and did, lose most of their value in the blink of an eye, and should therefore require a lot of back-up capital. But VaR was saying that no such capital largesse was needed. After all, hadn't those securities enjoyed a placid existence during their entire lifetime?

Would a VaR-less, math-less, commonsense-grounded approach have allowed such dangerous immense leverage? No, it wouldn't have. One hundred-to-1 or 1,000-to-1 leverage on portfolios loaded with very problematic stuff would have never been okayed by a thinking person. By letting an unthinking model dictate outcomes, the otherwise unacceptable is okayed.

By endowing VaR with the power to dictate the positions and the leverage that banks could take on, regulators effectively left the fate of the world in the hands of a tool with a natural capacity to severely underestimate risk. It is not only that VaR's internal plumbing can easily result in the underestimation of danger, as many problematic assets can present calm past periods, assets in the portfolio may have by sheer coincidence moved in an uncorrelated fashion, the Normal distribution assigns a probability to extreme events that is much lower than what is observed in reality, and past crises may not mirror the next unpredictable even bigger meltdown. Banks also have been allowed to calculate their own VaRs, pretty much any way they like. Given how bankers are incentivized to go for larger and more leveraged positions, they have a very good reason to churn out VaRs as low as possible and thus to manipulate the calculation method to that end. If we pair the structural deficiencies with the personal incentives, it seems clear that with VaR around, risk forecasts and capital requirements will tend to be subdued.

The VaR reign is thus almost a guarantee that the system will be more exposed and more fragile. There are simply too many conduits through which the model can deliver very modest numbers. Banks can employ an army of quants whose only job is to come up with the right combination of assets, the right statistical tricks, and the right calculation methodology so that their VaRs are optimized to be as small as feasible. The VaR reign allows punters to accumulate gargantuan amounts of risk under the veil of no risk.

If risk is underestimated, more risk and more leverage will be embraced and made possible. It is sadly ironic that all this was done in the name of prudence: VaR was supposed to help control risk, not to lead to more and more dangerous risk. The model-free old ways were tossed aside because the model was assumed to improve things and to make everyone safer. But a desire for prudence led to a very imprudent reality. The world's destiny was left in the hands of a device with an in-bred tendency to hide and augment risk. No wonder things turned out so badly.

■ ■ ■

Nassim Taleb was in a good position to understand from the get-go that VaR could result in destructive toxic risk taking if allowed to be influential. As a seasoned and successful options trader who had experienced several market roller coasters that had been prospectively assumed (by the same theoretical notions underpinning VaR) not to be possible, Taleb quickly realized that it is useless to try to measure that which does not lend itself to be measured. Market activity is simply too untamable, too wild, too undecipherable. In an environment where everything is possible and where the next unprecedented crash may be around the corner, it is hopeless to try to infer much from the historical record. As a quantitatively educated individual, Taleb knew only too well that the rotten math behind VaR only make things worse. For Taleb there was no doubt: rather than helping understand, control, and reduce risk, VaR will result in higher and worse risks. Bothered by such possibility, in the mid-1990s he embarked on a loud anti-VaR campaign. At the time, going at VaR was truly heretic. The acceptance of the tool within academic, theoretical, and regulatory circles was unassailably unquestionable, religiously so. Its defenders wasted no time in ruthlessly lambasting Taleb, dismissing him as a ranting worry-monger incapable of appreciating the magic that the mathematical risk technology could deliver. Financial risk, VaR fans declared, had been finally conquered, subjugated into a neat number by the unalterable precision of the precious analytics. How could anyone dare criticize such gloriousness? Had that Lebanese fellow gone mad?

Taleb was first vindicated in 1997 and 1998. As markets everywhere succumbed to the chaos ignited by the Asian crisis, first, and the disaster of mega−hedge fund Long Term Capital Management (LTCM) afterward, VaR was openly revealed as a gravely malfunctioning guide. As real trading losses climbed way above those predicted by VaR, the hitherto rock-solid reputation of the model began to suffer. Worse,

VaR itself had a large hand in accelerating those losses, by prompting banks to engage in sudden and massive liquidations of positions, fueling a devastating snowballing debacle. In a rehearsal of what would take place a decade later, VaR not only failed to warn of the upcoming danger but essentially contributed to the realization of such danger.

Despite the temporary tarnishing of its name, VaR was not discarded or abandoned in financeland following those nasty episodes (which, particularly in the case of LTCM, threatened the system's viability). Quite the opposite, actually. Not only did those regulators who had originally embraced the tool continue to do so, avoiding in the process a much-needed rethink of VaR's true value, but another, rather significant, one decided to join the party. In 2004, the U.S. Securities and Exchange Commission established a rule that allowed large Wall Street broker-dealers (the likes of Goldman Sachs, Morgan Stanley, Merrill Lynch, Bear Stearns, and Lehman Brothers) to use their own risk management practices for capital requirements purposes, recognizing outright that charges were destined to be lower under the new approach. VaR was predictably sanctioned as the main method of calculation, and as we know this implied that illiquid securities ("no ready market securities" in the jargon), which previously would have been subjected to something like 100 percent deduction for capital purposes (about 1-to-1 leverage, making it unaffordably expensive to buy billions and billions of dollars in those securities), were now afforded the same VaR treatment as more conservative and conventional alternatives: If the mathematically driven number happened to be low, the required capital charge would be low.

Engaging in unapologetically risky activities instantly became much cheaper and convenient for U.S. investment banking powerhouses. VaR numbers were unrealistically low back then, hiding a lot of real risk. The VaR-transmitted regulatory encouragement was probably too tempting to resist, as a return measured against a tiny capital base makes for very tasty quarterly results. The end result, of course, was a highly levered, undercapitalized financial industry whose fate was exposed to the soundness of subprime securities and other trading plays. Or, in slightly different wording, a ticking time bomb, which duly exploded not long after. The 2007 crisis was a crisis of toxic leverage, made possible by VaR's inexcusably low risk estimates.

By jumping onto the VaR bandwagon in 2004, the SEC allowed Taleb to enjoy a second, much stronger, vindication three years later. Had the SEC not adopted that policy, which some have salaciously termed "The Bear Stearns Future Insolvency Act," it is quite probable that the crisis would not have happened (as the lethal securities would either have not been accumulated, or would have been backed by a lot more cushiony capital) and that Nassim Taleb would not have had to don that bothersome tie that September morning.

The key question, naturally, is "Why?" Why did regulators choose to adopt a model that is so obviously foundationally flawed and that fails dramatically in the real world? What motivated the financial mandarins? Why was VaR allowed to become the most important financial metric ever? This book deals with those irrepressibly pressing issues, from which so many have tended to shy away.

■ ■ ■

In October 1994, JP Morgan flashily unveiled to the world something called *Riskmetrics*. The amalgamation of technical documents, software, and data became the equivalent of a global debutante ball for VaR. By popularizing its own internal procedures, the U.S. investment bank, one of the early pioneers in quantitative risk management, took VaR into the mainstream and solidified its role as the preeminent tool. In fact, it can be argued that without that display of generosity, the industry-wide adoption of VaR may not have proceeded in such a quick and profound fashion (if at all). By helping other less-resourceful financial institutions with the calculation of their risks, JP Morgan guaranteed that the same methodology would be adopted, concurrently, by all significant players. This, in turn, helped convince regulators that banks had found a magic way to tame exposures once and for all, and that the wise course of action would be to embrace, sanction, and enforce the use of such proprietary intelligence. Thus was born the modern trading regime that has dominated the market environment till our days.

The approach chosen by JP Morgan was particularly grounded in standard finance theory, with its belief in Normality and the power of historical precedent to indicate future asset volatility and correlations. That path has a high potential for leading toward modest VaR numbers, through a lethal combination of unworldly statistical assumptions and a naive confidence in the concept of diversification. JP Morgan's invention and its widely publicized spreading through financeland did wonders for the general reputation of VaR as a to-be-trusted measure; it endowed the construct with unlimited credibility, and those hundreds of equations-filled pages did the trick by terminally enchanting regulators and overwhelmingly impressing observers. It seemed implausible that anything other than saintly robustness and divine accuracy could emerge from such a potent display of braininess. Riskmetrics was the cherry on top that fully tempted policymakers into the VaR lovefest.

In this light, one could mark October 1994 as the true starting date of the 2007–2008 crisis. The coronation of VaR that took place back then ensured that, at some point in the future, the financial industry would be allowed to ingest vast amounts of securities (including very complex securities) in an impossibly geared way. It was just a matter of time for the stars of the VaR universe to align themselves right (a period of prolonged market calm, the imperial rise of an apparently risk-lite easily marketable toxic asset, low interest rates, friendly mathematical correlations) and unleash a torrent of cheap, leveraged, lethal speculation.

In fact, referring, as almost everyone did and continues to do, to the chaos of three years ago as a *mortgage crisis* or a *subprime crisis* appears less than accurate. It wasn't mortgages or CDOs, it was VaR. It was the inevitable arrival of the financial tsunami that a tool like VaR will inevitably unleash if given enough staying power among us. It was the inevitable *VaR crisis*, which could have happened a few years earlier or a few years later, but happen it was most definitely going to. The subprime stuff is just an anecdote, a simple momentary transmission mechanism, it could have been any other type of exotic asset, at any other time. VaR does not care about the exact nature of the asset as long as it fulfills the necessary conditions for it to be very low, thus excusing the reckless leveraged punting that VaR uniquely permits. It was only a matter of time before the VaR stars were aligned correctly and the right type of exotic punt showed up. It turned out to be housing-related securities, but it could just as well have been equity, or currency, or commodity related stuff behind a monstrous VaR-enabled crisis. As long as the asset has experienced quietness of late, as long as a sensible-sounding sales pitch can be built around it, and as long as financing the purchase of the asset is made easy by easy monetary policy, the reign of VaR as capital king can guarantee the emergence of an unseemly ultra-leveraged bubble, ready to wreak destruction as soon as the asset tumbles in value just a bit.

VaR waited patiently until the day when global blood could be shed. VaR always was a permanent structural flaw in the system, a terrible accident waiting to happen, a terminal cancer that would unforgivably catch up with the patient, and policy makers, rather puzzlingly, loved nothing more than promoting it and helping it become ever stronger, guaranteeing that the eventual pain would be maximum.

It is not exactly expected that the brains behind JP Morgan's VaR (which was first conceived around 1989) would have anticipated that their analytical creature would turn out to be irrevocably associated with tumultuousness and chaos, let alone envision its role as principal instigator of the mayhem. We would rather want to believe that their intentions were nothing but benevolent, and that they trusted that the quantitative and theoretical foundations of their beloved concoction would represent a welcome addition of rigor and concreteness to an otherwise slightly pedestrian financial risk management field. Few of the earlier VaR pioneers may have imagined that the life of the model would be surrounded by high-octane drama, mystery, and a first-row role in some of finance's most notoriously nasty episodes. And yet, that's what happened. VaR turned out to be a far more exciting and (often, negatively) influential invention than any of the inventors may have ever thought possible. As concerned inhabitants of the financial and economic spheres, we wish that things had evolved less noisily and that the crises had been less frequent. But that doesn't mean that, as people intrigued by the nature of the forces that truly shape our world, we should shy away from telling the story of the malfeasant. Though it may feel as scant compensation for the damage caused, we can at least be certain that the story of VaR will not be devoid of interesting anecdotes, important happenstances, intellectual accomplishments, eye-catching characters, and the drama of the monster market meltdown.

■ ■ ■

I have enjoyed writing this book quite a lot. If penning my prior tome, *Lecturing Birds on Flying: Can Mathematical Theories Destroy the Financial Markets?* (John Wiley & Sons, 2009), was the result of initial external encouragement (some very prominent people thought that I should do it and indicated me so), *The Number That Killed Us* was a project that I pushed for, energetically, before anyone could push me first. As I was completing *Lecturing Birds*, the role of VaR in the 2007–2008 credit crisis became unmistakably inescapable, and I thought that the analysis and the story deserved fully fledged treatment. I couldn't help but desperately realize that there was so much more to say. So I incessantly bothered my editors at John Wiley & Sons until they agreed to sign me on for this one, too.

There were plenty of books on VaR out there already, but they were all of a technical-descriptive nature (many of them highly mathematical). I wasn't interested in going that route, naturally. I am not particularly enchanted by the equations behind VaR (or most any other finance theory) but rather by the impact that VaR can have on the world. And, frankly, we don't need to become connoisseurs of all the geeky details behind VaR's precise calculation to understand said impact. In fact, all we would need to know is that VaR borrows from past data and from Normality-based statistical parameters. That gives us the requisite conceptual backing to argue that VaR will always, conceptually, tend to be an unreliable guide in the markets, and thus the wrong choice for risk radar and, especially, regulatory capital charge-setter. We can greatly improve our analysis by looking at actual banks reported results to comprehend how, in fact, VaR did churn out very humble figures and thus dangerously leverage and off-base loss predictions. That's all we really need to accuse VaR of inciting the crisis. We don't need to dig much deeper into the actual calculation technicalities.

Actually, we could have concluded that VaR created the leverage and the failed predictions even if we had no clue whatsoever as to how it is arrived at, simply by looking at the reported figures. This book could still have been written perfectly fine even if we didn't know at all where the VaR number comes from. Once we get a basic idea as to its analytical DNA we, of course, become yet more convinced of its guiltiness, but a basic idea is all we need for our purposes here. This tome is about how VaR contributed to sinking us, not about the minutiae of how VaR is precisely calculated. That makes it uniquely different and, I believe, uniquely relevant.

Writing a book on VaR and its responsibility for market crises was an obsession for me for the obvious reasons. Understanding what truly contributed to the carnage is understandably attractive, both as a theme to muse about and as a way to share impacting ideas. I have a demonstrable interest in how financial theorems can impact the markets and the world. I would too like to think that perhaps I could be making a contribution toward the prevention of similar future crises, at the very least forcing a rethink of the embracement of suspect technical machinations in finance, and their sponsorship by public servants.

But I was also seeking for vindication, and not specifically for me. I wanted to tell people how a (very) few freethinking skeptics had been warning for years that all this could happen, only to receive the opprobrium of the technical apparatchiks, only to see their platitudes ignored by policy makers and many financial pros. Those maverick contrarians had no other interest but to try to make the financial terrain a more robust one, less prone to murderous chaos, and they could see (more than a decade ago) that VaR had the capacity to wreak just such havoc. They tried to alert us. They tried to protect us. But the coalition of those who benefit personally from the reign of VaR and those who became bewitched by the endlessly advertised "scientificness" and "rigorousness" of the methodology (and who may have been intimidated into not raising too many concerns about the deified risk benchmark) closed ranks and fought mercilessly to prevent any of the sinful contrarianism from permeating too deeply. The world was thus prevented from hearing (and understanding) the warnings. The very small coterie of visionary "Noahs of finance," led as we know by Nassim Taleb, had seen the flood coming from miles away, and tried to save the planet from drowning. But those who provoked the life-threatening inundations stopped the message from filtering through, and no comprehensive preventive measures were taken (note that those investors smart enough to embark on Taleb's ark before the killing rains started found bountiful refuge from the malaise, not only avoiding a horrible death but actually enjoying a majestic existence; Taleb's crash-hedging fund made many millions for its backers in 2008). Those who ruthlessly censored intelligence that might have saved us, while relentlessly peddling the remedy that suffocated us, should be held responsible.

I wanted everyone to know that a band of contrarians had tried to prevent the great VaR flood from happening. I saw this book as, among other things, a conduit to that end. I thought that they deserved widely shared kudos.

April 28, 2004

Steve Benardete Gets His Wish; The World Suffers

I magine an escort service that offers two kinds of escorts. One is mildly attractive, with a boring personality, and overall not entirely arousing. The other is drop-dead gorgeous and undeniably enchanting. The discrepancies don't end there. The more desirable companion obviously charges a much bigger fee. Spending day after day with her comes at a price; if you don't want the, by comparison, boring alternative, you have to pay much more. But that's not all. Going with the queen of escorts would not only be more costly economically, but also maybe physically. For you see, the statuesque sophisticated bombshell dates a Russian mobster. He doesn't like to share. If he sees you frequenting his doll too often, he might just endow you with new concrete shoes and take you for a (rather deadly) aquatic adventure. So patronizing the comparatively more promising gal would carry lots of risk. Being content with her less-ravishing colleague, on the other hand, could be not only friendlier on the wallet but also easier on your sleep quality. She is single and while certain exposures may be inevitable, one could safely assume modest collateral damage. As they say in other fields, less return tends to be accompanied by less risk. Or rather, more return (in this case, enjoying top-shelf company) goes hand in hand with more risk (succumbing at the merciless whim of the enraged boyfriend). Even if you could afford the more titillating prospect, you may shy away on account of the accompanying threat. If you value your safety you may be content to spend time with the less attractive but also less potentially explosive companionship.

What the Securities and Exchange Commission (SEC; the regulator of securities firms in the United States) did in April of 2004, in a decision that would ultimately contribute to shaking the world to its knees, was the equivalent of financing endless adventures with the more attractive (market) escort for U.S. investment banks. The SEC made enjoying the better-returning alternative (read exotic, thus higher-yielding, high-risk trading assets) possibly as affordable, if not more affordable, as enjoying less-glamorous possibilities (read standard, typically low-yielding, low-risk trading assets). And banks rushed in as if there were no tomorrow, accumulating now-economical exotic assets in vast numbers. "You mean the charming bombshell now charges as little as the other one? Book me six weeks straight!" Some may ask: What about the Mobster? What about the dangers derived from selecting the most attractive choice? Didn't bankers care about ending up sleeping with the fishes at the bottom of the river? Was the prospect of amazing financial interrelationship really worth it?

The answers from Wall Street all too often were no and yes. There were several good reasons for this. For one, every time a trader was escorted by the more striking alternative (every time he accumulated higher-yielding daring assets) his bosses typically rewarded him with a point in the score blackboard. At the end of the year, the blackboard would be looked at and if you had scored a lot of points you would be paid huge amounts of money in the form of a bonus. So you have a clear incentive to pay up that sharply reduced fee for glamorous rendezvous (thanks, SEC!), over and over again. Of course, the more points for you in that board, the closer the day of reckoning when the Russian fellow loses his patience (the closer the day when your exotic riskier positions sink in value and blow you up). But you don't care much because in the Street the rules of the street don't always apply: Here if the risk materializes you don't necessarily have to die. The worst that may happen is that you have to seek alternative employment, comfily cushioned by all the millions you just earned. Hey, you may actually get to keep your job courtesy of the bailing-out government. Here it's other people who die at the hands of the brusquely enraged killer. You may be the one who forced the financial Mobster into the scene in the first place, but the real suffering is reserved for others, including plenty of unsuspecting bystanders.

What the SEC forgot is that if you charge the same for two financial assets, bankers (many, at least) will always gorge on the one offering the prospect of a far more pleasurable experience, return-wise, possibly disregarding entirely the (often, systemic) risks that such choice may entail. They may not care about the risk, only about its affordability. They may not care about the negative consequences from owning the asset, only about its costliness. Wildly asymmetric remuneration structures assure that the risk of sweet-looking plays is not feared; in fact, it is preferred. You get to enjoy and keep the returns; you don't suffer (much) if ugliness materializes. That type of one-sided bargain pushes bankers into frantically searching for the bombshells of finance, accumulating potential lethality for others. In the markets, as in our fictional escort service story, terrible danger can accompany the most attractive-looking of entertainments. Sophisticated, daring, high-stakes assets that deliver wonderful results for a while can abruptly sink in value as their inner riskiness unsurprisingly manifests itself fully, taking institutions into the abyss. If you set fees for those tempting toys that are so low that no-holds-barred munching within banking circles is guaranteed, you are essentially signing a death sentence down the road for the rest of the populace.

The SEC's April 2004 ruling effectively treated toxic, illiquid yet tempting punts (like subprime collateralized debt obligations [CDOs]) exactly the same as staid, boring plays (like Treasury Bonds) when it came to calculating the all-important regulatory capital to be prudently set aside for trading games. Regulatory capital is a mandatory cushion, ideally in the form of core shareholders equity, that aims at guaranteeing that banks will be, in theory, shielded from market turmoil; regulatory capital is supposed to be able to absorb possible future losses and protect banks from going under when severe setbacks take place. In effect, regulatory capital is the price tag that determines whether speculative activities are affordable or not as the lower the capital charge the cheaper trading becomes since the same upfront capital "deposit" can finance more punting. Most importantly, regulatory capital will determine the amount of leverage that a bank can take on (a capital charge of, say, 3 percent of assets allows the position to be financed with more leverage, i.e., debt, than a capital charge of, say, 10 percent), and thus its exposure to sudden market gyrations (the more your positions are financed with debt the more vulnerable you are to bad news, as your equity capital cushion will be "eaten" faster by the losses). Up to April 2004, obviously riskier stuff like subprime CDOs, which were made up of the worst kinds of mortgage loans, would have required a much higher capital charge than obviously safer T-Bonds, as leveraged punting on the former was commonsensically assumed to be way more dangerous than on the latter.

The new SEC rule now afforded both types of excruciatingly dissimilar asset families exactly the same calculation treatment. Under such unseemly level playing fields, the more daring punt could actually end up requiring the same or perhaps even *less* cushiony capital commitment. Punting on the riskier, illiquid alternative could well become less costly than punting on the much-sounder, liquid choice. The end result may not always be so, but the crux of the matter is that the new SEC ruling would in principle allow for such possibility (it is crucial to note that exotic trades did not have to cost the same or even less than Treasury Bonds in regulatory capital terms for bankers to create a gold rush in the former; it was more than enough that their particular capital charge was vastly reduced and this the SEC ruling definitely guaranteed, thus making it much cheaper for traders to gorge on such potentially lethal asset class). The SEC's 2004 change of heart aided the lascivious accumulation of troublesome assets on Wall Street's balance sheets, which predictable unraveling generated the billionaire write-downs that gave way to what is known as the 2007–2008 credit crisis.

If you want to preserve global calm you can't make speculating on highly tempting, highly dangerous things like subprime CDOs irresistibly economical. If you facilitate a bubble in enchanting yet danger-promising beauties, don't be surprised by the subsequent destruction.

■ ■ ■

On December 31, 1996, Steven M. Benardete wrote a letter to the SEC. Addressed to the Honorable Arthur Levitt, the SEC's chairman at the time, the missive's heading read "Re: Possible Amendments to the Net Capital Rule." Mr. Benardete (a very senior Morgan Stanley derivatives executive when he penned the note) was communicating with the SEC in his capacity as chairman of the then recently formed Risk Management Committee of the Securities Industry Association, a trade body (lobby) for Wall Street traders. What did Benardete want, and why should we care today? Well, he wanted a very special favor from Levitt and the SEC: the regulatory adoption of VaR models for trading-related capital charge determination purposes. Again, capital charges determine how much banks have to put up-front in order to play the trading game; the lower the mandatory charge, the more they are allowed to finance their trading activities through debt rather than equity. The letter was, in effect, a determined lobbying effort. It asked the chief of financial police to, please, just let Wall Street dealers use VaR to determine the capital costliness of their market activities. "Other regulators already allow commercial banks to use VaR, so why can't we, Mr Levitt?" went the spirit of the petition, "Come on, let us Wall Streeters join the VaR party."

There are several reasons why the Masters of the Trading Floor in New York would want to have VaR crowned capital emperor. But besides specific nit-picking, we can be irrepressibly adventurous and conclude that if Wall Streeters wanted VaR to replace the old capital order then perhaps, just maybe, Wall Street thought that VaR could help it achieve its goals better than the old ways ever could. If Mr. Benardete and his crowd wanted VaR so bad we have to assume that they saw something in VaR that could truly make them happier. Just like someone who marries for money, the object of adoration might be honestly adored for their intrinsic qualities, but that was not the main reason behind your romantic overtures; rather, you were seeking a material benefit that only that particular partner could satisfy.

Wall Street may have truthfully loved VaR for its inner beauty, but that was likely not the main reason why Benardete sat on his desk and scribbled his letter. He most likely did so because he thought that VaR could uniquely help him and his friends achieve something golden.

Why did Wall Street court VaR so passionately? What was Wall Street truly after? Keep this particular rationale firmly in mind: VaR, by, as we know, tending to be unrealistically low, can dictate very humble capital requirements for trading activities, including the most toxic kind. And there can be few things more generally loved by punters than being able to punt on the cheap, in a highly leveraged way, especially if the punt is exotic and thus higher-yielding. Why? Because the higher the leverage, the greater the returns on capital for every increase in the value of the positions; a highly leveraged play that goes well can translate into record results and compensation (of course, leverage works both ways: If you have a large portfolio backed by little equity, when your positions fall in value, even a bit, you may be wiped out as your tiny equity base can't cope with the losses). We further elaborate in later pages, but let's first concentrate our attention on Benardete's actual words, how he peddled his adored VaR to the regulators. Let's see how Wall Street asked the SEC for VaR's hand.

> As you know, VaR models are increasingly used by major banks and securities firms as an internal tool for managing market and credit risk. We believe that these models hold promise as a methodology for determining regulatory capital standards, as indicated by the actions of bank regulators to permit banks to utilize models in assessing their capital requirements.

Translation: I want to marry VaR for capital purposes, please let me. Further down the missive, Benardete referenced several studies that suggested that the ability of the SEC's Net Capital Rule, the set of policies dealing with broker–dealer capital requirements, to judge the capital adequacy of securities firms has been surpassed by other methodologies. These studies concluded that the prevailing ways (the so-called *comprehensive approach*) worked much less satisfactorily than a VaR-based approach would, since, as the researchers posited, "*under the former methodology there was no correlation between the relative riskiness of a portfolio and the amount of capital required.*" VaR, it was implied (then as nowadays), was a great improvement on things because of its ability to match capital requirements to an asset's "true" risk, as expressed by its volatility, obtained through the model with the help of past market data and statistical trickeries. As is thoroughly analyzed in this book, such claim is in fact of suspect validity: What VaR calls *risk* is usually nothing but dangerous make-believe. But it has nonetheless tended to work quite well as a sales pitch for VaR promoters.

Yet further down in his letter, Steve Benardete sang VaR's praises again when it came to another desirable potential application, the posting of margins (collateral) between trading counterparts; here, too, Wall Street wanted the prevailing rule firmly replaced by its ever-so-useful tool.

> We believe that the same principles that apply to questions of capital adequacy should also apply to margin questions. . . . The portfolio margining approach (i.e., VaR) is a much more efficient system for collateralizing risk exposures and achieves substantially the same market risk protection as the strategy based on Regulation T (an approach similar to that of the Net Capital Rule) but with collateral levels that are mere fractions of those required by Regulation T. In light of the greater statistical rigor that VaR models introduce into efforts to measure risk, we hope that the Commission will look favourably upon the attempts to amend the rules.

This last sentence is critical. This is Wall Street employing VaR's scientific-looking "rigorousness" as a promotional pitch, another traditional practice by VaR lovers. VaR's analytical glamour can be used to tear down obstacles to its spreading. VaR's quantitative complexion could be employed to intimidate others into giving in (who but an uncouth hick would dare oppose such sophistication? Embrace VaR and join the ranks of the smart people!). Whether Wall Street honestly bowed at the altar of VaR's statistical foundations or rather was concurring in naughty deceit wouldn't be the key issue, what really mattered is that said quantitative adornments sufficiently impressed *other* people. Given folks' general tendency to slavishly submit to anything laden with mathematical symbols and backed by serious-looking holders of prestigious academic degrees, the fact that VaR was, in its origins at least, a profoundly analytical construct (take a look at VaR-inventor JP Morgan's original documentation if you don't believe me) quite possibly scored lots of brownie points for the device. It is a safe bet that had VaR not been technical, the Street's peddling efforts may have been less successful. Complex math sells well in the markets.

The 1996 communication concluded by reinforcing the declaration of love, "*We believe that VaR modeling is the most powerful tool presently available for quantifying market risk in a portfolio of diverse financial instruments, allowing for comprehensive risk assessment across different risk types and markets.*"

And then doubled-down on its lobbying efforts: "*Integration of VaR models into the regulatory scheme for broker-dealers would have the important benefit of creating closer links between internal risk management and supervisory standards, and could establish a consistent framework within which regulators, traders, and risk managers could examine and discuss questions of risk.*" Translation: We have already developed and fine-tuned a risk guide that works well for us, now adopt it for policy purposes, make it the law of the land and we can all become best of friends.

■ ■ ■

On April 28, 2004, the SEC finally obliged. The marriage to VaR was finally okayed. In return for agreeing to more intrusive supervision, the five big American investment banks saw their fantasies come true. From then on, VaR would be used to calculate the costliness, and thus affordability and leverage of their trading rendezvous. With Arthur Levitt no longer at the helm, a response to Benardete's plea fell to one of his successors (former investment banking godfather Bill Donaldson). If Benardete's request had been compressed in exactly three pages, the SEC's delayed complaisance, at 100-plus pages, was decidedly richer in details.

The 2004 reply, titled "Alternative Net Capital Requirements for Broker-Dealers That Are Part of Consolidated Supervised Entities," began matter-of-factly by confronting the main issue head on:

The Commission is amending the "net capital rule" to establish a voluntary, alternative method of computing net capital for certain broker-dealers. Under the amendments, a broker-dealer that maintains certain minimum levels of net capital may apply to the Commission for a conditional exemption from the application of the standard net capital calculation. As a condition to granting the exemption, the broker-dealer's ultimate holding company must consent to group-wide Commission supervision. The amendments should help the Commission to protect investors and maintain the integrity of the securities markets by improving oversight of broker-dealers and providing an incentive for broker-dealers to implement strong risk management practices. Under the alternative method, firms with strong internal risk management practices may utilize mathematical modeling methods already used to manage their own business risk, including value-at-risk ("VaR") models, for regulatory purposes.

Translation: You let us be more snoopily supervisory and we'll scratch those bothersome old market capital rules; what's more, we'll let you substitute the disliked ancient ways for the ones you truly prefer.

And the SEC's accommodativeness went further than that: Not only did the financial police officers agree to hand Wall Street its capital weapons of choice, it went as far as to openly admit the benefits to be derived from such armory, "*A broker-dealer's deductions for market and credit risk probably will be lower under the alternative method of computing net capital than under the standard net capital rule.*" In other words, indulging in all kinds of trading should result cheaper going forward; the lower the capital haircuts the more bang for your buck, the more positions you can take for a given level of net capital. This point is driven home even more profoundly later in the document, as if to try to dissipate any doubts Wall Street may have had as to the SEC's utter willingness to give it want it wanted: "*The mix of positions held by the broker-dealer may change if the regulatory cost of holding certain positions is reduced. We estimated that broker-dealers taking advantage of the alternative capital computation would realize an average reduction in capital deductions of approximately 40%.*" Whatever the actual accuracy of those estimates, there can be no doubt as to the aroma scenting from the regulators' message: we firmly believe that VaR will result in sizably diminished capital charges and subsequently altered portfolio compositions. Let the reign of cheap trading begin!

We'll probably never know how critical Steve Benardete's particular letter was in helping steer the regulators toward compliance, but we are certain that the Morgan Stanley bigwig got his wish granted on a silver platter. At last, Wall Street could afford endless adventures with the most desirably exotic financial fare; at last, gone were the days when mesmerizingly attractive financial toys were unaffordably expensive, when beyond-average entertainments cost way too much. Under the previous VaR-deprived, "comprehensive" regime punting on nonstandard assets tended to be prohibitively taxing, capital-wise. Building a mountain of exotic positions would have required a similarly sized mountain of protective equity (this seemed only prudent, given how fast and hard nonstandard securities can sink in value). With VaR imperial, Wall Street was allowed to support that trading mountain with potentially just a few grains of equity, with massive borrowings making up for the rest. Amassing vast amounts of risky stuff became extremely convenient for banks, making it much easier for those entities to go under all of a sudden, thus posing a lethal threat to global economic and social stability.

■ ■ ■

So why did Wall Street lobby so stringently for VaR? Really, why the obviously intense infatuation? Was it true love or interested love? Let's be benevolent first. Perhaps Steve Benardete and others honestly believed that the "intuitional" approach to financial risk needed (no, demanded) a healthy dose of curative "rigorousness." The old ways may simply have looked exceedingly rusty in the brave new world of super-size bets and complex derivatives. It was urgent that risks be measured more accurately. A math infusion was in order, according to this argument. Capital charges, the storyline would go, could no longer be based on inflexible preset fixed numbers dependent on an arbitrarily selected list of different asset families (x charge for equities, y charge for corporate bonds, z charge for government securities, and so on), as was the case under the standard approach. Modern Wall Street, VaR cheerleaders would have sincerely postulated, could not afford to let the old pedestrian ways go on ruling supreme; they just couldn't cope with exposures anymore. The new analytical high-tech was required to tame risks more efficiently and wisely. That would be, roughly, the more innocent version of Wall Street's VaR pitch. Those of a more merciful bent may choose to fully buy into it.

But even the most charitably indulgent have to admit that there are plausible, less puritanical, alternative explications behind the VaR wooing. What if the VaR marketing campaign launched almost two decades ago was a conscious effort to have inscribed into law edicts that would let financial dealers insatiably guzzle leveraged exotic punts, like, for example, those that would give rise to the 2007 credit crisis?

Under this naughtier version of the story VaR is not espoused and forced onto the world due to its (purported) magical capacity to improve our lot by mapping financial risks in a grander fashion than previously existing alternatives. Rather, it was endorsed as a once-in-a-lifetime vehicle to improve the lot of Wall Streeters beyond the wildest of dreams. You badly want the humble capital charges and the humble risk estimates that VaR can uniquely deliver, especially if they can make trading on higher-return assets much cheaper, so even if you may not believe in its analytical foundations you forcefully endorse it nonetheless. Maybe Wall Street looked at VaR and didn't see (as advertised) the new golden paradigm of risk management that could, through its magic wand, warn us and protect the system by forever preventing the manifestation of crises. Perhaps what it really saw was a powerful alibi that could be profitably milked into untold millions. The key question, of course, becomes: Did someone, somewhere on the Street understand from early on that something like VaR did not only present a less-than-rosy report card when it came to structural soundness but would also tend to encourage the kind of misguided and reckless trading that could steer the system into breakdown? Did some Wall Streeters peddle as crisis-preventer a gadget they knew contained the seeds of out-of-control turmoil? Did they push into law a device they knew could open the fences of hell down the road?

Even if that was the case, was it an entirely unexpected one? Wall Streeters, like any businesspeople, are typically looking for any advantage that may yield additional profits and enhanced compensation. And it's not like endorsing VaR in search of personal advantages, and maybe under false pretenses, was illegal, or even fraudulent. It was a self-servingness that served the world badly in the end, but, if we are fair, not outrageously unbecoming. Wall Street is a place that attracts people who want to make money, and if they find (actually invent, in the case of VaR) a mechanism that assists them greatly in that respect don't be entirely surprised if they fall head over heels. If Wall Streeters reached the conclusion that VaR could help multiply their earnings, are we to show utter shock when they abandon all promotional restraints and present the tool as the best thing since sliced bread?

The real unexplainable conduct surrounding the VaR saga lies not so much with the bankers but rather with the regulators. Much as we can try to make sense of it, a scarcity of reasonable reasons dominates the atmosphere when attempting to comprehend why the financial police backed a flawed methodology, which potential for disruption was so easily detectable. The sight of the market police, paid to rid us of crime, consciously arming the Wall Street gangs with weapons of mass destruction surely must rank as one of the most puzzling happenstances in financial history.

Frankly, few things could go so contrary to the public mission of the regulators as their embracement of VaR as capital emperor. It's not so much that the April 2004 rule gave unfettered carte blanche to Wall Street gearing and yielded higher leverage ratios. Much more important than the overall leverage itself was, once more, the *kind* of leverage that the inscribing of VaR into law helped produce. Bad leverage, of the toxic kind. Not the one that you would expect policy makers to be helping spread around. Giving the same capital treatment to a very risky asset and to a very safe asset can generate untold economic tremors, not the kind of outcomes that politicians should be encouraging.

Under the old rules that Wall Street so desperately wanted scrapped, very bad leverage was impossibly expensive, under VaR very bad leverage can be very economical. If you dangle such incentives in front of bonus-hungry traders, chances are that banks will take full advantage and load up their balance sheets with toxic assets. Eerily enough, the regulators admitted themselves to be fully in-the-know as to the likely consequences of having VaR enthroned those years ago. It's not just that, as we have seen, they happily conceded that leverage was bound to climb as the costs of trading were sharply reduced across the board; creepily presciently they went further and even foresaw the possibility that that enhanced leverage would now be allowed to alter its composition. Let's recall what could well be the most dangerously prophetic sentence ever uttered in finance: "*The mix of positions held by the broker-dealer may change if the regulatory cost of holding certain positions is reduced,*" the SEC admitted on that fateful April 28, 2004. Did no one at the Commission realize that "certain positions" may grow up to mean poisonous system-threatening garbage?

Great love affairs have often resulted in tragedy and pain (think Romeo and Juliet). The SEC and Wall Street's torrid VaR affair honored that tradition. We are all for love, but the ill-fated VaR romance between regulators and bankers has cost the world dearly. For the future sake of the world's economic and social health, it would have been better if the courted SEC had resisted the advances by the trading floor heartthrobs. Steve Benardete's insinuations should have not been acceded to.

Chapter 1

The Greatest Story Never Told

The Leverage That Killed Us ▪ *The Number That Leads to Toxic Leverage* ▪ *Financial Risk Mismanagement* ▪ *Too Many Exceptions* ▪ *Lessons Unlearned*

A mid all the pomposity that surrounded the analysis of the 2007 credit crisis ("Capitalism is over!," "The American way is doomed!," "Hang anyone with a pinstriped suit!") it was easy to forget what had really happened, and what truly triggered the malaise. Simply put, a tiny bunch of guys and gals inside a handful of big financial institutions made hugely leveraged, often-complex, massively sized bets on the health of the (mostly U.S.) subprime housing market. In essence, the most influential financial firms out there bet the house on the likelihood that precariously underearning mortgage borrowers would honor their insurmountable liabilities. As the subprime market inevitably turned sour, those bets (on occasions many times larger than the firm's entire equity capital base) inevitably sank the punters, making some of them disappear, forcing others into mercy sales, and sending all into the comforting arms of a public bailout. As these global behemoths floundered, so did the financial system and thus the economy at large. Confidence evaporated, lending froze, and markets everywhere became uncontrollable chute-the-chutes. Investors lost their shirts, workers lost their jobs.

It wasn't a failure of capitalism or a reminder that perhaps we had forgone socialism a tad too prematurely (so far, we haven't yet heard calls for the rebuilding of the Berlin Wall). The crisis did not symbolize how rotten our system was. While certain bad practices were most certainly brought to the fore by the meltdown, and should be thoroughly corrected, the crisis did not symbolize the urgency of a drastic overhaul in the way we interact economically or politically. What the crisis truly stands for is the failure to prevent a tiny group of mortgage and derivatives bankers (I'm talking just a few hundred individuals here) from recklessly exposing their entities to the most toxic, unseemly, irresponsible of punts. The fact that Wall Street and the City of London were allowed to bet, via highly convoluted conduits, their very existence and survival on whether some folks from Alabama with no jobs, no income, and no assets would repay unaffordable, illgotten loans is the theme that should really matter, and not whether we should hastily resurrect Lenin. If capitalism was fine (overall) in May 2007, it should be just as fine today.

Rather than try to fix beyond recognition an arrangement that overall has served humanity quite well, why not focus on understanding what truly happened and on making sure that it can never happen again? If we don't address the heart of the matter, instead devoting all our time to distracting platitudes, we may be condemning ourselves to a repeat down the road. We surely don't want to go through this capitalism-doubting song and dance again five years from now, do we?

So the key questions throughout should have been: What really allowed those insanely reckless bets to take place? Several factors were and for the most part have continued to be held responsible for allowing this very specific mess to take place.

The conventional list of culprits typically has included the following key malfeasants: a less-than-perfect pay structure at banks, the use of deleteriously complex securities, asleep-at-the-wheel regulators, fraudulent mortgage practices, blindly greedy investors, and ridiculously off-target rating agencies. It is clear that each and every one of those factors played a substantial role and deserves a large share of the blame. But the familiar list has tended to leave out what I would categorize as the top miscreant. While the more conventionally acknowledged elements were definitely required, the carnage would not have reached such immense body count had that prominent, typically ignored, factor not been present. I put forth the contention that that one variable (a number, in fact) ultimately allowed the bets to be made and the crisis to happen.

That number is, of course, VaR. In its very prominent role as market risk measure around trading floors and, especially, the tool behind the determination of bank regulatory capital requirements for trading positions, VaR decisively aided and abetted the massive buildup of high-stakes positions by investment banks. VaR said that those punts, together with many other trading plays, were negligibly risky thus excusing their accumulation (any skeptical voice inside the banks could be silenced by the very low loss estimates churned out from the glorified model) as well as making them permissibly affordable (as the model concluded that very little capital was needed to support those market plays). Without those unrealistically insignificant risk estimates, the securities that sank the banks and unleashed the crisis would most likely not have been accumulated in such a vicious fashion, as the gambles would not have been internally authorized and, most critically, would have been impossibly expensive capital-wise.

Before banks could accumulate all the trading positions that they accumulated in a highly leveraged fashion, they needed permission to do so from financial regulators. Whether such leveraged trading is possible is up to the capital rules imposed by the policymakers. Capital rules for market risk (under which banks placed those nasty CDOs) were dictated by VaR. So by being so low ($50 million VaR out of a trading portfolio of $300 billion was typical), VaR ultimately allowed the destructive leverage.

Had trading decisions and regulatory policies been ruled by old-fashioned common sense, the toxic leverage that caused the crisis would not have been permitted, as it insultingly defied all prudent risk management. But with VaR ruling, things that should have never been okayed got the okay. By focusing only on mathematical gymnastics and historical databases, VaR turned common sense on its head and sanctioned much more risk and much more danger than would have been sanctioned absent the model. VaR can lie big time when it comes to assessing market exposures, unseemly categorizing the risky as risk-less and thus giving carte blanche to the no-holds-barred accumulation of the risky. By disregarding the fundamental, intrinsic characteristics of a financial asset, VaR can severely underestimate true risk, provid-ing the false sense of security that gives bankers the alibi to build huge portfolios of risky stuff and regulators the excuse to demand little capi-tal to back those positions. VaR allowed banks to take on positions and leverage that would otherwise not have been allowed. Those positions and that leverage killed the banks in the end.

Thus, we didn't need all that pomposity calling for all-out revolu-tion. What was, and continues to be, needed is to target the true, yet still wildly mysterious to most, decisive force behind the bloodshed and wholeheartedly reform the fields of financial risk management and bank capital regulation. The exile of VaR from financeland, not the nation-alization of economic activity or the dusting-off of *Das Kapital*, would have been the truly on-target, preventive, healing response to the mess.

And yet few (if any) commentators or gurus focused on VaR. You haven't seen the CNBC or Bloomberg TV one-hour special on the role of VaR in the crisis. This is quite puzzling: The model, you see, had already contributed to chaos before and had been amply warned about by several high-profile figures By blatantly ignoring VaR's role in past nasty system-threatening episodes as well as its inherent capacity for enabling havoc, the media made sure that the populace at large was kept unaware of how their economic and social stability can greatly depend on the dictates of a number that has been endowed with way too much power by the world's leading financiers and policymakers. VaR, in fact, may have been the greatest story never told.

■ ■ ■

Imagine that someone has just had a terrible accident driving a bright red Ferrari, perhaps while cruising along the South of France's coastline. Not only is the driver dead, but there were plenty of other casualties as the recklessly conducted vehicle crashed into a local market, at the busiest hour no less. The bloodbath is truly ghastly, prompting everyone to wonder what exactly happened. How could the massacre-inducing event have taken place? Who, or what, should be held primarily responsible? Public outrage demands the unveiling of the true culprit behind the mayhem.

After a quick on-site, postcrash check technicians discover that the Ferrari contained some seriously defective parts, which inevitable malfunctioning decisively contributed to the tragic outcome. So there you have it, many would instantly argue: The machine was based on faulty engineering. But wait, would counter some, should we then really put the blame on the car manufacturer? What about the auto inspectors, whose generously positive assessment of the vehicle's quality (deemed superior by the supposedly wise inspectors) decisively encouraged the reckless driver to purchase the four-wheeled beast? In this light, it might make sense to assign more blame onto the inspectors than on the manufacturers.

However, this is not the end of the story. Just because automobile inspectors attest to the superior craftsmanship of the Ferrari doesn't mean that you can just own it. While the (misguidedly, it turned out) enthusiastic backing by the inspectors facilitated the eventual matching of driver and car, it wasn't in itself enough. Necessary yes, but not sufficient. Unless the driver positively purchased the red beauty, he could never have killed all those people. And in order to own a Ferrari, you absolutely must pay for it first.

It turns out that our imaginary reckless conductor had not paid in cash for the car as by far he did not have sufficient funds, but had rather been eagerly financed by a lender. He had bought the Ferrari in a highly leveraged (i.e., indebted) way under very generous borrowing terms, being forced to post just a tiny deposit. Now, this driver had a record of headless driving, having been involved in numerous incidents. It appeared pretty obvious that one day he might cause some real trouble behind the wheel. And yet, his financiers more than happily obliged when it came time to massively enable the purchase of a powerfully charged, potentially very dangerous machine. Without such puzzlingly friendly treatment and support, the future murderer (and past malfeasant) would not have been able to afford the murder weapon.

Yes, he was obviously personally responsible for the accident. Yes, the manufacturing mistakes also played a decisive part. Yes, the okay from the inspectors mightily helped, too. All those factors were required for the fatality to occur. But, at the end of the day, none of that would have mattered one iota had the Ferrari not been bought. So if you are looking for a true culprit for the French seaside town massacre, indiscriminately point your finger at the irresponsible financiers that ultimately and improbably made possible the acquisition of the dysfunctional vehicle by the speed demon who, having trusted the misguidedly rosy expert assessment, inevitably took his own life and that of dozens of unsuspecting innocent bystanders.

This fictional story serves us to appreciate the perils of affording excessive leverage to purchase daring toys, and so to illustrate why the 2007 meltdown took place. If you substitute the reckless driver with investment banks, the red Ferrari with racy toxic securities, the auto inspectors with the credit rating agencies (Moody's, Standard & Poor's), and the eager financiers with financial regulators, then you get a good picture of the process that caused that very real terrible accident. In order for the wreckage to take place you obviously needed the wild-eyed bankers to make the ill-fated punts, the toxic mechanisms through which those punts were effected (you can't have a subprime CDO crisis without subprime mortgages and CDOs), and the overtly friendly AAA ratings (without such inexcusably generous soup letters the CDO business would not have taken flight as it did). But at the end of the day, the regulators allowed all that to matter explosively by sponsoring methodologies (VaR) that permitted banks to ride the trading roller coaster on the cheap, having to post up just small amounts of expensive capital while financing most of the punting through economical debt. Such generous terms resulted in a furious amalgamation of temptingly exotic assets. And when you gorge on such stuff in a highly indebted manner the final outcome tends to be a bloody financial crash.

If VaR had been much higher (thus better reflecting the risks faced by banks), the positions would have been smaller and/or safer. This was a subprime CDO crisis because VaR allowed banks to accumulate subprime CDOs very cheaply. Without the model, the capital cost of those intrinsically very risky securities would have been higher, making the system more robust.

Why exactly can sanctioning leveraged punting be so dangerous in the real financial world? What's so wrong with gearing? Why can an undercapitalized banking industry pose a threat to the world? In short: It is far easier for a bank to blow up fast if it's highly leveraged. Given how important and influential banks tend to be for a nation's economy, anything that makes it easier for banks to go under poses a dire threat to everyone. The bad thing about leverage is that it substantially magnifies the potential negative effects of bad news: Just a small reduction in value of the assets held by a bank may be enough to wipe out the institution. Conversely, the less leverage one has the more robust one is to darkish developments.

A bank's leverage can be defined as the ratio of assets over core equity capital (the best, and perhaps only true, kind of capital, essentially retained earnings plus shareholders' contributed capital). The difference between assets and equity are the bank's liabilities, which include its long-term and short-term borrowings. For a given volume of assets, the higher the leverage the less those assets are financed (or backed) by equity capital and the more they are financed by debt. That is, financial leverage indicates the use of borrowed funds, rather than invested capital, in acquiring assets. Regulated financial institutions face minimum capital requirements, in essence a cap on the maximum amount of leverage they can enjoy. A bank with $15 billion in capital may want to own $200 billion in assets, but if policy makers have capped leverage at 10 (i.e., a 10 percent capital charge across the board) the bank must either raise an additional $5 billion of capital (so that those $200 billion are backed by a $20 billion capital chest, keeping the leverage ratio at 10) or lower the size of its bet to $150 billion; under such regulatory stance, $15 billion can only buy you $150 billion of stuff. Were regulators to become more permissive, say increasing the maximum leverage ratio to 20 (from a 10 percent to a 5 percent minimum capital requirement), the bank could now own as much as $300 billion in assets without having to raise extra capital. It is clear that minimum capital rules will impact the size of a bank's balance sheet: If those rules are very accommodating, a lot of stuff will be backed by little capital (we'll see in a moment how accommodating a VaR-based rules system can be). VaR can easily lead to a severely undercapitalized banking industry; few things can create more economic and social problems than a severely undercapitalized banking industry.

If an entity has no equity it is said to be worth zero, as the value of its assets is equal to that of its liabilities (i.e., everything I own I owe). If assets go down in value, those losses must be absorbed by the equity side of the balance sheet (equity is actually defined as the over-all amount of an entity's loss-absorbing capital, or the maximum losses an entity can incur before it defaults on its liabilities); if those losses are severe, the entire equity base may be erased before there's time or chance to raise some more, leaving the bank insolvent. Therefore, the more equity capital (i.e., the less leverage), the more a bank can sustain and survive setbacks.

Shouldn't then banks try to finance their assets with as much equity as possible? After all, bank executives are supposed to be trying hard to preserve their firms' salubriousness. Well, it's not that simple. Banks, almost by definition, must run somewhat leveraged operations, oth-erwise making decent returns might be hard; after all, the prospect of such positive results is what attracts equity investors in the first place. At the same time, equity capital can be expensive (since equity inves-tors, unlike creditors, have no claims on a firm's assets and are first in line to absorb losses they would demand a greater rate of return) and inconvenient (as new shareholders dilute existing ones and may imply a redesign of the firm's board of directors) to raise, especially when debt financing is cheap and amply available. So banks will almost unavoidably have x amounts of equity backing several times x amounts of assets. Leverage, in other words, is part of banking life. Gearing needn't be destructive as a concept.

But if the size of the gearing and/or its quality get, respectively, too large or too trashy big problems could beckon. If a bank has $10 million in equity backing up $100 million in assets (a 10-to-1 lever-age ratio), a 1 percent drop in the value of the assets would eat away 10 percent of its equity, an ugly but possibly nonterminal occurrence. However, if those same $10 million had now to sustain $500 million in assets (50-to-1 gearing), for the same decrease in assets value the decline in equity would be 50 percent, a decidedly more brutal meltdown. The key question, naturally becomes: What's the chance that the assets will drop in value? If we believe it to be zero, then per-haps a higher leverage would be the optimal choice even for those banks most eager to run a safe and sound operation: If assets are not going to fall by even that modest 1 percent, I would rather go with the 50-to-1 ratio, as any increase in assets value will yield a greater return on equity (in this case, plus 50 percent versus plus 10 percent). Thus, if the assets being purchased are iron-clad guaranteed to never descend in worth, more gearing will be no more harmful, return-wise, than less gearing while offering more juice on the upside.

Leverage, in other words, can be a great deal when asset values go up all the time (or almost all the time) since for every increase in value, I get wonderful returns on capital. That is why banks often prefer a lot of leverage rather than just a little bit of it. It is obviously better to make 50 percent positive returns on capital than 10 percent positive returns on capital. Traders and their bosses get bigger bonuses when they are generating 50 percent returns on capital than when they are generating 10 percent, so building up massive leverage is a big temptation for them. VaR can be wonderful for those purposes, given how easy it is for the model to churn out very low capital requirements. But this only works fine if your trading portfolio is behaving well, otherwise the plus 50 percent bliss could quickly transform into a minus 50 percent nightmare.

Of course, in real life few assets (if any) come with a guarantee never to lose value. Since even the soundest-looking possibilities can be worth less, more leverage can be safely ruled as more daring than less of it, for a given asset portfolio. Having said that, the nature of the portfolio can also dictate whether the leverage ratio is prudent or not. Whether a larger leverage ratio will be a more harmful choice will depend on the quality of the asset side of the balance sheet. A 10-to-1 ratio can seem wisely conservative or recklessly wild, depending on what type of assets we're talking about. Illiquid, complex, toxic assets that can sink in value abruptly and very profoundly may render the $10 million cushion extremely insufficient, extremely rapidly. Relatively more trustworthy and liquid plays, like Microsoft stock or World Bank bonds, should (in principle) be more foreign to sudden debacles, rendering the $10 million grandiosely sufficient. In fact, a, say, 30-to-1 gearing ratio exclusively on standard assets may be considered a safer, more insolvency-proof capital structure than 10-to-1 gearing exclusively on toxic assets, as it could be deemed more likely to witness a 10 percent tumble in the weird stuff than a 3 percent decline in the vanilla stuff (of course, this cuts both ways: During good times, a rapid 10 percent rise in complex securities may be more feasible than a 3 percent vanilla uplift, which is naturally why the nasty stuff can be so tempting).

Naturally, the very worst thing would be a higher leverage structure comprised largely of high-stakes punts; essentially, a recipe for sure disaster. Encouraged and enabled by the low equity requirements sanctioned by VaR and other tools as well as by the very economical access to short-term credit, most of the world's leading financial institutions spent the first years of the twenty-first century hard at work arriving at such a perilous state of affairs. Banking leverage was not invented by VaR; it existed before the model showed up. Not even very large leverage was invented by VaR (in the pre-VaR days, the rules essentially allowed banks to build unlimited leverage on debt securities issued by developed countries, an asset class that, as more recent events have showcased is not exactly devoid of problems). But VaR did signify a revolutionary, potentially very chaotic development, pertaining to banking gearing: thanks to VaR, vast leverage on vastly toxic assets was now possible, something that the pre-VaR financial police did not allow.

■ ■ ■

The mayhem that officially started in the summer of 2007 was the inevitable result of a regulatory structure that had allowed too many influential players to afford too many financial Ferraris too cheaply. For the past 15 years or so, worldwide financial institutions (to a greater or lesser degree) have enjoyed extremely generous financing terms from the markets' policemen whose job description supposedly includes the safeguarding of the system. The rules have actively encouraged wild leveraged punting, and not just on semi-safe assets like government bonds (the Volvos of finance) but also on impossibly exotic, accident-prone stuff. Negligible regulatory capital requirements were demanded from banks in years prior to the meltdown when it came to obviously lethal assets, both trading-related and credit-related; and given how easy and economical it was to obtain borrowed funds, bankers found it irresistibly convenient to load up on subprime CDOs and other trading stuff. Without the humongous losses suffered on such largesse, there would have been no farewell funerals for Bear Stearns, Lehman Brothers, or Merrill Lynch. In other words, no real crisis.

How can we be so sure that the regulatory measures abetted bankers' ferociously enthusiastic embarking on the leverage express, which eventual derailment sank the world? Among other things, because the numbers dictate so. The proof, if you want, is in the pudding. As of August 31, 2007, for instance, the $400 billion–strong asset side of Bear Stearns balance sheet contained $141 billion in financial instruments, $56 billion of which were mortgage-related. All those billions were supported by just $13 billion in equity. That means that at the outset of the crisis, Bear was leveraged more than 30 times over (the ratio for November 2006 was pretty similar). Or consider Lehman Brothers. As of May 31, 2007, $21 billion supported $605 billion in assets, half of which were of the financial instruments variety ($80 billion mortgage-related). Similarly, on September 31, 2007, Merrill Lynch's balance sheet showed $1 trillion in assets ($260 billion trading assets, $56 billion mortgage-related, $22 billion subprime residential-related) on top of just $38 billion of equity. That's three for three so far when it comes to Wall Street powerhouses leveraged 30 times, with trading positions outnumbering equity by around 10 to 1, and with mortgage positions (including very nasty stuff) by themselves way above the entire equity capital base. If losses exceeded just 3 percent of assets value, the entire equity cushion would be gone and the firm would collapse; given how many of those assets were suspect and how low the value of suspect assets can go in a short period of time, it seems clear that those Wall Street giants were sitting on dynamite.[1]

But wait, there's more. Swiss giant UBS was on September 28, 2007, the proud owner of assets worth $2.2 trillion ($39 billion in U.S. subprime residential-related garbage, $20 billion of which were mega-toxic CDO tranches), backed by $42 billion of equity. That's right, the Helvetian entity had not only been allowed to gear itself 50 times over, but, apparently not content with such feat alone, had decided to make bets for an amount equal to its whole equity base on the likelihood that a bunch of poorly employed, income-challenged, assets-deprived faraway Americans would repay their (mostly ill-gotten) unaffordably inflated home loans.

Even the most notorious white-shoe legends incurred in geared action. As of November 2007, Goldman Sachs' $42 billion equity base shouldered $452 billion of trading assets ($1.1 trillion total assets). Coincidentally in time, Morgan Stanley's $31 billion equity capital resourcefulness carried the burden of $375 billion in financial instruments ($1 trillion total).

It is abundantly clear that banks had become amply leveraged, overall. But it gets worse. Those figures don't reflect the vast gearing that was allowed specifically for trading games. The prior analysis reflects banks' equity levels as a whole. Capital charges for market risk-specific were far smaller preceding the crisis, making the leverage experienced on trading activities alone sordidly unbounded, way beyond the already highly geared ratios implied by the all-encompassing (trading assets plus all other kinds of assets) above data. That is, the leverage enjoyed by investment banks on their trading activities (usually their riskiest activities by far) was immensely larger than those overall, by themselves headline-grabbing 30-to-1 ratios.

The Bank for International Settlements (BIS; the Switzerland-based central bank for international central bankers) studied the trading-specific capitalization prowess of a group of banks for 2007 and found that although trading assets accounted for between 27 percent and 57 percent of total assets, trading risk capital only constituted between 4 percent and 11 percent of total capital requirements (and yes, the bank with 57 percent of its possessions into trading was the one boasting the gargantuan 4 percent trading/total capital ratio). In other words, capital requirements against trading books (precisely where asset growth was taking place, and where the toxic waste was mostly being laid) were extremely light compared to those for (in principle, more solid) banking books. In further words, required trading book capital was obscenely insignificant, morbidly inadequate. And (hold on to your seats), the BIS found that market risk capital requirements as a percentage of total trading assets were in the range of between 0.1 percent and 1.1 percent (only one of the banks had posted capital in excess of 1 percent of all its trading positions).[2] Yes, that would be between 1,000-times leverage and 100-times leverage. If assets go down by just 1 percent or even by just 0.1 percent the capital allocated to those trading positions would be wiped out. Pretty leveraged, if you ask me.

Especially when a lot of those trading assets are junk, as (thanks to yet more permissive regulation) banks had been parking billions and billions of dollars in subprime CDOs and related securities inside their VaR-ruled trading books (as opposed to inside their banking books, where as credit-related illiquid positions they truly belonged; capital requirements for trading books have traditionally been assumed to be lower than for banking books).

By crowning VaR as the capital-charge king, financial policy makers pretty much assured banks that they could, very economically and basically worry-free, fool around with even the most adventurous of financial fare. That VaR can produce tiny capital charges, and thus encourages and affords risk-taking beyond common sense, is borne out by the numbers exposed above. VaR demanded only $1 or even just $0.1 for every $100 in trading assets that a bank would want to accumulate; it is clear that the model can make it extremely easy for massive risks to be taken on in an incredibly unprotected manner. VaR allowed banks to expose themselves to being blown up if their positions went down by less than 1 percent. That is, VaR made it essentially certain that those banks would blow up. Prevalent regulatory rules for trading-related capital requirements resulted in massive speculative gearing up to the 2007–2008 massacre. VaR was the prevalent regulatory rule. VaR, thus, resulted in massive speculative gearing.

And as was just said, the resultant leverage ratios on illiquid complex assets alone may be deemed intolerably reckless. As famed fund manager David Einhorn put it,[3] if Bear Stearns' only business was to have $29 billion of illiquid, hard-to-mark assets, supported by its entire $10.5 billion of tangible equity that by itself would be an aggressive, very risky strategy; were the high-risk positions to sink they could well lose half their value (or even all of it: toxic financial stuff has been known to be worth zero on occasions), wiping out the bank's capital. But on top of all that, that sliver of equity also had to support an extra $366 billion of other assets, making it essentially improbable that the firm could survive even the slightest of setbacks. That is, a tool that allows you to accumulate illiquid exotic assets three times over your entire equity capital resources would be dangerous already; one that lets you add 12 times that in other financial stuff is lethally permissive. A ticking time bomb, patiently waiting to detonate a casualties-infested bloodbath.

As 2006 ended and 2007 approached, Merrill Lynch and Lehman Brothers had one-day 95 percent VaR of $50 million, while Bear Stearns disclosed a 95 percent VaR of $30 million. Regulatory capital requirements were roughly defined as 10-day 99 percent VaR multiplied by a factor of three, which (again roughly) would imply multiplying one-day VaR by 9. That would be the amount of capital that would have to be committed by the banks. Let's say, roughly, $470 million in the cases of Merrill and Lehman, $280 million in the case of Bear Stearns. Merrill at the time owned $203 billion of on-balance-sheet trading assets, Lehman $226 billion, and Bear $125 billion. $1 billion equals $1,000 million. This would yield market risk capital requirements equal to 0.23 percent, 0.21 percent, and 0.22 percent of total trading assets respectively. Am I the only one who would categorize such cushions as insufferably small? Certainly, my off-the-cuff calculations are bound to be less than exact, but it is interesting to note that even if we doubled the nominal size of those capital requirements the trading-specific leverage ratio would be remarkably in line with the results outlined in the BIS study highlighted earlier. Even if we doubled them again, none of the three institutions would have presented, barely six months before the unleashing of the mayhem, market-specific capital charges of at least 1 percent of (on-balance-sheet) trading positions. I think this is again more than enough to allow us to say that VaR wildly erred on the side of excessive gearing.

We can do similar calculations for other banks. Take UBS, for instance. In June 2007, the venerable European institution was the proud owner of CHF950 billion in on-balance sheet trading assets, backed by a 10-day 99 percent VaR of CHF455 million.[4] Let's then do the math once more: This yields a capital requirement of (again, roughly) CHF1.365 billion, or 0.14 percent of total trading assets. Want to double that number, just to be on the safe side and correct for any unacceptably erroneous calculating on my part? Okay, let's say 0.28 percent of total trading assets. That would still be an awful lot of leverage, wouldn't it? Especially when UBS at the time had accumulated truly vast amounts of subprime junk in its trading book. Just like at many of UBS's peers, VaR was allowing unheard-of-before gearing on portfolios containing unheard-of-before amounts of financial trash.

Or take Citigroup. Its December 31, 2006, one-day VaR was $98 million, measured over trading assets worth $394 billion. Thus the corresponding rough capital charge of $882 million would amount to only 0.22 percent of trading positions. Clearly, trading books all around had been allowed to gear themselves up enormously. Thanks to VaR's permissiveness, the area where banks kept the riskiest and wildest stuff had been allowed to operate essentially with no capital. VaR's insultingly low estimations permitted banks to play the trading game almost for free, precisely at the time when such entertainment was becoming both more voluminous and dangerous than ever before.

Would a thinking person have considered 100-to-1, 500-to-1, or 1,000-to-1 leverage on trading portfolios loaded up with nasty subprime securities prudent? Of course not. It would not have been allowed.

Given how dominant the trading division had become inside banks, an extremely leveraged trading book naturally translates into an overall extremely leveraged banking industry, translating into an extremely fragile financial, economic, and social system. Now we better understand why the banks had large total leverage ratios. VaR was simply too little relative to trading assets, leading to very humble VaR-total assets ratios. For instance, the 2007 year-end levels of that ratio for JP Morgan, Citigroup, and Goldman Sachs were, respectively, 0.006 percent, 0.007 percent, and 0.012 percent. The 2008 year-end levels, with VaR figures that had gone considerably up due to the setbacks and turbulence caused by the financial meltdown, the ratios were still just between 0.015 percent and 0.016 percent for JP and Citi and 0.028 percent for Goldman. While the trading component of a bank's overall activities was increasingly sizeable, trading added little to the overall capital pot. By year-end 2007, the contribution of regulatory VaR to total equity capital was 0.75 percent at JP Morgan, 1.30 percent at Citigroup, and 2.93 percent at Goldman.[5] The corresponding figures for UBS and Merrill Lynch as of late September 2007 were 3.66 percent and 2.02 percent. Not too high, right? Particularly, again, given how much smelly mortgage-related stuff these and other firms held as market assets (on December 31, 2007, Citigroup held $40 billion in gross subprime CDO tranches, which it kept in its trading book; one year later the exposure was still sizeable at $19 billion. UBS and

Merrill Lynch held similar amounts). It seems obvious that the contribution of the trading book to the overall equity base was negligible, completely out of tune with how big and how daring those trading activities were. Something funny was definitely going on inside those trading books, something that was very unrealistically saying that the stuff inside them was nothing to be worried about and therefore nothing that warranted even a mildly decent capital cushion against. Balance sheets across Wall Street and the City of London had a lot of toxic waste because VaR made it very cheap to have toxic waste.

Once you have let the toxic leverage dynamite in, you are doomed. You've irremediably poisoned yourself. Once that junk inevitably takes a dive, you are a goner, fast. If you have financed a lot of trading bets with a lot of very short-term debt and very little equity as soon as your bets turn a bit sour no one believes you can save yourself and your very short-term financing lines are rashly cut off, instantly preventing you from surviving as a going concern. And that is precisely why VaR can be so destructive as a capital-charge setter. A VaR-less system would have essentially forbidden the billionaire trading orgy, as much more capital would have been required to back up such unbounded speculating, especially in the case of the smelliest assets. Once those billions found a home inside Wall Street's institutions, the game was up. The tiny capital cushions could not even begin to cope with the precipitous fall in value of those punts. VaR opened the gates to the destructive stuff. It let it in. That's what sealed our fate, and the pre-VaR universe would not have allowed it.

Institutions with the power to ignite global tremors (the kind that result in bankrupt companies and lost jobs all over the world) played for several years a game of Russian roulette, with the gun loaded with not just one but several bullets, manufactured in the famously lethal subprime mortgage factory. VaR allowed them to rabidly imitate Christopher Walken's suicidal character in *The Deer Hunter*, by making sure that the gun and the ammo would be affordably economical. The fate of the globe was left in the hands of a clique of traders that were given unfettered permission to gamble our well-being on the (implausible) chance that the CDO gun would not fire. VaR made that happen, by persistently denying that the gun contained any bullets. Akin to Robert DeNiro telling his pal Walken to go ahead and keep pulling the trigger in that last movie scene at the shady Asian parlor; go ahead, shoot, there's no risk.

■ ■ ■

Even without hard cold numerical evidence, we could have easily guessed that VaR would have a weakness toward tiny capital figures and risk estimates. Besides the empirical evidence, we would have conceptual backing. VaR's structural foundations dictate that the concoction would tend to disappoint those with a predisposition for conservative risk management. It is very likely that VaR, by design, will tend to underestimate true risk.

First, and for the umpteenth time, VaR heavily borrows from historical data. This is particularly true in the case of possibly the two most popular methods for calculating VaR, so-called *Historical Simulation* and *Covariance*. Historical Simulation, which became the favorite of banks leading up to the crisis, literally simulates how a current portfolio would have behaved during a preselected past period and builds estimation of future losses based on those results. As simple as that. It's interesting to note that while VaR was promoted and embraced by bankers and regulators largely due to its perceived sophistication and high-tech engineering, in the end, the number was calculated with the simplest, most rudimentary of methods: Take a look at a database of past market prices and manually select the worst loss that took place; not a lot of high-tech sophistication there. Covariance was the original methodology and is much more mathematically and computationally intensive, and also resorts to past market data for the purposes of estimating the future volatilities of and correlations between the portfolio's components. If during the selected sample market volatility was tame and the presence of extreme negative events was limited or nonexistent, then the risk estimates and the amount of required capital churned out from the model will be in accordance with such an apparently placid environment, that is, a pretty lenient number. If the past was calm, VaR will be tiny. Of course, the opposite holds true: sometimes VaR may be quite large rather than quite low; in fact sometimes VaR may be overestimating real risk, for instance if the market for certain otherwise sound securities just experienced nastiness; so the true problem with VaR is not that it will perennially underestimate risks but rather that it is very easy for VaR to underestimate risks, in particular those of the intrinsically most risky assets; VaR will not always understate upcoming danger, but as long as VaR is around there's a big chance that upcoming danger will be understated.

In finance, the past behavior of an asset and the true riskiness of that asset need not be perfectly correlated. Just because an asset behaved well during a certain past period doesn't mean it will always behave well. Many times, an apparently well-behaving asset suddenly becomes much naughtier and losses ensue "unexpectedly." In fact, and as anticipated earlier in the book, it could be said that, conditional on existing, highly risky assets will only present a rosy past. Given the nature of those plays, they just don't tumble a bit in value if a market correction takes place. Rather, they sink all the way to zero and are never traded again. So those daring assets are either worth a lot (as a bubble in them is created and sustained) or nothing (as the bubble inevitably blows up). VaR would analyze those positions and proclaim that everything is fine, based on the rosy performance. But in reality, the trades couldn't be more dangerous. A clear example of how the model can hide true risk. In abiding by historical financial evidence, VaR follows a mischievous and untrustworthy guide. Blinded by what happened yesterday, VaR can be very deceitful about real risk. In markets, the rearview mirror often lies about what lays ahead.

Even if the past did contain tumultuousness, who is to say that such agitation would be a good predictor of future, yet-to-be-seen, perhaps doubly (or more) agitated developments? Financial markets are simply dominated by monstrous rare events for which there tends to be little historical precedent, so chances are that when such freakish events present themselves capital levies calculated by looking at the past would be rendered exceedingly inadequate.

In the run-up to summer 2007, markets had been trotting along calmly (recall, for instance, the notorious, widely reported, death of volatility in years prior? Or the never-ending mentions to the "great moderation"?), making sure that VaR would be very small. VaR was saying, "There's no risk!," all the while letting banks accumulate as much risk as possible. When VaR declares the nonexistence of future risk the opposite may well be true, courtesy of VaR's very declaration.

VaR would not only be lying (by denying the existence of present danger) but would itself have created the lie (by encouraging the trades that guarantee that the future will not be as tame as the past). A low VaR can help fuel a trading bubble through the complacency, false sense of security, and humble capital requirements that such modest number enables; by denying the existence of risk, the glorified risk radar can create risk out of thin air, making VaR a tool that can transform tranquility into chaos.

Secondly, the probabilistic foundations on which the tool typically rests don't assign large odds to the extreme materializing out there (while the Covariance method does assume Normality, the Historical Simulation method doesn't make any initial assumption as to the portfolio's probability distribution; rather, it lets the market reveal its "true" distribution through its past behavior). By endowing VaR with Normality, the tool's engineers condemned it to being unrealistically small. Financial markets are simply not Normal, and extreme moves and big losses take place quite a lot and quite severely. The Normality straightjacket introduces two highly suspect statistical parameters into the calculation: standard deviation (or "sigma") and correlation. Sigma is supposed to measure turbulence in a given asset, and correlation is supposed to measure co-movement between different assets. But these variables are in themselves calculated by looking at the rearview mirror, and so will only reflect upcoming chaos and joint dependencies accurately if those statistical siblings display the same behavior going forward as they did before. However, time after time, the markets behave in a rebellious nonstationary fashion: what was volatile (timid) yesterday can well be timid (volatile) tomorrow, what moved together (disparately) yesterday can well move disparately (together) tomorrow. This is, by the way, what took place before the credit crisis. The statistical guidance on which VaR is built was again proven to be less than worthy, precisely at the time when such steering was most urgently needed.

Naturally, it doesn't take a genius to understand that a tool based on "the past is prologue" and "Normality rules" can't deserve to be considered inalterably trustworthy. Many may have been fully aware of VaR's deficient foundations but chose to keep their doubts to themselves as they had more to gain from the preservation of VaR as a relevant tool. Bankers have been basically allowed to calculate their VaR in any way they wanted, using as much past data as they see fit, employing the mathematical trickeries of their choice, and even choosing which financial assets should be included in the calculation. Essentially, a bank's VaR will be whatever that bank wants it to be. And the temptation to have a VaR as low as possible can be difficult to fight: For many financiers, more leverage and more risk-taking can be the path to untold quick riches. So what do you do? You can search for the most favorable historical time period: If the past two years contain too much volatility you may want to also borrow from the three years prior, which happened to be quite sunny and tranquil, so as to compensate and obtain an overall sample that will paint the desired not-too-turbulent picture that can yield a not-too-abundant VaR. Or you can search for the most desirable combination of assets that happen to display the right type of historical correlation (i.e., no or negative co-movements) that, through the diversification effects allowed by the model, can deliver a tamed VaR. Definitely another strong argument for concluding that VaR will tend to be too low. And bank leverage and risk-taking, thus, a tad too overextended.

To illustrate the reductions in overall VaR (and thus in risk estimates and capital charges) that the use of correlation can yield, take a look at the table below, which indicates asset-specific and firmwide VaR levels for Merrill Lynch at several dates.

(dollars in millions)

	Sept. 28, 2007	June 29, 2007	Dec. 29, 2006	High 3Q07	Low 3Q07	Daily Average 3Q07	Daily Average 2Q07	Daily Average 2006
Trading Value-at-Risk[1]								
Interest rate and credit spread	66	48	48	77	55	63	61	48
Equity	27	36	29	47	13	27	31	19
Commodity	17	21	13	25	17	20	20	11
Currency	5	5	3	11	3	6	4	4
Subtotal	115	110	93			116	116	82
Diversification benefit	(33)	(39)	(41)			(40)	(39)	(32)
Overall	82	71	52	92	60	76	77	50

[1] Based on a 95% confidence level and a one-day holding period.

As can be seen, overall VaR can be reduced by almost 50 percent as a result of including in the calculation estimated co-movements among asset families (what Merrill called "diversification benefits"). Where do those diversification figures come from? Historical evidence. Here is Merrill's literal justification for enjoying a sharply reduced final VaR: *"The aggregate VaR for our trading portfolios is less than the sum of the VaRs for individual risk categories because movements in different risk categories occur at different times and, historically, extreme movements have not occurred in all risk categories simultaneously."*[6] But what if the future betrays the (selective) past and asset families that were not supposed to move together begin to naughtily move together? What if assets that were not supposed to move againts Merrill at the same time begin to move against Merrill at the same time? Then the correlation argument would have turned out to be a hoax, a conduit to hiding true risk, and to produce undercapitalized banks incapable of coping with real danger when it materializes.

If you think about it, the entire notion of basing bank regulation and risk management practices on the arbitrary personal selection of a bunch of historical data is childish, and prone to generate dangerously silly results in areas that are anything but child-play. To base outcomes as critical as bank capital and bank risk-taking on whether, say, two or six years of data are selected is astonishingly short-sighted. Keep in mind that you could achieve VaR numbers that are completely different based on the chosen sample: The two-year VaR may be twice or half as big as the six-year VaR, thus giving rise to twice or half as big leverage and risk taking. But nothing about the bank or its trading portfolio or the markets or the economic environment has changed one bit. Just because someone arbitrarily decides to calculate VaR with two years or with six years of data doesn't mean that more or less leverage or more or less risk should be automatically welcomed. Whether X amount of leverage and X amount of risk are acceptable or not should depend on more robust fundamental analysis, not on the arbitrary technicalities of a statistical analysis. Let's illustrate with an example.

Imagine that you are using the Historical Simulation method. If you select the past six years, the 99th percentile loss was $50 million, but if you select just the past two years the 99th percentile loss was $1 million. So what do you do if you want much lower capital requirements? You select two years and churn out the much lower VaR. Just like that, by simply making the internal voluntary decision of using two years of data, a bank is allowed to be immensely more (50 times more) leveraged on its trading portfolio. Just like that, trading desks are allowed to accumulate lots more positions. As a result of those capricious decisions, the system becomes much more leveraged and exposed, thus much more prone to accidents. Nothing else has taken place that would justify such increase in danger. All that has occurred is that a few risk managers inside a handful of big institutions have selected more or less cells in their historical price data Excel spreadsheets. Is that an adult and responsible way to determine factors as influential as bank capital and bank risk? Why not leave it all to coin-tossing? "How much leverage should the banking industry enjoy? How much risk should banks take on? Uh, let me see. . . . Heads we use two years of data to get VaR; tails we use six years of data. Flip it up!" Call me crazy, but I suspect there must be sounder approaches to dealing with issues that affect the lives of millions around the globe.

I personally learned of the flakiness of making financial estimations based on past data more than a decade ago, when I was trying to build a VaR system for a corporate treasury department. All the quantitative technicalities, all the advanced statistical indoctrination stopped to matter about one minute after I opened the spreadsheet containing all the historical price series. A decidedly much more plebeian, much less scientific issue took center stage: How much data, exactly, should I use to get the volatility, the correlations, the loss percentiles? Two years? Five? Ten? The myriad of technical documents and books piled on my desk and of quantitative risk management lectures attended ceased to matter one iota. High-minded considerations of probability distributions and econometric models were suddenly swept aside. At the end of the day, and when confronted with the inescapably practical decision of how to actually arrive at a VaR number, the only thing that truly mattered was how far down I should drag my computer mouse so that the Excel column housing the past data used for the calculation would contain more or fewer cells. Should I drag it down a lot or stop midway? Whether I went one way or another, I began to notice, my results could be excruciatingly different: Based on how I operated my mouse, my company's interest rate risk could be $100 million or $35 million or $234 million. This made no sense to me. After all, my company's exposure to interest rates should be a fixed quantity (whatever that was), not a roller coaster that goes up by 100 percent or down by 50 percent based simply on my capricious dragging of the cell selection. How can my company's perceived risk, and thus the perceived appropriateness of its policies, ultimately depend entirely on how many Excel cells I arbitrarily feel like selecting? I began to wonder how the big boys were dealing with this. I realized that far from laughing at such flakiness, they seemed to take the data selection thing quite seriously. I found that different banks used different rules: One went for two years of data, another for five years, and so on. I was perplexed. Why two years? Why five years? What's the basis for such decisions? I now knew that said selection could yield completely differing risk estimates, so why even attempt to follow such fishy guidance? Historical counsel can be such an unreliable grey area that perhaps it would be much better to not rely on it too much.

When presenting my VaR calculations, I was left with no option but to illustrate several possible scenarios, based on several different data selections (I wasn't pretentious enough to assume that I could precisely select a single unalterably superior period with perfect forecasting powers, even if such thing existed at all). My bosses received several, widely different, risk estimates. They, too, grew skeptical of the results. I don't think they fully bought into the "scientificness" of modern risk modeling.

In essence, by basing banks' trading decisions and regulatory capital requirements on past market behavior, the fate of the system was determined by how far down risk managers felt like dragging their computer mouse. How's that for a rigorous, solid structure?

Having a regulatory capital measure that is calculated by looking at the data rearview mirror can be a uniquely permissive enabler not only of overall leverage, but in particular of toxic leverage. For here is where the cost savings in terms of capital can become incredibly large with respect to a VaR-less, fundamentals-based regulatory system. When it comes to vanilla financial plays, VaR can still likely result in sizably reduced capital charges, but the play may nonetheless still have been put on under the more conservative alternative policy: If you want to accumulate standard assets, the pre-VaR capital requirement (based on rather commonsensical assessments of an asset's intrinsic and fundamental riskiness) would still have been relatively permissible (in fact, some government bonds were assigned a capital charge of 0 percent, a feat that not even the most generously accommodating VaR figure may be able to accomplish). So the punt on, say, bonds issued by an Italian bank would likely still have happened, even if perhaps in less substantial volumes than under a VaR system, as the latter may deliver a number below the 1.6 percent mandatory charge (20 percent risk weight times the 8 percent minimum mandatory capital levy) that was typical for claims on developed countries' banks under the old, so-called *Basel I*, international bank capital regulatory regime. Even if VaR-based figures would at times have allowed cheaper punting on vanilla assets, the older methods possibly were permissive enough to not entirely deter trading in those assets. Large-scale vanilla speculation by banks did not necessarily have to wait for VaR to show up.

But the same can't be said about nonstandard punts. Here, the old policies were quite taxing, reflecting among other things the need to make sure that obviously riskier stuff should demand more cushiony capital backing than obviously safer stuff. Anything too exotic was made very expensive capital-wise by the regulators. If you were a bank in the pre-VaR days, it was tough for you to fool around with adventurous fare, forcing you to either limit the size of those nonvanilla bets or to raise tons of additional capital, which may be costly or even well nigh impossible. In this case, the older methods did most possibly act as strict deterrent, preventing the accumulating of too many weird securities.

Once VaR showed up, things changed drastically. Since VaR has no idea whether an asset is intrinsically daring or not, it does not discriminate between asset families and can't place those families in different risk buckets according to fundamentals. VaR can't say outright that Treasury Bonds should automatically be cheaper than complex mortgage derivatives. VaR doesn't know what a Treasury Bond is. All VaR knows are blips of historical data, thus leveling the field for all types of securities, no matter their obvious intrinsic differences. Given that it is certainly not impossible for toxic securities to have behaved more placidly than sounder ones during a specific period of time, it is certainly possible for VaR to dictate that the former should require less capital commitment; and recall that the most toxic assets may always have low VaRs as long as they are trading. So a system based on past market data rather than fundamental analysis will structurally declare the most risky plays risk-free. If you can find a complex asset that happens to have enjoyed recent calm (and/or the right correlations with the other assets in your portfolio), VaR will allow you to trade it in a much more leveraged fashion than the preexisting system would. VaR can make the difference between not being able to afford exotic plays at all and being able to afford monstrous amounts of them.

This is most likely a side effect of VaR that did not go on unacknowledged by at least some of the original VaR-promoters within financial institutions; in fact, that has most likely continued to not go unrecognized through the years. Toxic leverage can be the most desirable kind for many a trader, as few things can lead to greater and faster profits and returns on equity than accumulating higher-yielding positions on borrowed money. The unique comparative advantage of VaR for traders is that it makes that kind of leverage possible; alternative risk methodologies, in sharp contrast, made it utterly impossible. The temptations that VaR makes uniquely possible can in fact be so irresistible that it may seduce bankers into creating bubbles on all kinds of convoluted funny-looking securities: Since toxic leverage can be so easy, why not make sure that the market value of that toxic stuff goes up and up and up and so reap enormous short-term rewards from our hugely geared positions? If VaR lets you accumulate, say, $100 billion in complex securities backed up by just, say, $1 billion in regulatory capital that's a great thing because the market value of said illiquid trades is (in good times, at least) controlled by you and a few other firms, and all you have to do is consensually decide that the stuff is worth 1 percent more for your returns to be a whopping 100 percent. So VaR may end up encouraging the development and pushing of less-than-sound financial products.

Is that a good thing?

■ ■ ■

It is critical to note that VaR can (and did) cause trouble via multiple conduits. Inconveniently smallish capital requirements for trading activities are not the only possible deleterious by-product of the model. It can contribute to havoc-wreaking by just playing its origi-nally conceived role, the part that it was intended to act since the very beginning, before policy makers picked it up and adopted it for regula-tory purposes. In other words, VaR can hurt us by simply being VaR. You see, VaR was not initially invented as capital-charge setter. That came later, as financial mandarins became irremediably infatuated. VaR was, and of course still is, designed as a measure of market risk, proba-bilistically speaking. VaR was invented so that bank executives could be told how much money they could lose, say, 99 percent or 95 per-cent of the time, according to the model's assumptions. That num-ber (e.g., $100 million) tells you the maximum market-related setback that you will experience, say, 99 or 95 days out of 100 (the confidence level can be whatever the user wants; 99 percent and 95 percent levels are the norm, with the former typically delivering a higher VaR figure than the latter). Or, more important, tells you that only on, say, 1 day or 5 days out of a 100 you will lose more than $100 million, without going so far as indicating the size of that isolated negative development (though, as we've seen, the model's engineering dictates that odds are that it won't be exceedingly large). Of course, "will experience" and "will lose" become truisms only if the model's underlying assumptions hold true out there in real-life finance.

VaR was then invented to measure in monetary terms what can happen to your trading positions, probabilistically speaking. Bank CEOs worried about the enhanced levels of their (increasingly com-plex, increasingly larger) market exposures apparently found such neatly presented numbers useful, and gave their quantitative analysts carte blanche to play with their VaR toys. And that's how VaR became, some 20 years ago, the worldwide market risk radar de rigueur. Inside Goldman Sachs, Morgan Stanley, JP Morgan, Deutsche Bank, Barclays, and the like, trading decisions began to be subjected to what VaR said, and with the rise of VaR came the general rise of financial risk man-agement as both executives and quants fully bought into the assuaging certainties that the model promised. It is no exaggeration to say that the advent of VaR produced revolutionary changes within the financial industry. Nothing would ever be the same.

VaR's impact as imperial risk beacon has not been neutral. By endowing VaR with acceptability, bankers gave VaR the power to affect their own actions, and therefore market activity in general. By judging trades (and traders) based on their VaR figures, by setting trading limits based on VaR, and by describing your exposures to the outer world via the VaR lenses, financiers allowed a stranger to influence their play and, most poignantly, all economic participants (many of whom, naturally, would not be expected to have a clue as to what that VaR thing is and how it works). Such influence can't be counted on to be magnanimous for two main reasons. One, by attempting to measure that (financial markets) which is not amenable to quantification, VaR encourages the development of misplaced confidence and an unfettered faith in complacency-building "precision." Clearly, those would not count as the strongest of foundations for financial decision making. With VaR, you may think that you know something about the future, but all you have is a description of the past (a subjectively selected subset, to boot) mixed in with inappropriate probabilistic assumptions. VaR's presumptuously precise take on future risks is bound to be woefully misleading. In the name of soothing concreteness, financial players (and their stakeholders) would be given a map replete with falsehoods. Second, its natural tendency to be unrealistically low and to hide true danger encourages reckless, even deceitful wild risk-taking, and can cause untold volatility both as the VaR–aided bubble collapses and as a result of forced (and typically en masse) liquidations directly mandated by VaR.

It is straightforward to understand how VaR can, besides its role as determiner of the capital cushion, encourage excessive risk-taking. If you are a punter, you may love nothing more than being able to collect rich returns (in the short term, at least) while giving the impression of running a robustly riskless operation. You are making good money in an apparently wholesome way. You are a hero inside the dealing room, and you are paid accordingly. Your trading limits are expanded. You make yet more money. You love your life.

How can VaR help you achieve such state of rapture? Easy. Just scour the financial world for assets that have the following attributes: (1) they are to a greater or lesser extent "trashy," and thus offer a good return; (2) they have enjoyed little volatility and negligible setbacks in the recent past; (3) you can attach some story to them, some feel-good argument for justifying your choice ("selling pet food online is the new paradigm," "Russia can't default," and "solid as house prices" are known to have been used at one point or another). It is not exactly impossible to find such golden combinations; plenty of nonstandard markets have enjoyed prolonged days in the sun throughout history. VaR, per attribute #2, will testify in court as to the Fort Knox–like safeness of the punt, and everything else will follow. When the glorified number claims to see no danger, who's to argue with such wisdom? "Punt, punt, punt!" would utter your bosses and your risk managers. Keep printing those risk-free profits.

Soon, many of your colleagues, jealously eyeing your fattened bank account, replicate your strategy. So do some of your rivals at enemy firms. Suddenly, VaR has helped you create a bull market in your chosen exotic product. As other traders join the bandwagon, values go up, and complacency gets further enhanced. The prospect of a surprise gets further diminished. VaR goes down, becoming even smaller. Yet more cash is showered on the punt, all across the Street.

Naturally, the fact that VaR says there's no risk does not eliminate real risk from the picture. Financial institutions in effect become concurrently exposed, in huge amounts, to a drop in the value of an asset of suspect fundamental soundness, notwithstanding its placid recent past. A monstrous bubble is created, but VaR is conveniently hiding the potential for trouble. VaR is in effect a risk-management device that can decisively contribute to creating, not controlling, risk. VaR's low numbers can be used as an alibi to initially take on the exposures and can add fuel to the fire progressively as more and more participants are attracted to the apparently-risk-lite high-return party.

The presence of VaR in finance can lead very influential and sizable players to own exactly the same positions, not only because they would all face the same VaR-stamped encouragement (if a bank can find an asset or group of assets with a placid past and accommodating correlations, so can all the other banks) but also due to the self-feeding effect that a VaR-based trading architecture can give rise to: A low VaR (especially in the case of an exotic play) will generate interest from traders in the asset and will make complacent risk officers and executives okay the trades, driving up the asset's value and thus attracting yet more traders and thus ever-lower quantitative risk estimates. After a few years of such juicy states of affairs, even the most skeptical and reluctant of players has no option but to join the party. Soon everybody is long Thailand bonds, or Mexican index volatility, or U.S. residential mortgages.

Given how low VaR numbers have become, the slightest of set-backs will result in internal VaR limits being breached across essentially all banks at exactly the same time. When a VaR limit is breached (i.e., when the real losses suffered by a trading desk happen to be higher than the maximum loss limit imposed on it by risk managers), trad-ers are typically asked to cut down positions until their exposures are reduced back below their VaR limit. In a quest to reduce risk, traders are forced to sell some of their portfolio into the market. If many firms do this concurrently, massive volatility and crashing prices may rap-idly ensue; if everyone (or almost everyone) is dumping large amounts of the same stuff, liquidity can quickly disappear as prospective buy-ers either shy away or bid their time waiting for prices to unavoidably tumble yet further. The end result: massive liquidations leading to addi-tional massive liquidations (as VaR gets breached over and over again), causing huge losses and potentially a system-wide breakdown (as after one point not only the more exotic stuff, but all types of assets get sold in a desperate search for liquidity). Market correlations go to one as every asset family is dumped, banks stop trusting each other, average investors lose their shirts (without knowing exactly why), short-term credit is constrained, and politicians may have to come to the rescue.

This type of phenomena is exactly what took place during the now legendary 1997 and 1998 market crises. When Asian economies ran into trouble and Russia defaulted, respectively, the complacent VaR numbers that had aided the big similar bets were quickly overtaken by the initial increase in volatility, kick-starting a liquidation cascade that led, among other things, to the blowup of mega–hedge fund LTCM and a government-coordinated intervention. For a few days, the viability of the financial system held in the balance.

With VaR as the preeminent risk management tool, volatile crashes may be easier because banks' trading decisions and policies become homogeneous, coordinated into consensus by the VaR beacon. It's as if all banks shared the same risk department, which counsel they all followed at once. Risk concentration becomes much more feasible this way, and risk concentration within banking circles can be a bad thing for the economy. What hurts one bank will hurt all the rest, in a self-feeding downward spiral. Not only can VaR make everyone own the same stuff at the same time, it can make them dump it at the same time too. And given how ridiculously modest VaR numbers can be, massive risk concentration and massive liquidations both become extremely likely. If VaR was more realistic and less unworldly, neither the concentration nor the liquidations would be so worrisome.

Unfortunately, nothing was learned from the 1997–1998 lessons and VaR remained the undisputable risk management paradigm. This allowed the model to have a starring role in the even more monstrous 2007–2008 cataclysm, an event that highlighted like nothing else how bad a risk manager VaR is.

■ ■ ■

Merrill Lynch's one-day VaR on December 29, 2006 was a paltry $52 million ($50 million average daily VaR for the entire 2006), implying mathematically projected one-year losses of around $800 million (with 95 percent probability), not a devastatingly large amount for such a towering firm. In those pre-crisis (crisis-manufacturing, in fact) days Merrill's VaR endowed the firm's trading operations with sublime complacency. Bear Stearns' November 30, 2006, VaR was not only typically modest at $28 million ($440 million annual projection, 95 percent probability), but was actually slightly higher than the one prevailing on February 28, 2007, and exactly the same as May 31, 2007. The complacency inside the firm was kept unchecked literally until seconds before the explosion. Lehman's average daily VaR for the quarter ending on November 30, 2006, was $48 million, which also appears a tad appeasing. All those humble analytical estimates of losses turned out to be exaggeratedly off the mark. Real losses turned out to be excruciatingly larger than what VaR had predicted. The 2007 year-end one-day VaR for JP Morgan, Citigroup, and Goldman Sachs were respectively $103 million (99 percent), $163 million (99 percent), and $134 million (95 percent), implying projected annual 2008 trading setbacks of, respectively, $1.62 billion, $2.57 billion, and $2.12 billion. Contrast this with real credit crisis-related write-downs for the three firms for that year of $41 billion, $102 billion, and $8 billion.[7] Merrill Lynch's maximum daily VaR for Q3 2007 was $92 million (average $76 million), and yet the firm suffered a trading-inflicted $8.4 billion write-down,[8] rather above the $730 million projected annual loss that one would obtain by scaling that $92 million figure three months into the future. VaR proved to be a very unreliable risk estimator, across all banks. VaR's "predictions" are bound to be off-base, but what happened during the crisis was flat-out obscene. The analytical misfirings were monumental. Take Swiss giant UBS, a prominent victim of the crash. It reported 50 VaR exceptions for 2008 and 29 for 2007. At the 99 percent confidence level chosen by UBS, there should have only been about 2.5 exceptions (trading days when actual losses exceeded VaR's predictions; 1 percent of roughly 250 trading days per year in this case) per year. Or take local rival Credit Suisse. The Zurich powerhouse experienced 25 and 9 VaR exceptions in 2008 and 2007, respectively; also at 99 percent confidence, this implies above six times more real losses than theoretically forewarned. It seems unnecessary to state that VaR did not properly warn the Helvetians during the unfolding of the bloodbath.

You didn't need to be based in a neutral country with magnificent ski slopes and exquisite private bankers in order to experience your own dose of VaR disillusionment. Being American, for instance, would also do. Perhaps it shouldn't be exceedingly surprising that Lehman Brothers and Bear Stearns witnessed less-than-glorious VaR behavior, particularly in the latter case (around 30 exceptions during its last three quarters as a living independent entity, more than three times the predicted number for the adopted 95 percent confidence level, which allows for only 12 yearly exceptions or 5 percent of 250 annual trading days); but they were not alone by any means, with Morgan Stanley, JP Morgan, and Bank of America (BoA), for example, similarly witnessing the breakdown of the theoretical dogma (BoA 14 violations in 2007 at 99 percent, JP Morgan 8 in 2007 at 99 percent, Morgan Stanley 18 violations in 2008 at 95 percent). And other Europeans can boast plenty of misguiding, too. Mighty Deutsche Bank, for one, was surprised to observe 35 VaR violations in 2008 and 12 the year before, in all around 10 times higher than theory would dictate.

By pulling together all the institutions listed above, we would roughly have about 120 VaR exceptions for 2007. Those banks' VaRs (using differing degrees of confidence) would have altogether allowed for some 50 exceptions annually. So that would amount to something like two-and-a-half times more real setbacks than theoretically predicted. But because basically all the breaches took place in the second half of the year, we could state that when it came to crisis time, the theory actually underperformed five-to-one (120 real violations versus 25 allowed). And this analysis crucially does not include Merrill Lynch or Citigroup, which don't seem to have reported their own figures for breaches. It is highly feasible that they posted huge exceptions during the fall and winter of 2007, given that they shouldered monstrous losses. Also, don't forget that the real/theoretical exceptions ratio only conveys the magnitude of VaR's disappointing performance, not its size. Many of those exceptions were brutally large. We are not talking here about real losses overtaking theoretical projections by just a few dollars (in which case, frankly, who would care much?). The reality check was expressed in the millions. For instance, of UBS's 30 breaching days, more than 10 saw setbacks in excess of CHF150 million over VaR. That is, it's not simply that VaR failed; the real drama is that it failed by a lot. And keep in mind that all those scandalously prevalent violations were taking place as VaR (drinking from the enhanced volatility) was itself growing substantially; that is, VaR was unveiled as vastly underestimating even as it was going up! In fact, for those of the above-listed institutions that made it through 2008, the ratio of actual exceptions to allowed-for exceptions was 133–134 (a fourfold theoretical underperformance) even though VaR, on average, was in most cases approximately twice that of 2007.

When Merrill Lynch inaugurated its descent into meltdown by posting trading-originating losses in excess of $2 billion in Q3 2007, it was quick to publicly betray the tool that had given it so much for so long, by openly finger pointing:

> VaR significantly underestimated the magnitude of actual loss from the unprecedented credit market environment, in particular the extreme dislocation that affected US subprime residential mortgage-related and Asset-Backed-Securities CDO positions. In the past, these AAA ABS CDO securities had never experienced a significant loss of value.[9]

Merrill's statement is a double-blow to VaR, and serves well to highlight why its presence among us can be so pernicious. First, the befallen Wall Streeter reminded the world, the tool can't be even in the vicinity of predicting turmoil when it truly matters. Second, the tool can itself help create the turmoil in the first place. Keep these words in mind: "In the past, these AAA ABS CDO securities had never experienced a significant loss of value." That is, it was VaR heaven for all those punters wishing to earn good money (temporarily) on the wager that subprime borrowers may be able to meet their mountainous obligations. The rearview mirror swore that those bets (impossibly toxic to anyone with half a brain) could not be expected to sustain heavy losses. Here is Merrill mercifully letting us know how VaR abetted it, and its cousins, into succumbing to multibillion dollar write-downs. The toxic stuff had never seen cloudy days (among other things because it had been invented two minutes ago, a commonsensical individual might opine), so in VaR fantasyland that translates into unfettered permission to ride the CDO roller coaster.

Merrill, of course, learned about VaR's deceitful limitations the hardest way. Even though it had one of the lowest VaR numbers on the Street, it became one of the largest sufferers from the cataclysm. For instance, while Goldman Sachs, with a VaR double in size, went as far as posting record earnings, Merrill saw a net downfall of $8.5 billion in 2007, which contrasts sharply with the theoretical "prediction" of just $800 million discussed earlier.

Some may wonder how seriously financial pros really took VaR as guide through the market jungle. Perhaps they voiced to the world that they followed VaR for risk-management purposes, but they didn't entirely abide by the tool when making risk-based decisions, such as trading. Banks may report VaR religiously, but how obediently do they actually listen to it? How intensely do they actually let it influence their decisions? This is admittedly a potentially gray area. Traders are assumed to be restricted by internal VaR limits, so, yes, a low VaR will always tend to help those eager to punt and punt and punt. A low VaR will always assist those eager to take risky bets in the name of risklessness. But it is not incontrovertibly clear how each institution truly lets its internal trading wishes be affected by its VaR numbers. Some may postulate that such grayness may diminish the charge that VaR caused the crisis; perhaps banks would have acted just the same in the absence of low VaR figures, even in the absence of VaR itself.

Of course, we know that not to be the case because there is nothing gray about VaR's prominent role when it came to determining capital requirements for trading activities. Its presence in the formula was indelible. There's not a shred of doubt as to VaR's decisively deterministic role there. Banks' individual preferences and intrinsic ways of doing things don't matter one iota in this case (except when it comes to the actual chosen methodology behind the calculation of VaR, naturally). Whatever your trading preferences, whatever your risk appetite, your final actions would be hostage to the capital price tag dictated by VaR. You will only be able to leverage yourself to the hilt if VaR lets you. You may not have cared much for what VaR says about future danger, but your trading prowess would be ultimately determined by VaR. You may want to trade a lot but only VaR would tell you if you can afford it.

There's no controversy whatsoever about the requisiteness of low VaRs before banks could afford the leverage that sank the world. In order for VaR to help cause the crisis it wasn't an absolute requirement that bankers listened to VaR (though they did, and many were mightily glad to hear the model condone wild risk-taking). The only true requirement was that the capital price of their trading lottery tickets would be set by VaR. That's the ultimately incontestable, unquestionable conduit through which VaR aided mayhem. What are we saying here? That while banks' use of VaR as an internal risk beacon can indeed have problematic repercussions, VaR's real threat to the world lies in its other main role. Perhaps it wouldn't be unjustifiable if financial entities kept calculating and following their VaR (provided that they don't abide too much by it), as long as the tool is irrevocably abandoned by regulators. Although we may be able to live with VaR as a risk-management instrument, we may not be able to survive with VaR as a bank capital utensil.

So the truly key questions concerning VaR are: Will policy makers continue to embrace such an inaccurate and potentially deleterious concoction? Why did they fall in love with such a visibly flawed tool in the first place? How was this allowed to happen by the financial police?

■ ■ ■

One of the most puzzling developments to take place in finance over the past 15 years or so has been the overenthusiastic embracement of VaR by international regulators. The tool, as we've said, was initially developed by banks themselves, not imposed from above by intruding policy makers. By the late 1980s and early 1990s, financial institutions were starting to run inundating amounts of trading-related exposures in a myriad of different markets and through an intoxicatingly diverse family of products. This put risk measuring at the top of the to-do list inside dealing floors and Wall Street executive suites. The technical resources to embark on the task had also become conveniently available, with fast-delivery computer power and long databases of historical prices now within easy reach. Banks wanted a risk measure that was easy to understand and interpret and that could be equally applied across all asset categories. VaR dutifully obliged, and could be mathematically and computationally tamed with the help of the hundreds of PhD-endowed scientists that had been progressively invading the financial industry for the prior few years. Soon, trading firms began to experiment with their own proprietary creations for internal use. All that was now required for VaR to become prevalent was a little push, an incentivizing propellant that directed banks toward no-holds-barred, even fanatical adoption of the tool.

Bureaucrats provided that necessary jolt. In 1993 the Basel Committee[10] decided to add market risk to its mandate and put forward a proposal for measuring trading-related capital requirements. While the recommendations may lack force of law, countries implicitly commit to adopting them into their domestic rules book. Confrontingly, though the U.S. SEC initially refused to give up its own cherished method for calculating the capital charges of Wall Street broker-dealers for the one preferred by the Committee, thus guaranteeing that, in the case of the United States, banking (regulated by the Basel-abiding Federal Reserve) and securities requirements would remain, in principle, not harmonically homogeneous (as was the case in the European Union) but rather distinct.

By the time the Basel market risk proposal was released, tons of financial institutions were already using their own proprietary, and typically quite complex, versions of VaR. Banks liked their beloved tools much more than the methodology initially put forward by the regulators, the so-called *standard model*, which was a building block approach that assigned fixed predetermined arbitrary capital charges to each different asset class. In essence, Basel was attempting to treat market risk just like it had been treating credit risk, with very little flexibility, no equations, and no allowance for historical data–driven volatility or correlation effects. To the banks such an arrangement seemed inhospitably archaic (and, quite possibly, also too expensive; VaR, by allowing you to select the data sample of your liking and to make friendly mathematical assumptions, can be made to be much less taxing on your capital wallet).

Soon, banks began to lobby to have things changed. The "science" of risk measurement would have to rule supreme over more boorish proposals. The first big lobbying salvo came in July 1993, when the influential Group of Thirty (G30; an assemblage of top bankers, academics, and regulators) released a report on derivatives best practices that included as the main recommendation the adoption of VaR as the most appropriate measure of market risk.[11] Interestingly, this document may be the first time that the term *Value at Risk* appeared in print. The G30 backing of VaR put substantial pressure on the Basel Committee to endow VaR with capital powers. It took a little while for the financial mandarins to finally succumb. The definite convincing moment probably came in October 1994, when JP Morgan released unto the open world its *RiskMetrics* system, symbol-filled documentation and data-inundated software describing and facilitating the calculation of the bank's version of VaR (deeply rooted in the math-heavy, hypothesis-inundated Covariance methodology).

Why was this a seminal moment? Because it gave a tremendous popularity boost to the model (a public relations firm placed ads and articles in the press, JP Morgan staff went on a multicity promotional tour[12]) and because it made it much easier for any type of entity to calculate their own VaR. JP Morgan's VaR provided a one-two punch to any reluctance to bring the model into the regulatory fold: It looked intelligently complex and sophisticated, but at the same time it could be very easy to compute. The best risk-measurement techniques that elite Wall Street brainiacs can devise within convenient reach? Who could resist that? VaR became unassailable gospel.

Whether or not JP Morgan's 1994 move was self-interestingly aimed at knocking down any resistance to the global imposition of the VaR regime (maybe the bank was engaging in a selfless act of community service?), that's exactly the effect it had. So as not to disrupt things too much and in order to avoid being perceived as promoting backwardness, the Committee did in January 1996 flexibly accept the use of banks' internal VaR models, subject to its veto, through the famous Market Risk Amendment to the original 1988 Basel Capital Accord (interestingly, the regulators favored the banks twice, with the introduction of a strange thing called *Tier 3 capital* that banks could use to satisfy market risk requirements; Tier 3 was not really capital, as it was composed not of hard-core equity but of subordinated debt; so the 1996 policy U-turn not only delivered a tool that was almost certain to enable lots of high-risk leverage but also lowered the quality of the capital supporting all that trading, something that would come to bite the banking industry severely some 10 years later). In the words of an expert witness, "*This was a significant step forward. Prior to this, regulatory requirements and internal risk calculations had been diverging at an increasing rate. The 1995 Internal Markets Proposal, for the first time, represented a significant convergence between banking regulation and internal practice.*"[13] By the way, that expert, when analyzing the bank capital regulatory arena in VaR-crazed 1998, outrightly recognized that the arrival of VaR on the scene meant substantially lower market risk capital charges. Banks could choose whether to employ the standard model or VaR (an early study showed that VaR could deliver capital savings of as much as 85 percent when compared to the standard model[14]). Should they, as has tended to be the case ever since, select the latter, the minimum daily market risk capital charge is to be calculated as the maximum of the previous day's VaR or the result of multiplying the average VaR for the past 60 days by a multiplication factor (typically equal to three, maybe higher if VaR behaves badly as an estimator of losses). Banks were free to select any VaR calculating method they wanted and any historical data sample beyond one year.

This arrangement is the one that essentially prevailed for more than a decade, until the 2007–2008 crisis prompted regulators to introduce some add-ons and twists to the formula described above. As we know, even U.S. securities regulators eventually became enchanted when in 2004 the SEC developed an enhanced sense of international solidarity and decided to join the Basel bandwagon by allowing Goldman Sachs and its domestic siblings to compute capital charges according to VaR.

What explains the regulatory lovefest with VaR? Anyone who spends a few minutes thinking about it would understand that there is something very fishy about assuming that when it comes to the markets Normality rules, or that the past is prologue. Financial regulators are smart people, typically with tons of years at the job, so how could they miss such no-brainers?

Though it is true that some financial mandarins have now shown some (atonement-seeking?) contrition and some desire to correct for the tool's failures—all the while refusing to do away with it—it all feels like too little too late. No amount of atonement may be able to compensate for the fact that for so long the watchdogs that we trust to take care of our system encouraged, promoted, and endorsed the peddling of airbags that won't inflate if we hit a wall.

■ ■ ■

The response of many (nonregulatory) VaR-lovers to the VaR crisis that unleashed the 2007 subprime crisis has been, in general, quite disturbing. Rather than admitting to the utterly visible failures that have produced so much wreckage, they cling to old, tired, empty arguments in a desperate attempt to preserve the tool, at all cost. Although disappointing, said response is welcomed for one key reason: It allows the world to contemplate, now without any shred of doubt, the dogmatism of these people, as well as their allergic relationship with empirical truth. Empirical evidence (all those exceptions, all those stupidly insufficient capital charges, all those huge trading-related losses, all those failed measurements and predictions) is a nuisance, to be radically discarded at the slightest sign of VaR-negating proof. They just don't care if the thing works out there or not. They just want it to remain alive, forever.

The postcrisis tactic appears to have been to try to confuse with the ultimate goal of erasing from the debate any discussion on the actual performance of VaR and the actual consequences of having VaR around. Many VaR defenders have taken to lecture people on how, whatever the circumstances, you must definitely go on using VaR because it wasn't VaR, it was the mishandling of the poor analytical baby by impudent rogues inside trading floors and policy-making circles! That's it, that's right, VaR doesn't kill people, people kill people; VaR wasn't the problem, it was people who never understood VaR, they were the problem; poor misunderstood VaR was manhandled, it wasn't VaR it was those idiotic people! After years of excitedly calling it the golden new benchmark for risk, the new paradigm that would change the world, the arrival of the Chosen One, many VaRistas have suddenly developed a weird tendency to belittle the model; (it is true that VaR has been disclaimed about in the past by its more ardent peddlers, but those statements were rather mild compared to the postcrisis belittling; in any case, warning about the model's shortcomings should not earn VaR and its fans brownie points: the point should not be to employ flawed models which weaknesses are adequately warned about, rather the point should be to stop using flawed models, no matter how intensely the flaws have been emphasized; a model that has to be disclaimed about all the time should not be used, period). You can't just convert to sincerity and admit that you had been peddling a deleteriously fallible tool that just happened to help cause the worst crisis ever. But at the same time, you badly want to preserve the model, and in the face of bloodshed and unremitting criticism you may have to talk-down VaR a little, so as to keep it around, in a diminished form perhaps, but alive nonetheless. The reputation of your tool may suffer a slide, but you can live with that. What you surely can't live without is VaR. So you do whatever it takes to keep VaR around, and if that includes publicly betraying the thing a bit, that's okay.

Of course, in reality VaR was used exactly as it was intended to be used. As it had always been used. There was no confusion here. There was no mishandling. No misunderstanding. If anything, it could be posited that VaR (and what it can do) had been understood all too well by financial players. VaR was not embraced under false pretenses by confused pros and policy wonks. They knew exactly what VaR is about. VaR failed because that's its nature, not because folks used it inappropriately.

Soon after the credit crisis materialized, a public debate on VaR's strengths and weaknesses broke out. As was mentioned earlier, this had the beneficial side effect of unveiling VaRistas' way of thinking, openly showing how detached from terra firma many of the analytical risk managers can be. As an illustrative sample, consider the following statement by an enthusiastic VaR defender participating in one of those debates:

> We can improve our "weather forecast" methods and it would
> be a real mistake to abandon all the work done and leave again
> risk management to the common sense of the practitioners.[15]

It can be said louder, but not clearer. For such VaR espousers the "common sense of the practitioners" is nothing more than a mistake. Something to be avoided at all costs. The opposite of goodness. The enemy.

To all those financial professionals who have dared toil the markets for centuries (millennia?) unassisted by the holy quantitative scriptures and drawing only on their experience-honed common sense, let me tell you what VaRistas think you are: a big mistake, an unacceptable aberration. How dare you try to act on your own freethinking intuition and on the accumulated practical knowledge of your peers rather than blindly follow the dictates of a failed quant dogma?

■　■　■

A big problem for those quantitative risk managers and academics (let's call them *QuAnts*) denying VaR's capacity for destruction and for malfunctioning is that even the regulators have, rather rashly, left them behind. The hopelessly in-denial QuAnts may end up like those WWII Japanese soldiers who were left stranded in the jungles by their retreating, defeated generals; believing the conflict to still be going on, trusting their contribution to still be required, hoping that victory is still within reach. Long after the divine Emperor signed the concession papers aboard that U.S. ship, some of his soldiers were still thinking that they were fighting His war. Now that the regulatory demigods have (to all effects) conceded defeat, will the jungles of finance be filled with disoriented, lost VaR soldiers still flying the flag?

In essence, regulators have decided to kill VaR without going as far as definitely removing it from the land. What have they done? They have modified the formula for setting trading-related capital charges in such a way as to basically guarantee that going forward requirements will be several times above what VaR alone would have traditionally dictated. In other words, they are recognizing that the prior arrangement (i.e., VaR alone) had delivered unrealistically low charges, especially, naturally, in the buildup to the crisis. They are recognizing, in fact, VaR's crucial role in fueling the leveraged fire that engulfed us all. Through their actions, regulators are saying that VaR was dangerously inappropriate. Guilty.

They still keep VaR around (perhaps so as to avoid hard questioning on their loving adoption of the tool all those years; brusquely dumping the model may unwelcomingly cause some to wonder why it was ever embraced in the first place). But the new formula clearly shouts that VaR is wrong, and can't be trusted with as relevant a task as setting bank capital charges.

VaR is still in the formula, but its influence has been noticeably diminished. Regulators no longer want VaR to be the sole determiner of market risk regulatory capital, of trading-related leverage. So they've made up something that achieves such goal without having to actually send out invitations to VaR's official burial ceremony.

The new Basel capital formula, as was mentioned, adds several add-ons to the prior method. The new capital levies required for market punting would be the number that the previous VaR-only methodology would have churned plus the add-ons. One of those add-ons is something called *Stressed VaR* (sVaR), introduced in 2008 and that is calculated by selecting a historical time series from a particularly, well, stressful past market period; kind of a parallel VaR where the data used for the calculation is the most volatile possible for each asset, thus in principle guaranteeing modest estimations of future losses. VaR + sVaR, thus, should be expected to yield far more conservative capital requirements than just VaR, in line with the regulatory desires to never again err on the side of undercapitalized banks and excessive leverage.

Another postcrisis add-on to the Basel capital formula is the so-called *Incremental Risk Charge* (IRC), introduced to better capture some risks not well covered by VaR and which importance was indelibly highlighted by the 2007–2008 meltdown. IRC applies only to non-securitized positions, and deals with default risk (direct and indirect losses derived from an obligor's default) and credit migration risk (losses due to other credit-related events, such as a rating downgrade). The IRC model estimates expected losses over a one-year horizon and with a 99.9 percent confidence interval. Just like with sVaR (and, naturally, VaR), banks can use any analytical methodology they wish to calculate IRC.

Finally, international regulators have dictated that securitizations (things like mortgage-backed-securities) and re-securitizations (things like CDOs made up of mortgage-backed-securities) should carry the same capital charge whether a bank includes the position in its banking book or its trading book, thus eliminating the possibility of "regulatory arbitrage" whereby bankers would shift an asset from one type of book to the other depending on which imposed a cheaper capital requirement at any point in time (precrisis banking book requirements depended on more or less fixed credit ratings, precrisis trading book requirements depended on much more volatile VaR; if market developments rendered the latter lower than the former, a bank could punt in a more leveraged way via the trading book and vice versa).

Some studies have estimated that under the revised, new methodology capital charges could be increased as much as three- or fourfold. It seems obvious that the hastily-put-together fixes were an unmitigated declaration by regulators that they had got it exceedingly wrong for so many years, that their beloved tool can't cope with reality, and that they eagerly want to make amends with a victimized world. Only problem is that we had to be killed by VaR before VaR could be killed.

Those QuAnts desperately hanging on to VaR may not want the world to know about VaR's perilous deficiencies, but their erstwhile allies from the public sector have already taken to the megaphones and let the populace know. One of the globe's most important financial regulators, the U.K.'s Financial Services Authority, stated its view rather unshyly as part of its widely circulated and influential Turner Report in February 2009. When discussing the problem of enhanced banking leverage from 2003 onward under the heading of "What

Went Wrong?" the FSA declared that, "It is clear in retrospect that the VaR measures of risk were faulty and that required trading book capital was inadequate."[16] It continued, "Mathematical sophistication ended up not containing risk, but providing false assurance that other prima facie indicators of increasing risk (e.g., rapid credit extension and balance sheet growth) could be safely ignored." So there you have it: The mandarins (the ones who endowed VaR with unlimited power in the first place) are saying that VaR delivered the leveraged punting and the faulty risk assessments. In other words, the crisis.

Will the QuAnts now show repentance, too? It's unlikely, I fear. If, as VaRistas tend to believe, history is any guide, it's a safe bet that they'll keep skirting the issue, ignoring the empirical evidence, and blaming those using VaR (the traders and the executives that give them shelter inside financial institutions) for not being intelligent enough to truly comprehend how to use the poor misunderstood tool. They'll keep proposing to badmouth the users, never the instrument (and those who manufacture it). Akin to someone saying that nuclear bombs had nothing to do with Hiroshima and Nagasaki, that only those flying the planes should be held responsible; that nuclear bombs don't kill people, only people who drop nuclear bombs kill people; that nuclear bombs were never meant to be nuclear; that if we want a mushroom cloud-free planet we should get rid of all the military pilots, but not get rid of the bombs (and those who manufacture them). Just because some physical person must eventually use the destructive instrument (be it a real or a financial bomb) does not diminish the intrinsically destructive nature of the device; stop using such toys and nuclear winter (real or financial) will be instantly avoided.

To QuAnts, VaR is never the problem, those who (to the delight of QuAnts) used VaR are. QuAnts are like engineers who build an arsenal, sweet-talk the generals into using it, and then blame the inevitable unpleasant consequences on the men in uniform, while lobbying furiously for the continuing preservation and manufacturing of the bombs, and denying that they were ever supposed to act like bombs.

There is a key reason why the above analogies may be less than perfect (and not only because, as some may posit, military weaponry may oftentimes serve honorable purposes). With nuclear weapons, there's no deceit. No one is claiming the bombs to do anything but cause destruction. No one describes them as, say, fertilizer from which flowers will blossom. Everyone involved in the nuclear discussion understands that the bombs are made to destroy stuff. The same, of course, can't be said of VaR. We were never told by those promoting VaR that VaR could enable destruction; we were rather told that VaR could save us from destruction. VaR was imposed on us in the name of tranquility, a device that would prevent the shedding of blood in finance. The tool that (rather inevitably) claimed untold casualties was peddled on us as the tool that would deliver us from evil. We were, now we know, misled. As much as if an army general would sell us the benefits of nuclear armory by arguing that before they hit ground the bombs will morph into a sea of peaceful white doves.

■ ■ ■

What would a VaR-less world look like? Well, we may be already living in a VaR-lite universe given how policy makers have semi-abandoned the model, so the query may best be posited as: What *should* a VaR-less world look like? If VaR does in fact get killed, or terminally marginalized into irrelevant obscurity, what should replace it?

I am of the opinion that simply getting rid of a bad solution is in itself a valid solution, so answering "No VaR" to the question sounds optimal to me: First and foremost, let's make sure that we appreciate the benefits of not living under flawed practices (quitting cigarettes is no less healthy because you don't offer to do something alternative to puffing). By just erasing a bad model from financeland, we would make tremendous strides. No-VaR in itself would be a wonderful improvement over VaR.

Having said that, financial risks would continue to need managing and bank capital would continue to need regulating even in a post-VaR order so it probably doesn't hurt if we make tangible proposals as to how such system should operate. In a nutshell: Going forward let's do less mathematical financial risk analysis, please. Softer sapience based on traders' war scars, experience-honed intuition, historical lessons, and networking with other players will not only typically beat quant sapience when it comes to understanding and deciphering exposures (we humans can't be that bad!), but most crucially should be far more effective in preventing obviously lethal, chaos-igniting practices. Commonsensical, rather than analytical, counsel ought not only identify risks much better, but especially keep toxicity at bay much more resolutely. And, at the end of the day, what's risk management if not the prevention of the worst kind of ills? With VaR as king, it can be quite easy for the system to drown in destructive lethality. With commonsensical steering at the helm, it can be quite difficult (if not well nigh impossible) for such a nightmarish outcome to materialize. Results that would be deemed outright lunacy under the commonsensical lens (say, 1,000-to-1 leverage in a trading portfolio that contains lots of nasty stuff) are accepted and encouraged if churned out from the analytical strainer. Recommendations that would have never been arrived at under the rule of common sense can be easily put forth when analytics reign.

The gargantuan toxic leverage that VaR did sanction and can sanction was the type of aberration that can result when common sense is dilapidated under the weight of the analytical rock. A commonsensical way of doing things would not allow the crazy, trading that VaR did and can so uniquely allow. Reckless actions by financiers and reckless policies by regulators, forbidden under commonsensical decision making, are permitted by VaR. Commonsense decision making makes terrible market crises much *less* likely. Models-based decision making makes terrible market crises much *more* likely.

It all comes down to how risk-blind VaR can be. VaR doesn't know anything about the true riskiness of an asset, only about soulless data series. Without models, we would have no option but to think about the actual risks of a portfolio. Our conclusions may not always be on the mark, but it would surely beat flying blindfolded. Any risk analysis of subprime CDOs by a flesh-and-bone trader that is at the very least slightly aware of the nature of the underlying mortgages making up the structure runs circles around an analysis based exclusively on how the security happens to have behaved of late. While past data can hide true risk, it's much more difficult for thoughtful introspection to do so. While VaR can take an obviously trashy asset and label it as risk-free, thoughtful introspection won't. By choosing common sense over VaR we at least manage to avoid such idiotic dictates from permeating the economy, and the pronounced bloodshed that would surely follow.

Shouldn't that be the main goal of risk management and prudential regulation? First and foremost, make sure that the obviously unacceptable is not possible. Then you deal with the other stuff, but first implacably forbid the dangerously unacceptable from rearing its ugly head. Any risk system that sanctions 1,000-to-1 (even 100-to-1) gearing on banks trading books is unacceptable. Any risk system that allows banks to own more super-toxic assets than their entire equity base is unacceptable. Any risk system that predicts placidity days before giant legendary banks sink into oblivion is unacceptable.

While commonsense-grounded Basel I blockaded the unacceptable, its later models-based siblings Basel II and Basel III happily permitted the unacceptable. Under Basel I, financial mandarins chose to use their brains and come up with fundamentals-based risk rankings, making sure that capital requirements rose as the nonstandard character of a particular asset family is enhanced (i.e., government bonds required less capital than claims on banks, which in turn required less capital than municipal bonds and much less capital than underdeveloped-countries debt, and so on). It's well known that those risk buckets were far from perfect, but at the very least it made it hard for illiquid, complex assets to be relatively very cheap capital-wise. Under Basel II and III, regulators put their brains under lock and key and outsourced risk control to the fancy VaR and credit models developed internally by banks. Fundamentals stopped playing any role whatsoever. This made toxic leverage suddenly economical and possible, especially because traders could now effectively calculate their own capital requirements. The old, imperfect risk buckets that discriminated between quality and trashy assets would not have allowed the 2007 crisis to take place. VaR, in contrast, is much less discriminating. By welcoming the unacceptable in, modern risk rules sealed our fates.

So let's use the latest market crisis and the latest VaR disaster to redefine risk management and risk regulation as the prospective prevention of the unacceptable. It's clear that no risk management-measurement system and no risk policing mechanism will get it right 100 percent of the time: Many exposures will be underestimated or overestimated, regulatory capital will end up being a bit too taxing or a bit too scarce. It will always be an inexact art, full of uncertainty. But we do have the capacity to ex ante identify intrinsically daring securities, and to make them apart from naturally safer alternatives. While no one can guarantee that punting on the latter will perennially be setback-free, it seems clear that global stability is much better served if we discourage the massive accumulation of weird assets that can lose their entire value on a whim. The rule should be never to endow relevance on risk tools and policies that have even the slimmest chance of yielding such results. As simple as that. If there is a possibility that a risk mechanism can deliver toxic leverage, then such mechanism should be banned from the premises, immediately. It is true that, as was said earlier, regulators seem to have learned the key lessons from the latest market debacle ("VaR can kill," "Metrics-based financial policing can kill," "Toxic leverage can kill"), but their response has not been exactly the most appropriate one (as long as VaR is kept around in the regulatory capital formula it remains influential; besides, all those post-crisis add-ons to the formula could be quietly removed in the future, perhaps following a prolonged turmoil-free period that seduces policy makers into imposing less restrictive rules on bankers, essentially taking us back to the explosive precrisis VaR-only system). The current regulatory architecture still requires further, more radical tweaking, notwithstanding the reforms undertaken. Even those who are willing and able to learn some of the important lessons still have lessons to learn.

Many experts will tell you that risk management is about risk measurement and loss prevention, but those things are not attainable: We can't map markets probabilistically, and bad news will always be indelible possibilities. There's not much we can do about all this. We shouldn't be judged too harshly for not anticipating all that "day-to-day" stuff. But we should be penalized ruthlessly if we fail to do the one thing we can definitely do, and the one thing that truly matters: Make obviously reckless behavior (i.e., that which has consequences that are destined to be catastrophic with almost total, or indeed total, certainty) impossible. Crises may still happen through other conduits, but the by-far potentially more lethal paths (the insane leverage, the insane toxicity) would have been roadblocked.

(Good) bankers and (good) politicians would benefit from this proposed new risk paradigm. As many healthy financial institutions can attest, toxic leverage is not a requirement for a bank to deliver attractive results and generate investor interest; there are plenty of other, much more system-friendly, conduits through which positive (and long-lasting) performance can be obtained. Those bankers disproportionately interested in the survival of their firms and of the financial system should welcome with open arms any risk policy that decisively curbs leverage madness. Similarly, any policy maker bent on safeguarding national stability should be in favor of rules that clamp down on destructive bank behavior, given how the latter tends to give raise to mass unemployment and unsustainable public deficits. The coalition of good bankers and good politicians should push for the banning of the unacceptable, and help make that the central target of risk policing.

There'll always be a chance that banks and other players suffer some types of setbacks in the cold hard markets; and as long as humans shape the action, those events will be pretty much unpredictable. Risk control shouldn't be judged on its capacity to eliminate or foresee such pretty unavoidable outcomes. Risk control should be about the doable task of making sure that the odds of such setbacks being destructively monstrous are not guaranteed to be 100 percent. In that light, VaR was the worst possible contribution to risk control imaginable. The number that ruled the world should never be given such powers ever again.

Chapter 2

Origins

History Lessons ▪ *The Unknown Inventors of
VaR* ▪ *Till and His Band of Correlated Brothers* ▪ *Number
Crunching* ▪ *The Dangerous Charm of Lazy Precision*

L et's dwell a little bit more on VaR's nature. In prior pages we
touched on some of the essential key points. We got some historical background: We amply know by now that JP Morgan
is credited with having invented the thing in the late 1980s, that the
model was quite mathematical in its early days, that it was very publicly
spread to the rest of the populace in the mid-1990s. We got an idea as
to how the risk number is calculated. But let's now act more snoopily
and pry more intensely into VaR. Let's find out more about its past.
How did the whole thing begin? In so doing, we get a better idea as to
how the tool was and is calculated (while reminding ourselves that the
particular technicalities are not our main concern in this book; compre-
hension of the basics is more than enough). Let's, in sum, know more
about what VaR is and where it comes from. This will help us not only

to better understand the model's insides and thus to appreciate why it can underperform, but will also put a human face to the whole affair. Aren't you intrigued to find out the names and surnames of those who gave birth to the analytical maven? Who first invented the most powerful and influential machine ever to trot the financial landscape, and why? What type of people were they? Where did they come from? Where did they go? One of those pioneers (Aaron Brown, to this day a top risk manager) regales us with an essay-length contribution at the end of the book. But VaR had other fathers, and we will present them here. Some of them have been often profiled and are well known. Others have remained anonymous beyond the small circle of VaR cognoscenti; they will be properly unearthed here, doing justice to their pioneerism. Ready to learn more about the history of the model that has ruled the world for the past 20 years and that may continue to do so for a while longer?

■ ■ ■

Kenneth Garbade is most likely not a household name for most people. And yet for the purposes of this book he is an important figure, for he may have been the first person inside a bank to concoct VaR-type models. The former academic and current Federal Reserve of New York economist spent several years in the 1980s at then derivatives powerhouse Bankers Trust (now a long defunct institution, after the very daring strategies pursued by the famously aggressive firm backfired drastically in the mid-1990s) where he put together several research studies dealing with statistical measures of market risk, bringing on board many of the same tools behind the version of VaR that later became popular. Assets were assumed to be distributed Normally, standard deviation was used to represent risk, and 99 percent confidence intervals were chosen. These reports were meant as components of the marketing efforts to Bankers' clients, and do not seem to have been distributed externally with any particular zest or to have gathered much attention. Bankers Trust (already a pioneer in risk management methods) may have had the chance to be widely known as the true father of VaR, but it may not have been much interested in that. Kenneth Garbade could have been globally famous, but he may not have pursued that type of stardom too eagerly (some years later he assembled in book form a compilation of some of his research pieces; the ones related to VaR were not included).

If the cowboys at Bankers Trust gave up on VaR glory, the same can't be said about their cross-town rivals at JP Morgan. They grabbed the opportunity with both hands. Not only did the firm enthusiastically embrace the model for internal purposes, it very eagerly shared it with the outside world, engaging in the most notorious and loud VaR marketing campaign ever launched. And that is why everyone has always regarded JP Morgan as the inventor of VaR. It simply made too much noise for someone to conclude otherwise. But if the role of JP Morgan is well understood, what may have been less accurately told is the story of how things enveloped inside the legendary Wall Street giant. Two individuals (Dennis Weatherstone and Till Guldimann, then the firm's chairperson and head of research, respectively) have been traditionally credited with the original manufacturing of VaR inside JP Morgan. Every single source (every single source that I was aware of, which includes all the well-known sources and then some) unfailingly tells the same tale: It was Weatherstone and Guldimann. If you want to praise, or blame, someone for the initial design and push to the model that would come to rule the land, those two individuals would be the main targets. And yet, it seems that the conventional story might be woefully incomplete. There is an unsung hero. The real inventor may have gone externally unnoticed and unrecognized all these years. Someone else inside JP Morgan did at least as much, if not more, to lift VaR off the ground. The true architect of VaR has remained in the shadows.

■ ■ ■

Raymond May was born in a remote farm in Kenya, as close to the middle of nowhere as you can get. He describes the experience as equivalent to living in Nebraska in 1830: no electricity, no running water, no TV, no radio, no outside influences. He was raised by his mother and grandmother, his father having died when he was six months old. He grew his own chickens and sold rabbit meat, in an early sign of the entrepreneurial spirit that would be fully unleashed in later years. At the age of 17, May ran away from Kenya and joined the British Army, rising to the level of lieutenant. He soon decided that such a life was too constraining, heading to the University of Exeter for a physics degree. A desire for a business career led him to one of the big accounting firms, where he spent four years, and then to the City of London, starting at JP Morgan as an accountant. There, opportunity knocked. Best-selling author Malcolm Gladwell has stated that success in life is often the overwhelming result of being in the right place at the right time,[1] and this dictum seems to fit Raymond May to a tee. Just as Microsoft's Bill Gates' stroke of fortune was to attend in the late 1960s one of the few high schools in the world that at that time provided students with access to computers (thus affording him a unique global competitive advantage among his age group), Raymond May was fortunate to get into banking just as the swaps business was being developed. In due course, swaps would, of course, become the most voluminous members of the derivatives family, in essence one of the biggest markets in the world. But in 1986, when May joined JP Morgan, swaps were still very much nascent and infant, allowing him to get in on the ground floor of a financial revolution. In Gladwellian terminology, this made Raymond May an "outlier": someone whose success is explained as much by chance and external opportunity as by talent and hard work. Raymond May invented VaR because Raymond May happened to be hired by a financial firm exactly as the new breed of exotic financial risk products that would eventually dominate the markets was being developed. Had he joined a couple of years earlier, it might have been too soon, swaps and derivatives still too youngish to warrant special attention. Had he joined a couple of years after, it might have been too late, the position already filled. But mid-1986 was about right: swaps were promising enough to matter but also small enough to need people that would lift them off the ground. An unexpected opportunity opened up, and Raymond May took it.

He became JP Morgan's internal accountant for swaps and other derivatives. As he tells it, the business was run by half a dozen dealers who cared "only about the deal, not about the shop." May's job was to care about the shop. He approached JP Morgan's technology department and asked for help to support the derivatives area. He was given a $15 million price tag and a two-year timeline. He offered to do it himself for half a million and in six months. May and his small team engineered what may have been the first derivatives technological platform ever built by a bank. As he tells it,

> My first project was to build a Back Office System for swaps. This allowed us to process, make payments and account for swaps. My second project was building a Mark to Market accounting process for swaps. Once this was completed I was asked by the business to move from accounting to the business and develop systems to the front office. The needs were limitless— they had nothing but a calculator. First was a position management and pricing (what we called an unwind model), then came credit and end-of-day profit and loss. We imported a Sun from the US. The principal tool was Lotus.[2]

The entrepreneurial spirit honed by a childhood spent selling rabbit meat was now proving all its worth. The Kenyan farmer had become an indispensable member of an elite investment bank.

Much more was to come. Soon, he was asked to calculate the risk of all those swaps:

> In 1989 Connie Volstad who had started the swap business at JPM was replaced by Michael Eindhoven—Michael had no previous knowledge of swaps—his previous role was as a senior banker. After a while Michael asked me into his office and told me he needed a method to understand the risk being taken—with spread, basis, delta, vega, gamma, and curve, how could he get a handle on what everyone was doing? I left his office and began to think about the problem.[3]

That meeting may have been the true genesis of VaR. Raymond May got to work and delivered:

> The first simple model was to create three simple scenarios—a parallel move of the yield curve, a steepening of the yield curve and "humping" of the curve (note: the value of an interest rate swap, those by far most popular back then and today still market dominants, varies when the yield curve, a depiction of interest rates across many maturities, moves). This was applied

to the positions and a single number calculated—we tagged this Value at Risk. It was a fairly meaningless number but it had value in the relative risk in different books, and we soon saw it as value in setting trading limits.[4]

That is, what the inventor of VaR is saying is that the VaR number doesn't say much in itself but can be useful when comparing different positions. The VaR number doesn't say much about the risk of a position, but it may say something about whether that position is riskier than other positions.

In order to improve things, May needed more resources. If VaR was to grow up, efforts would have to be stepped up. He reminisces:

In order to do better I needed two things—data and a quant. For data I set up a Lotus spreadsheet and started collecting all the prices, rates, and spreads used in the swap business. I collected this at end of day London. For the quant I called the Research group in New York (read Till Guldimann) and asked if they had a resource they may lend me for the project. I was sent Gustavo Domingo. Gustavo came to London and sat next to me for three months and we developed the VaR model that everyone knows. By this time I had more than three months of good data. I developed the model in a Lotus spreadsheet. At this time it was only a single currency single portfolio model. In the swaps business at JPM at the time we ran a swap portfolio in all the major currencies, and we calculated an individual VaR for each. The option business had yet to really develop. I developed a position spreadsheet for each portfolio which allowed the trader to graph their positions and calculate their end of day profit and loss. I then spent all of 1990 and 1991 trying to get the traders to use my end-of-day spreadsheet![5]

What was Raymond May's VaR like? Its calculation assumed a Normal probability distribution and employed the Variance-Covariance method, the one also preferred by the Research team and, not surprisingly, the one that was initially most popularized across the industry. The confidence level was set at 95 percent, so that traders should not lose more than that number 19 out of 20 days. The "Ray May spreadsheet" was a huge one ("*I always believed it was the largest Lotus spreadsheet ever used*").

Tired of seeing how traders and dealers made all the money while he did all the work, Raymond May decided to switch hats. He asked his boss to move to trading, and was duly okayed and sent to New York in January 1992. He used his new home to convert the last holdout in his VaR quest, the U.S. dollar rates book, and to expand the methodology to indices and options positions. In 1994, he became head of New York trading for interest rate and foreign exchange derivatives.

By the end of 1989, there were two VaR tracks within the bank. One was the original Ray May spreadsheet. The other was the Research Group's, alerted of May's efforts by Gustavo Domingo. "*Gustavo had returned (to New York) and clearly must have told Till, who then took the idea and began to do a lot of research into the topic—none of this was I aware of at the time. I can't remember ever communicating again.*"[6] A naughty thought springs to mind: Was VaR internally stolen from Raymond May by Till Guldimann's team? This wouldn't be the first time in the history of financial markets that someone else appropriates a project from the original founder and then goes on to achieve fame and notoriety as the perceived inventor of an eventually highly popular endeavor. Something like that, for instance, took place at Morgan Stanley in the 1980s when it came to "statistical arbitrage," a widespread quantitative trading technique; conventional wisdom held for years that Nunzio Tartaglia had been the indisputable father of the sophisticated and potentially very lucrative strategy, and yet a 2007 book written by an eyewitness openly revealed to the world that the real inventor had in fact been a guy called Gerry Bamberger (whom Tartaglia, apparently better connected inside the firm, ruthlessly elbowed out). So, was Till Guldimann the Nunzio Tartaglia of the VaR saga?

Raymond May doesn't seem to think so. He is not aware of any internal VaR competition, and he only found out about Research's efforts when they released their model to the world in 1994 amid great fanfare. While he admits that the limelight may have been taken away from him, he has praiseful words for what his JP Morgan colleagues were doing. "*They did a lot of work and the final documentation they generated was high quality and I would never have gone to such lengths—I am a*

practical type—I was about building models not writing research documenta-
tion. It needed their work to take it to the next level," he says today.[7]

What's more, Ray May's VaR continued to be internally relevant throughout. Even as Research was working on its VaR version,
some higher-ups inside the firm still wanted to rely on May's figures.
Recounts the unsung VaR hero:

> I can't remember when the next step happened—'93 or '94—but
> by this stage Peter Hancock ran Derivatives at JP Morgan.
> Peter called me into his office and said he wanted a con-
> solidated single VaR for all currencies and he wanted it by
> 4:15 PM—the time all the senior managers met to discuss
> "risk." I would guess this was a lot about one-upmanship.
> Initially I looked for a technical person to come and help
> me—but after three weeks of endless meetings I decided to
> do it myself! All portfolios under Hancock used my spread-
> sheet. And the last in the timeline was NY which I managed.
> I embedded a macro in each to export the end of day results to
> a server. I then developed a master VaR spreadsheet which ran
> individual and consolidated results. I had this all done inside a
> week while running the U.S. Dollar business. I had my assis-
> tant then run this and distribute the reports for the 4:15 meet-
> ing. It almost needed no effort to operate and no one knew it
> was going on.

He kept supporting the Lotus spreadsheet even after switching to
trading, and the 4:15 report (the one that found its way daily to the
firm's chairman) was, according to May, still being fed with his model
by the time he departed from JP Morgan in 1997.

What does Raymond May today make of VaR's role in the 2007
crisis? Is it fair to blame the model? *"I don't think VaR caused this,"*
comes the blunt response. He thinks it unfair that VaR is fingered
because, at the end of the day, it didn't matter that much anymore: Risk
management, he asserts, had in recent years moved on, relying little on
VaR. His conclusions are based on practices at his old employer (which
almost uniquely managed to escape the crisis pretty much unscathed,
a testament, May says, to the firm's solid risk culture). *"By the mid
2000s at JPM VaR was a much less used risk management tool than stress*

testing as everyone knew that what really mattered was what was lurking in
the wings of the distribution. VaR was still calculated, but I think it's doing
a big injustice to the industry to suggest that's how risk was still being run in
the 21st century. Maybe other institutions misused it—but I don't think that
was the case at JPM." This may be so (though in this book we provide
evidence that VaR in fact did overwhelmingly guide trading and risk
decisions inside many banks in the run-up to the crisis) but it is crucial
to keep in mind that the main indictment against the model lies on
its role in bank capital regulation, not so much on its role as trading
floor risk radar; and, again, there's absolutely no doubt that when it
came to determining trading book leverage VaR was the one and only
thing that determined the, eventually very sad, outcome. Even if VaR
deserved (because, as Ray May argues, the model's counsel may not
have been what really mattered for internal decision making) to be
acquitted of the charge of providing the bad risk guidance that led
banks to accumulate toxic assets, that still would not acquit it from the
charge of having enabled the crisis.

After departing Wall Street, Raymond May tried to become Wall
Street's competitor. He decamped to North Carolina and began to
develop a start-up company charged with the mission of designing
an alternative electronic trading platform for derivatives. Ray May in
essence decided to bring efficiency and transparency into the derivatives business by offering an open alternative dealing route, in the
process locking horns with the over-the-counter derivatives industry.
Three years and $40 million in raised capital later, Blackbird was ready
to go. Soon, obstacles presented themselves. First came the regulators,
who were not sure whether they should police the new venture
(Was it an organized exchange like those in Chicago? Was it over the
counter?). The banks lent their support in the joint aim of keeping
regulation at bay. But soon, the same banks turned against Blackbird.
They were making too much money trading derivatives in an "inefficient
and opaque" way to risk the arrival of such a competitor. Blackbird's
launch was blocked.

In later years, he continued on an entrepreneurial quest. He
started a headhunting firm. He started an education-services company. What about VaR? Does Ray May ever reminisce about the "Ray
May spreadsheet"? Does the past ever show up in his mind? Well, the

credit crisis did rekindle old memories, and brought the inventor of VaR back face-to-face with his invention, almost two decades after the fateful meeting where Michael Eindhoven asked him to come up with a single risk number for JP Morgan's derivatives business. *"Since 2008 I have joked to friends that I was responsible for the blow up of the world because I never managed the 20th day—and left that to managers on Wall Street—they would take max advantage of that hole! My friends did not take me seriously—they had no idea what I was talking about."*[8]

■ ■ ■

After acting unconventionally by introducing the story of VaR through Raymond May's lens, let's now embrace orthodoxy and tell the conventional tale behind VaR's birth. In this tale, Ray May is nowhere to be found. He is not mentioned. He doesn't exist. In this tale, Dennis Weatherstone and Till Guldimann are the only names mentioned. They are the unique inventors, the only pioneers. Upon listening to Ray May's story we doubt that conventional line, but it is nonetheless quite useful to direct our attention toward it, for it helps us understand the role of two people that, indeed, had a very big part in VaR's nurturing and development. Ray May might have been the true original technical architect, but we can't talk about VaR's early life without talking at length about Weatherstone and Guldimann.

Let's begin with the chairman. In recent times it's almost become de rigueur that a bank's CEO would come from a trading floor background. Credit Suisse, Morgan Stanley, Citigroup, Goldman Sachs, Deutsche Bank, Lehman Brothers, and Bear Stearns are examples of very big firms that at one point or another in the past decade were (and are) run by people with a financial products past, rather than an advisory or commercial banking one. But when British-born Dennis Weatherstone became chairman of JP Morgan in 1990, his appointment seemed out of the ordinary. He had been a trader, not a traditional banker, throughout his career, rising to head the foreign exchange desk. Given such background, it is not surprising that market risk management was prioritized inside the firm during his mandate. Weatherstone had firsthand knowledge of how critical it was to keep a lid on things in the brave new world of derivatives and financial engineering. JP Morgan, like its competitors in general, was by that time engaged more and more in trading-related activities, and Weatherstone was bent on pushing that trend even further. But such boldness would have to be accompanied by stronger risk controls. When you are doing a lot of swaps and selling a lot of options, simple and naive approaches to risk won't cut it. Innovations in risk management were needed to safely navigate the waters of financial innovation.

Weatherstone, the conventional storyline goes, picked Till Guldimann to lead that effort. Produce something fancier than what we currently have, were the marching orders. Guldimann would have been an obvious choice. As head of research he would have had a predisposition toward big-thought projects and a team of highly trained quanty types at the ready. He also knew the bank well, from the inside, having previously held several senior risk-related roles. A Swiss national with an engineering degree from the prestigious ETH institute in Zurich (where Albert Einstein studied) and an MBA from Harvard Business School, Guldimann found the pre-VaR ways sadly rudimentary. *"How should I know if a trader should get an increase in his limits? All I could do is ask around. Is he a good guy? Does he know what he's doing? It was ridiculous."*[9] Guldimann was itching for something more scientific. He and his team focused (just like Ray May had already been doing for a while) on a Covariance approach to VaR. The model was unveiled at the bank's 1993 client conference, with market risk management at the height of fashion, and many attendees showed lots of interest in the device. In October 1994, Guldimann's team's RiskMetrics VaR methodology was made public to the outer world. Why? Why not keep proprietary techniques and information secret and away from competitors? Why give up on charging fees for the thing? According to Guldimann, JP Morgan decided that sharing its VaR would make everyone better off by reducing risk in the system. *"It popularized a methodology, and it enhanced the reputation of JP Morgan,"*[10] came the summation.

RiskMetrics documentation stated three reasons behind the unseemly sharing of knowledge and intelligence: One, JP Morgan was interested in promoting greater transparency of market risk since transparency is the key to risk management; two, JP Morgan aim's was to create a benchmark for market risk measurement since the absence of a common point of reference makes it difficult to compare different approaches to and measures of market risks; and three, JP Morgan intended to provide its clients with sound advice on market risk management, with RiskMetrics being an aid in such pursuit.

The bank noted that the methodology behind RiskMetrics was similar but not exactly the same as the one it internally used. So RiskMetrics VaR was not exactly the same as JP Morgan's VaR (Ray May's VaR?). And it warned of the model's limitations, "*We remind our readers that no amount of sophisticated analytics will replace experience and professional judgment in managing risks. RiskMetrics is nothing more than a high-quality toolkit for the professional risk manager involved in the financial markets and is not a guarantee of specific results.*" As you can see, VaR was disclaimed about from the very beginning. If even JP Morgan doubted the reliability of the thing, one wonders why just a few months after the public launch of VaR regulators endowed the model with the ultimate power and influence (much greater than that of just a risk radar). If VaR, according to its very parents, was not exactly foolproof for the relatively less relevant tasks of setting trading limits and determining staff compensation, why should it be considered reliable for the much more important role of bank capital regulation?

The gift of RiskMetrics most certainly made it easier for VaR to spread around. JP Morgan's analytical child was an invitation to calculate VaR, it made it so convenient. Not only was the math thoroughly explained in a thick user manual, but JP Morgan gave away the data, too. Generation of the statistical inputs needed to obtain a Covariance VaR is no picnic, and the daunting effort may have held many institutions back. But now that the estimations of volatilities and correlations derived from reams of historical prices were given away (accessible daily through the Internet), anybody with a computer could calculate their own VaR. A diskette (this was the 1990s!) with spreadsheets showing examples of VaR calculations was included. JP Morgan went as far as providing a list of specialist companies that could calculate your VaR using RiskMetrics, in case you didn't want to do it yourself. VaR was God and Till Guldimann was His Prophet. The world had to be converted and what better way than giving away thousands of RiskMetrics Bibles and helping a crop of VaR priests spread the gospel around.

RiskMetrics was a global sensation from the get-go. By October 1994, everybody and their brother was focused on risk, following a spate of continuous derivatives disasters (the very enthusiastically reported cases of Japan's Showa Shell oil company, Germany's Metallgesellschaft, Chile's Codelco, and Orange County, Procter & Gamble, Gibson Greetings, and others in the United States). The world was thirsty for a remedy, or for something that could be sold as a remedy. JP Morgan was a top firm, VaR looked impressively intelligent, and you had lots of help calculating it. It may have seemed impossible not to be seduced.

Originally, RiskMetrics technical document was 50 pages in length and the volatility and correlation data covered about 20 markets. By mid-1998 the document had been updated three times and run at almost 300 pages, while the free dataset had expanded to cover foreign exchange, equity, fixed income, and commodities in more than 30 countries. That year, as outside demands for JP Morgan's risk expertise became overwhelming, RiskMetrics was spun off into a different company. It was also successful as a stand-alone entity. By 2001, 1,000 copies of the technical document and 6,000 datasets were still being downloaded each month from its web site. In early 2008, the RiskMetrics Group listed on the New York Stock Exchange, a testament of how far VaR had come. Two years later, it was acquired by MSCI, a leading financial indices and analytics firm founded by Morgan Stanley.

By then, Dennis Weatherstone and Till Guldimann had long departed JP Morgan. On leaving the firm in 1994, Weatherstone (who had joined JP Morgan as a bookkeeper when he was 16) assisted the Bank of England's supervisory activities and served on several corporate boards. He died in Connecticut in June 2008. The *New York Times* obituary spoke of him as a "banking sage" that helped usher a new era of banking by realizing that the future laid in trading and securities.

Guldimann left JP Morgan in June 1995, departing for Infinity, a financial software company. He was excited about the opportunity to develop new risk gadgets. In his farewell e-mail to his JP Morgan colleagues, he certainly sounded upbeat: *"Their products are terrific, the troops are half my age and twice as smart (thus equal) and they will conquer the world even with me hanging on (jealous?)."*[11] At Infinity, Guldimann relished the chance to go beyond derivatives and trading risks to focus on firm-wide risk management covering all positions and asset classes, *"I don't want to sit in long meetings and manage a lot of people any more, I want to focus on advancing the craft of risk management and building new products,"* he explained. *"This is my second life."*[12] He retired in May 2011, having risen to vice chairman of the company. These days, Till Guldimann owns and runs Chateau Hetsakais, a winery in the San Francisco area.

■ ■ ■

Aｓ we've said, the Variance-Covariance method was originally the most widely used way of getting to the VaR number. RiskMetrics became useful precisely because it produced the analytical information needed to use that method. Variance-Covariance must have impressed people, since it looked impressive: The documentation was inundated with statistical and mathematical symbols and its foundations borrowed from revered classic financial theory principles. If you wanted to peddle the new science of financial risk management, Variance-Covariance was a great tool. Particularly in those early days, when the financial industry was still predominantly dominated by innumerate chums and innumerate practices, VaR looked as unassailably sophisticated and as undoubtedly superior as an alien spacecraft.

How does Variance-Covariance work? Roughly, you need the following pieces of information: the size of the positions (naturally), the volatility of the assets-risk factors, the selection of a statistical degree of confidence (implying the selection of a probability distribution), and the correlations between the different assets-risk factors making up the portfolio. Mixing all those things together, and with the help of some historical data, you arrive at your VaR number. The techniques have evolved through time, adding extra layers of complexity as more quants joined the risk world and as more academics focused on VaR (for instance, very advanced models were developed to forecast volatility; one of those approaches received a Nobel Prize), but the essence remains unaltered.

Let's start with a very simple case. Imagine a portfolio consisting of one single position on a single asset. The size of the position is

$1,000,000. We look at our selected historical data (going back several years) and see that the volatility (standard deviation, sigma) during the period was 0.55 percent. If we multiply $1,000,000 times 0.55 percent (if we multiply the position by its volatility) then we obtain the one-standard deviation VaR, $5,500 in this case. That is how much you could lose tomorrow. With what probability? According to the Normal distribution typically underpinning the Variance-Covariance method, an assumption that in fact allows us to use standard deviation as proxy for volatility, one standard deviation covers 68 percent of the entire "probability mass" inside the famous bell curve that describes how probable each particular outcome is under Normality (this bell-shape curve accumulates most of the total probability mass around the center, or the mean value, with events to the left and to the right of that center progressively receiving less and less probability, until they get a negligible portion of probability; the Normal curve, thus, is a curve that assigns a lot of chance to habitual events and very little chance to nonhabitual events, whether to the left or to the right, and thus is very appropriate to model things like human height that are dominated by the absence of outliers). That is, there would be a 16 percent chance of seeing values greater (right-hand side of the bell curve, or positive deviations) than the one-sigma value and a 16 percent chance of seeing values lower (left-hand side of the bell curve, or negative deviations) than the one-sigma value. So a single sigma delivers a two-tailed 68 percent statistical confidence interval: It tells you what can happen inside that 68 percent probability mass, but not what lies outside. Since VaR only concerns itself with losses, we focus only on the left-hand tail. Everything to the right of that area is now "worth" 84 percent of probability mass (the bell curve's entire right-hand tail plus its center plus part of the left-hand side). With 84 percent confidence, bad news should not be greater than the one-sigma value. So the one-sigma VaR is the 84 percent confidence VaR. That is the risk measure that we need. Now we can complete our analysis: for that particular $1,000,000 portfolio, one-day losses should not exceed $5,500 with 84 percent probability.[13]

What if we want to fine-tune things and get a higher confidence level? Easy. The Normal distribution playbook conveniently gives us very precise numerical guidance. If you want to go from 84 percent confidence to, say, 95 percent confidence you just multiply sigma by 1.65. (Why? Because 1.65 times the standard deviation happens to cover 90 percent of the bell curve, leaving just 5 percent of probability mass on each tail; we only care about one tail, so it becomes a 95 percent confidence level.) So the 95 percent VaR would be $5,500 * 1.65 = $9,075. That's the most you should lose 95 percent of the time. Want to fine-tune even more and jump to a 99 percent confidence? Then multiply sigma by 2.33 (2.33 times the standard deviation covers 98 percent of the bell curve). Our 99 percent VaR becomes $12,815. You should be expected to lose more than that amount only one day out of a hundred. Not surprisingly, as we reduce the probability that the loss would be superior to VaR, VaR becomes greater (it owns a larger share of the entire curve, thus a larger number of possible negative outcomes). As can be glanced, a loss beyond 2.33 sigmas is pretty much assumed not to take place (less than 1 percent chance). The problem, of course, is that in real life markets regularly register moves way beyond that (5 sigmas, 10 sigmas, 20 sigmas). A 5-sigma or 10-sigma VaR is not supposed to happen, but it does happen. If we are calculating our losses or capital with a 2.33-sigma tool and then much more extreme things take place often, then obviously our risk estimates and capital levels will prove very insufficient. If you guide yourself by a 1.65 or 2.33 sigmas radar in a 5- or 10- or 20-sigmas universe, you will be hopelessly lost.

What if my portfolio has more than one asset? How do I obtain the portfolio's volatility and thus its VaR? Here is where the math gets interesting. Devices known as *matrices* make an appearance. A matrix is a combination of rows and columns containing a bunch of different numbers. You can perform arithmetic operations between matrices. Matrices in essence allow you to collect bunches of numbers in big groups and then perform multiplications, or additions, or subtractions between those big chunks. They are a great way of dealing with calculations where a lot of numbers and variables are involved. And the great news is that the result of all that amalgamation of calculations may be a neat single number. You could start with thousands of figures grouped in several chunks and, after much toiling, end up with a single number as the final result.

So if you have several assets in your portfolio and you want a single portfolio VaR, you don't just calculate the individual positions' VaRs and add them up. Rather, you go with matrices. Why? Because this allows you to take account of the statistical correlation among the assets, a key component of the Variance-Covariance methodology. Correlation is useful because it may allow for diversification bene-fits and thus yield a lower (perhaps much lower) overall VaR number than if you simply added individual VaRs. The magic of Variance-Covariance for those praying for low VaR estimates lies not only in those unrealistically low sigmas, but also on the blessing of correlation: If assets happened to be uncorrelated or, better, negative correlated in the selected past period, the total VaR will be much lower than oth-erwise as assets are supposed to not move in tandem or even to match each other off (the chance of them crashing all together, your worst case scenario, would seem greatly diminished). The correlation param-eters can make a huge difference. For instance, in a three-asset port-folio example[14] total VaR can go from $41,000 to $66,000 if all assets are assumed to be perfectly correlated with each other (i.e., all the numbers in the Covariance matrix are 1), or down to $31,000 if just two of the assets are perfectly negative correlated with each other (i.e., −1 numbers in the relevant row-column spaces in the matrix). The premia of negative correlation can be vast. The drawbacks of positive correlation can be painful.

Drinking from Modern Portfolio Theory (the one famously invented in the early 1950s by a man named Harry Markowitz who went on to receive the Nobel Prize in Economics), two matrices are built. One contains the individual VaRs, at the chosen level of confi-dence, for each asset-risk factor in the portfolio. The other contains the different correlations between all assets–risk factors (how asset A correlates with asset B, how asset B correlates with asset C, how asset A correlates with asset C, how asset C correlates with asset D, and so on). Obviously, if you have a lot of assets, the Covariance matrix will be enormous. These two matrices are then multiplied, and, voila, you get a single number: VaR.

Obviously, the more components (assets, risk factors) the portfolio holds the more sensitive your calculation is to the assumptions behind Variance-Covariance. The greater the chance that the past volatility of some assets–risk factors will not be an accurate depiction of future volatility, and (specially) the greater the chance that the Covariance matrix would be unreliable: Correlation is a knowingly tricky concept in financial markets, with past guidance not exactly fully trustworthy; pretending to precisely map how dozens, let alone hundreds or even thousands, of individual assets are going to co-move together may be closer to voodoo than to real science.

While Variance-Covariance was the predominant methodology and to this day is probably the approach most closely associated with VaR (seems hard to think of VaR without thinking of sigma, correlation matrices, and probabilistic hypothesis), in time banks appear to have migrated toward the Historical Simulation alternative. The latter presents a few key advantages: It is model-independent (you do not have to make assumptions about the statistical behavior of the assets), it is conceptually extremely simple so anybody can understand it (the insides of Variance-Covariance can be indigestible for nonquants), it represents actual market behavior, and it copes well with any type of financial product (some derivatives can be hard to deal with via Variance-Covariance). Most of the banks involved in the 2007 crisis were using Historical Simulation, so understanding this method is key to understanding why those banks took on so much leveraged risk. Lehman Brothers, Goldman Sachs, Morgan Stanley, JP Morgan, Bear Stearns, Credit Suisse, Société Générale, and UBS all relied on Historical Simulation for their VaR calculations during the critical period.[15]

How does Historical Simulation work? You take a portfolio of assets and using a history of market prices for those assets revalue the portfolio, seeing what kind of performance today's portfolio would have enjoyed during those past data points. That is, you want to see what type of gains or losses your current portfolio would have registered had it been "alive" in each and every one of the trading days in your historical sample. Armed with that information, you proceed to generate a distribution of profits and losses from which the VaR at any given confidence level can be obtained. So-called *percentiles* are created, each containing 1 percent of the portfolio value changes. Instead of making theoretical assumptions about the probability distribution governing markets, you would imply the "true" distribution from actual market action. That's the main difference with Variance-Covariance, and from which platform the confidence levels are obtained. If we work with theoretical distributions (such as the Normal) then we have a precise rulebook that tells how to arrive at a given statistical estimation (say, multiply volatility by 2.33 or 1.65). If we instead work with "real" distributions then rather than borrow from an analytical guide, we look at actual money results that would have been experienced by the portfolio. We don't need to calculate volatilities or correlations, they are already embedded in and reflected by those past market prices. For example, the 95 percent VaR is the number corresponding to the 95th percentile worst performance that the portfolio would have registered using past prices. Imagine that the worst 95th percentile daily return for the portfolio in the preselected time frame (say, two years of data) would have been, say, −2.3 percent equivalent, given the notional size of each of the assets in the portfolio, to, say, −$1,250,000. That is your one-day 95 percent VaR. We didn't need sigma, we didn't need a Covariance matrix, we didn't need the Normality hypothesis. Just a plain simple look back through the market rearview mirror, to see how our portfolio would have fared back then. Of course, we are being very presumptuous and assuming that the road already traveled is a good indication (as good as 95 percent or even 99 percent) as to the road ahead. We are assuming that the probability distribution and statistical properties that held in the chosen sample (that were "revealed" by the chosen past) are the true ones and thus can be safely extrapolated into the future. Just like Covariance is way too cocky by pretending to know what is the right distribution, Historical Simulation is way too cheeky by pretending that the market knows what is the right distribution.

Historical Simulation may have seemed too provincial a method to impress anybody in the early days of VaR. Variance-Covariance (and Monte Carlo Simulation, another complex tool based on computationally randomly generating a lot of possible future outcomes and then applying those to the portfolio to get a estimation as to its possible future values) likely appeared as a much more powerful and impressive presentation card for the model. A better way to convince regulators and investors that the banking industry had finally subjugated the age-old beast of market risk. Sophisticated volatility and correlation mathematical exercises look more reassuringly high-tech than just collecting a bunch of old data and scouring for the least favorable days in the sample. While you may need high-powered science PhDs for the former task, a high-school dropout may be able to perform the latter. So maybe banks embraced the most complex VaR models first and then, once the royal dominance of the tool had been assured thanks to the complexity disguise, switched to more simplistic ways. Notice, poignantly, how JP Morgan itself eventually went Historical. Raymond May, for one, recognizes the PR value that the RiskMetrics Covariance-heavy exercise delivered at the critical beginning:

> In 1994 the Derivatives (Swaps) Business in the US hit a really nasty bump. Procter & Gamble and Gibson Greetings took huge losses from derivative trades executed through Bankers Trust. Congress went into high gear and regulation became a real possibility. Till and JPM came to the rescue—they released VaR and Risk Metrics as a model for how well JPM managed this complex business, and as part of a campaign to persuade Congress that derivatives where not a risk to the system. The rest is history.

■ ■ ■

Why did VaR catch on? JP Morgan was obviously enthusiastic from the get-go and VaR had a glorious launch, but the model could have died a quick death. Why didn't it? What made it stick? Well, VaR had several things going for it. First of all, it was a single figure that any-body could understand. The alternative to a firm-wide consolidated VaR was a messy myriad of risk reports pertaining to each product line, to each trading desk, and to each geographical location. Also, VaR was (duh!) numerical: The risk of a giant bank could be looked at in five seconds, rather than the hours and hours that it may take to obtain detailed verbal explanations as to the different market risks that were being run. So VaR was easy and comfortable. It also provided a bench-mark for managers to evaluate their underlings: traders and risk man-agers could now be judged according to the same tool, their actions and compensation linked to the same neutral (i.e., nonpersonal, non-emotional, nonsubjective) parameter. VaR, too, allowed different banks to be compared in a similarly objective manner; to this day, many ana-lysts and reporters would consider Bank A more daring than Bank B if the former's VaR is above the latter's. VaR was also assumed to be smarter than the previous status quo: It drew on actual market signals and rewarded portfolio diversification (in itself, a good way to reduce a bank's risk; something to be deservedly prized). An easy, comfortable, convenient, smart benchmark. No wonder it was a hit inside dealing floors worldwide.

Of course, we are leaving out the cynical reasons for loving VaR. Maybe bankers understood from the beginning how low VaR can be or can be made to be, a great thing if you want to run risks and (once you've sold the model to the regulators) build leverage. VaR also gave banks the ultimate word on their riskiness: If Bank A's VaR is low, any external complaints that it is nonetheless running a very risky operation may be drowned and silenced by the model's sanctified edict. VaR allowed a lot of people to make a living as VaR operators, lending golden respectability and scientific cred to the risk management profession.

Besides all the above rationales (both purist and cynical), there's quite likely another key reason why people fell head over heels: VaR offered a dream. An irresistibly enchanting promise: the promise of precision. And in an effortless fashion. Just pay some people to collect some data, run some computer programs, and every day after markets close your exposures are distilled precisely. No need to laboriously argue about risks, to pore over positions, to get a feel for things, to think about fundamentals. Those actions, you say to yourself, may in any case lead to inconclusiveness, to the vagueness of human opinion. Not to concrete specific dictums. Lost in the sea of information and opinionated takes, you may pray for conclusive unequivocal guidance. Even if you doubt that something like that could ever exist in the markets, the temptation to fool and delude yourself is ample. What's the risk of a portfolio comprised of gold bullion, currency options, and interest rate swaps? You could go the thinking way and slowly analyze the prospects for inflation, economic growth, global trade imbalances, the future path of Libor, and the inexhaustible list of other variables that could affect the value of your holdings. Or you can just press the "calculate VaR" key on your computer.

Chapter 3

They Tried to Save Us

Not Everyone Loved VaR ■ *The Lebanese Seer* ■ *The Man from Barbados* ■ *The Icelandic Professor* ■ *Lost Prophecies*

From the late 1980s to mid-2007, VaR was generally deeply loved and highly respected. Bankers were proud of their invention (and thankful for the beautiful things it could deliver), quants were enchanted by the technical possibilities it afforded and the legitimacy it showered on their skills, software vendors and risk consultants were in awe as to the commercial opportunities the model provided, financial theoreticians applauded the analytical conquest of finance that the model symbolized, the specialist media enthusiastically devoted pages and pages to its calculation methodology, and regulators couldn't wait to bow at its altar. Famed economist John Maynard Keynes once talked of the difficulties of guessing other people's votes during a beauty contest; rather than focusing on which contest participant you consider to be prettier, the key, Keynes said, was to be able to predict which participant the other judges will consider prettier. Applying this logic to risk

71

management beauties, it seems hard not to conclude that during that two-decade period everyone would have guessed that everyone else's vote would have gone to VaR. The alternative (that someone would renege on VaR) just looked too unthinkable.

And yet, the VaR field in those days was not entirely devoid of rebel contrarians, more than willing to accuse the deified model of terrible shortcomings and of containing the seeds of chaos. Perhaps a ragtag bunch of misfits rather than a consolidated and coordinated movement, but still enormously noteworthy and telling. For, if VaR is really so great, why are these (quite high-quality and reputable) individuals so busy proclaiming the opposite message? We should be interested in what those mavericks had to say not so much out of an interest in two-sided debates or a belief in the benefits of diverse views. What should matter most to us is that the heeding of those bravely contrarian arguments could have prevented the 2007–2008 financial crisis. If VaR had been severely doubted and second-guessed following the warnings of the rebels, then maybe VaR's role in the markets would have been diminished, perhaps even into oblivion. The insurgents who refused allegiance to the VaR dictatorship first spoke their minds many years before anybody had heard of subprime CDOs. There would have been plenty of time to fix banks' internal risk management practices and bank capital regulation, so that they wouldn't abide by a tool that conveniently facilitates lethality and instead based themselves on commonsensical rules that don't lead to 1,000-to-1 toxic leverage and to proclaiming as riskless the riskiest securities ever conceived.

The truly sad aspect of the historically destructive 2007–2008 mayhem is that it could have been avoided had the world chosen to attentively listen to the heretical VaR dissenters who, out of nothing but concern for the system's health, tried to warn us.

■ ■ ■

In 1995, Nassim Taleb made his international intellectual debut. A very successful and veteran option trading professional by then, he had yet to amply share his views with the world. The release of a book called *Dynamic Hedging* (John Wiley & Sons, 1997) changed that. Widely considered the bible of option trading to this day, the book didn't just overnight make Taleb the indisputable authority in a complex and arcane field, but most crucially provided a platform for the expression and spreading of his views. Just like *Dynamic Hedging* contained ideas, insights, and language never seen before in such a tome, Taleb quickly showed himself to be a pioneer of unique ideas, insights, and language. Financial people became eager to listen to what this fiercely outspoken battler of conventional wisdom had to share.

One of Taleb's earliest public appearances was curiously one of the most relevant (for the purposes of this book, the most relevant in fact). In what remains the classic debate on VaR, now long defunct *Derivatives Strategy* magazine invited Taleb and a pro-VaR nemesis to lock horns on the model's reliability. The Lebanese-American went first, in the December 1996 issue.

"What do you think of VaR?" Taleb was asked back in those youthful times.[1] His answer set the tone not just for that particular interview but for a truth-spreading campaign that continues to the present day,

> VaR has made us replace about 2500 years of market experience with a covariance matrix. We made a tabula rasa of years of market lore that was picked up from trader to trader and crammed everything into a covariance matrix. Why? So a management consultant or an unemployed electrical engineer can understand financial risks. To me, VaR is charlatanism because it tries to estimate something that is not scientifically possible to estimate. It gives people misleading precision that could lead to the build-up of positions. It lulls people to sleep.[2]

But surely, Mr. Taleb, VaR must be better than what we had before, right? Wrong.

> You are worse off relying on misleading information than if you had no information at all. If you give a pilot an altimeter that is sometimes defective he will crash the plane. Give him nothing and he will look out the window. Technology is safe only if it's flawless. A lot of people reduce their anxiety when they see numbers. Before VaR we looked at positions and understood them. After VaR all we see is numbers, that depend on strong assumptions. I'd much rather see the details of the positions than some number that is supposed to reflect the risk.[3]

For instance, Taleb mentioned how the massive selling of options (a potentially very risky strategy that can send one to the cleaners very suddenly and dramatically should markets fluctuate) that would have been frowned on by the old risk management approaches could after VaR be condoned on account of the model registering no risk (perhaps because of a lack of market volatility, possibly due to the probabilistic assumptions behind the model). Just an example of how financial modeling can lead to the hiding and utter misinterpretation of risks (and keep firmly in mind that the 2007 crisis was essentially the result of a lot of important people massively selling optionality under the VaR-aided disguise of no-risk). Are you, Mr. Taleb, implying that VaR should not be used inside trading floors to measure risks? *"The risks that do not matter perhaps, but not those that truly matter. Moreover traders will find the smallest crack in the models and try to find a way to take the largest position they can while showing the smallest amount of risk."*

So what's going to happen as a result of everybody and their cousin adopting VaR in financeland? Since you are so opposed to the model, are you worried about its future side effects? *"VaR players are all dynamic hedgers (i.e. mechanically following certain model-dictated trading instructions) and need to revise their portfolios at different levels. VaR can thus make very uncorrelated markets become very correlated, by forcing people to dump assets at the same time."* In other words, if we all become VaR robots and VaR clones and automatically base our actions on the model's guidelines, big market shake-ups may ensue as we all liquidate at the same time once our VaR limits are all breached at the same time. Also, if people know that you will have to take certain actions in blind obedience to VaR, they will try to force you to take that action and front-run you so as to milk millions while bankrupting you. A bit less mathematically driven sectarian groupthink and a bit more intuition-driven individualistic decision making would be healthier and more effective as crisis preventer.

Smelling an exclusive attention-grabbing scoop, *Derivatives Strategy* proceeded to stir the pot by requesting academic Philippe Jorion (a staunch VaRista, then and now) to provide a reply to Taleb's unshy ruminations. Noting that Taleb's stance was "somewhat unusual given the widespread interest in VaR,"[4] the California-based professor proceeded to peddle the model by noting one of its most often cited advantages, namely how easy it is for anybody to understand its outputs. Anybody can get the meaning of "You won't lose more than $100 million 99 percent of the time" or "You will only lose more than $100 million twice a year." Even the most boorish of bank executives can understand what VaR says. This has traditionally been seen as a very potent selling point for the model (okay, we are all for clarity, but clarity is useless or worse if the $100 million 99 percent of the time storyline turns out to be a very false representation of actual risks; if VaR's numbers are structurally wrong I don't care how easy they are to understand).

Trotting along familiar VaR-endorsing paths, Jorion stated that without VaR it is not possible to get an estimate of the overall trading floor risks of a bank, that VaR would have prevented the derivatives disasters of the mid-1990s, that VaR, while admittedly a wobbly measure, is better than nothing and better than relying on "market lore"[5] (call me crazy, but it seems a bit disrespectful for a cloistered academic to belittle like that the actions of the real men and women shaping market activity through their hands-on activities, to demean the hundreds of thousands of pros who toiled and toil the markets without recourse to VaR as actors of "nothingness"; I wonder what pre-VaR market legends and masters of risk would think of the professor). Jorion, who seems to have done quite well for himself out of VaR's popularity and out of his carefully crafted position as the go-to VaR guru (I am told that he was in a real hurry 15 years ago to be the first to publish a book on VaR), concluded his rebuttal with the following words, "*It seems premature to describe VaR as charlatanism. VaR is an essential component of sound risk management systems.*"[6] I, for one, wonder how he views things after the VaR reign that he so fanatically advocated for has yielded a monstrous market crisis full of toxic leverage and irrepressibly obscene risk underestimations. How's that for robust?

Perhaps intoxicated by all the back-and-forth, the folks at *Derivatives Strategy* could not resist asking Nassim Taleb to rebut Philippe Jorion's rebuttal. The first thing the uncloistered trader did was remind people where each of the two protagonists stood: While he was for the suspension of VaR as potentially dangerous malpractice, Jorion was for the preservation of VaR and its supplementing with other methods. Proclaimed Taleb:

> I find that the risk managers I hear recommend a "guarded" use of VaR on the grounds that it "generally works" or "works

on average" do not share my definition of risk management. The risk management objective function is survival, not profits and losses. According to legend, one trader made $8 million in eight years and lost $80 million in eight minutes. According to the VaRista standards, he would be in general and on average a good risk manager.[7]

Sound familiar? It should. As this is exactly what happened to many banks up to and during the 2007 crisis. They made money consistently for several years and then got spectacularly blown up by the very same positions that had delivered the earlier windfalls (and that according to VaR were trouble-free and gloriously prudently managed). Would you catalog such conduct as commendable risk management?

After pointing out that the fact that VaR was embraced by all major financial players does not grant it instant credibility, as banks have been known to consensually make erring decisions before, Taleb delivered the truly gifted insight, the truly memorable line, the truly for-the-ages prediction,

> I believe that VaR is the alibi that bankers will give shareholders (and the bailing-out taxpayer) to show documented due diligence, and will express that their blow-up came from truly unforeseeable circumstances and events with low probability not from tak-ing large risks that they didn't understand. I maintain that VaR encourages untrained people to take misdirected risks with shareholders', and ultimately the taxpayers', money.[8]

It is almost insultingly prescient. Taleb nailed the 2007 crisis 10 years earlier. I guess it pays to keep an open mind and to refuse to be fooled by quantitative snake oil.

Taleb could have stopped right there and the 1997 debate would have already been sufficiently legendary. But he still had time to offer some extra pearls: the applications of engineering methods to the social sciences in the name of progress has led to economic and social disaster; no self-respecting scientist would ever think anyone would hold on to a falsified theory and VaR was falsified several times (via the prevalence of extreme market events, which likelihood is deemed impossible by the model); traders are trained to seek for truth and look into reality's garbage can, not the elegant idealized world of models; probabilities in the markets are unknownable and nonstationary (volatility and correlation can't be estimated reliably); and we can't learn much from past data (among other things, because traders adjust their behavior following market events).

The anti–VaR diatribe concluded by equating the model to the Maginot line. The more unpredictable something is, the more harmful it is. Or the most harmful events are unpredictable, as we learn from experience and correct that which caused harm in the past. VaR can't capture the German Army going around the "impregnable" fortifications because it had never happened. Thus, the Nazi advance (the crisis, the mega losses) is not prevented. That which was supposed to protect ended up making you vulnerable and led to your destruction. So much like VaR, indeed.

■ ■ ■

Avinash Persaud is a lucky man: He lives and works in the Caribbean. He is also a smart man: He was an early identifier of VaR's appetite for destruction. The grist of his year 2000 denunciation[9] was straight: Market-sensitive risk measures will lead to less stable and more crisis-prone markets. The more popular VaR is the less likely it is to work. Widespread use of VaR can lead to sudden snowballing asset liquidations across a myriad of apparently unrelated markets, as correlations among asset classes increase. Why? If large banks see their VaR limits breached because of some piece of bad news in a particular market segment (say, U.K. technology stocks), they may cut positions not only in that particular segment but also in other holdings so as to bring VaR numbers under control. This dumping can enhance volatility across different market sectors, which begin to move in tandem. Now smaller banks that may not have had significant (if any) exposure to U.K. tech stocks get impacted and see their VaR limits get surpassed, demanding that they engage in their own round of liquidation, possibly involving assets different from the ones the big banks are dumping. Now the number of asset classes and products behaving in a correlated fashion increases, in a self-feeding mechanism (large banks may be prompted into further liquidations in the type of assets that the smaller banks were forced to get rid of). Potentially, all the way to a major crisis.

This is compounded by what Persaud sees as a tendency among financial players to copycat each other and to build portfolios similar to those of their competitors, for several reasons. Thus, at any one point many firms would have identical positions. If one is forced to liquidate, that means all will have to liquidate. VaR forgot to consider the impact of having it around, giving orders. If one VaR-compliant institution is losing more than its specified limit, chances are that many firms will begin to suffer losses way above those previously indicated by their VaR models. As VaR becomes predominant, the fall of one bank can result in the fall of all banks. VaR may work for a single bank but not in a universe with many banks, particularly if there is herding behavior in position-building. VaR-dictated liquidations will impact market prices and volatility as long as VaR is widely employed and followed. Of course, the real issue is that VaR may force banks to liquidate *way too soon*, thus giving rise to a systemic catastrophe at the slightest increase in turbulence or losses. Given VaR's capacity for humble risk estimates, banks' limits may be too easily breachable and risk managers too easily scared into forcing a reduction of risk (especially following a complacency-building calm market period that yields very low VaR numbers while sanctioning the accumulation of large positions). So, many times a sharp increase in VaR following sudden market gyrations may not so much indicate a really troublesome situation as much as the fact that prior VaR figures were extremely underestimating true risk. If those figures had been realistically higher, the gyrations may be less impactful and the liquidations less urgent, making the snowballing disaster less likely. The key issue is that thanks to VaR relatively modest market developments can morph into a very big crisis.

Also, VaR may start to ascend for the *wrong reasons*. Just because an asset happens to experience some temporary convulsions does not outright imply that the asset has become intolerably daring and thus a portion of those holdings should be gotten rid of. Foundationally sound and robust securities can nonetheless waltz around, slaves to the whims of emotional investors and frantic opinion makers. Such waltz-ing need not be indicative of a decline in the safeness of the play, and yet that's what VaR would unfailingly proclaim. Reading from the tea leaves of ever-changing, never-stable, dubiously informative market action can indeed lead to abominably misguided risk assessments. Just like a decrease in volatility need not imply lower risk, an increase in turbulence need not beget danger. Data-driven volatility is simply not an accurate depiction of true risk. That is, those massive snowballing liquidations that take place in the name of risk reduction may have been instigated by numerical instructions that have nothing to do with real risk (in fact, the liquidated asset could well be in the midst of a de-risk-ification process; for instance, as the value of corporate bonds may, for whatever reasons, be fluctuating a bit economic growth and consumer confidence may be on the rise, thus lowering the chance that companies won't repay their debts and reducing the real risk of owning those bonds). Subjecting traders to VaR limits is odd because VaR may have absolutely nothing to do with real risk. In their desperation for measurable concreteness and precision, banks have allowed a meaningless ghost to shape markets and to determine whether crises happen or not.

According to Persaud (a globally recognized guru who at the time was a senior buy-side analyst, following a long stint at JP Morgan), *"The predominance of herding behavior and its lethal combination with the practice of VaR limits may explain why the 1990s have been a decade of such financial dislocation: the financial system has been in crisis for 40 out of the 120 months."*[10] In light of this, Persaud found it quite paradoxical that regulators would actively support the adoption of VaR.

Almost a decade later, and motivated by a financial cataclysm several notches more intense than those that prompted him to first denounce VaR, Persaud revisited the issue.[11] Reminiscing on the 1998 Asian Crisis (when VaR was for the first time publicly unveiled as flawed and problematic), Persaud reminded us of a crucial point: VaR may make people sell even when they don't want to and when they would otherwise not have sold. He recalls the explications given back then by one reluctant liquidator: *"I wanted to hold on now that prices had fallen so far, but my risk systems pushed me out and kept me out."*[12] It was inevitable then that market prices would drive market prices, in a vicious circle. Writing in mid-2008, Persaud recognized the chaos afflicting markets at the time. He had seen it before, a decade earlier.

He knew what VaR was capable of: the unleashing of a "liquidity black hole" with price declines triggering not bargain hunting but further selling. And all this caused by a mechanism that was supposed to help financial institutions control risks.

As the Caribbean sage understands only too well, VaR encourages traders to scour the financial planet for punts that appear risk-free, statistically speaking. It is not just that by doing so VaR may end up on occasions discriminating against fundamentally sounder investments and in favor of naturally shakier ones (remember, volatility is not risk), but that VaR is a tool that transforms calm into chaos. Placidity into war. Once the model that every bank is using detects the placid spots in the market jungle, every bank will be motivated into settling in those spots, eager to gorge on "no-problem" fare that requires very little in the way of capital commitments and that contains the promise of lascivious returns on equity. The more exotic the game to be found in those soothed places the greater the motivation. Such communal, model-directed actions can end up ugly. "*The observation of safe sectors by risk models turns them into risky sectors: increasingly overvalued, highly correlated, and prone to volatility,*" posited Persaud.[13]

It is highly interesting that Persaud learned firsthand of VaR's troubling impact while being employed by the firm that invented and, most crucially, provided the key initial marketing push for the model. He worked for JP Morgan as the Asian debacle unfolded and as his views on VaR became indelibly formed. In 2008 he described his 1998 epiphany, and how his counsel was received:

> I had learned firsthand that whereas risk-sensitive systems may help banks manage their risks during quiet times, they are like seatbelts that don't work when you drive fast. They are not crisis-prevention measures: They make crises worse. This lesson prompted me to write my 1999 essay warning on the disturbing interaction of herding behavior and market-sensitive risk management practices. Mature risk managers found resonance in the story, but regulators queued up to dismiss the criticisms.[14]

So the front-row views of this battle-scarred practitioner went unheeded by the detached regulatory community. The skeptic's words could not prevent VaR from continuing to populate the rulebooks (in spite of the notoriety of Persaud's original critique; the essay won a coveted international prize). The VaR-incorporating 1996 market risk amendment to VaR-devoid Basel I was enshrined into Basel II, while in the United States the SEC modified its earlier stance and also fell for the model. If it was up to Persaud, bank capital regulations would have never been based on VaR. It must have been disheartening for the Barbados-born economist to witness how VaR's dominance and power became even more extended following the release of his warning. He is obviously not a fan of letting banks capture bank regulation,

> If the object of regulation is to align banks internal controls more closely with regulation, then why engage in extremely costly regulation in the first place? Leave it to banks' risk controls. If the purpose of regulation is to avoid market failures, we cannot rely on market prices as the instruments of regulation. Risk sensitivity as a regulatory principle sounds sensible until you think about it.[15]

The veteran market-trotter was not surprised one bit that the imperial reign of VaR led to a vastly undercapitalized banking industry, even while regulators, blinded by the models, had assumed it to be extremely well capitalized just as the nastiness arose. Market risk-based measures are just too lethally procyclical and lead to too lethally procyclical capital requirements, blindly fueling the boom and possibly prolonging the bust.

VaR and other metrics promote bad banking, argues Persaud, where decisions are not based on on-the-ground analysis by analysts with long knowledge of market and credit risk, but on the pseudoscience of data-driven computations that can lead all banks (all using the same publicly available information behind the calculation of those metrics) to own identical portfolios and "*herd in and out of markets eventually causing systemic collapse.*"[16] When diversity in risk assessment is eliminated by a flawed technical construct, bad things ensue. In closing his I-told-you-so post-crisis summation, Persaud could not resist delivering one final lashing: "*Let's not forget that the proponents of Basel II said that the criticisms were far-fetched and that the system was now safer than ever before.*"[17] Let's not, indeed.

Jon Danielsson is a cosmopolitan who suffered a double blow from the 2007 crisis. As a resident of London, he experienced firsthand the debacles of Northern Rock, Royal Bank of Scotland, and the myriad of large international investment banks with a heavy City presence. As a native of Iceland, he had to in parallel endure the personal pain of seeing his country sink into a financial and social abyss. The naive observer may even be tempted to argue that the London School of Economics (LSE) academic maven seems to have a habit of chasing crises around the world. He was a student in the United States during the period that saw the greatest one-day stock market drop in Wall Street's history, the chaotic disappearance of legendary bank Drexel Burnham Lambert, the meltdown of the junk bond market, and the collapse of the savings and loan industry, not to mention the first economic recession in a long time. And his 1997 arrival at the LSE coincided like clockwork with the unleashing of the Asian, and then Russia-LTCM, meltdowns.

In light of this biographical background, it may surprise few that financial risk counts among professor Danielsson's strongest interests. He has been opining on risk modeling and risk regulation for a long time. Such ventures inevitably put him face-to-face with VaR. And he didn't like what he saw. As far as I could tell, Danielsson began to muse on VaR as early as 1997. He seems to have originally been mostly interested in the statistical fine print of the model, rightly pointing out that VaR models (especially the earlier ones) suffer from the Normality affliction and thus are bad capturers of the non-Normal extreme events that characterize markets. Danielsson and colleagues consequently applied new quantitative techniques that attempted to tackle said issue. They heartedly recommended the use of those calculation tricks given how standard VaR models appeared to underestimate risk, making them ill-suited to the regulatory task. Interestingly (and cheekily), already in 1998 they expressed their doubts as to banks' eagerness to embrace their suggested approaches since the standard approach could yield so humble capital requirements. Even more intriguing was their wondering about regulators' motivations for imposing VaR as a regulatory measure. They didn't seem entirely convinced, "*In our opinion, the regulatory basis for VaR is not well understood and merits further study.*"[18]

The Icelandic and his team of accomplices may have been among the very first (if not *the* very first) hard-core finance theoreticians to focus on the economic and social rationale for the imposition of the model as risk and capital king. In other words, they focused on the truly critical questions. Which led them to the truly critical answers. Danielsson clarified:

> The measurement and implementation of VaR is an active and exciting area of research, with numerous contributions. This research has almost exclusively been concerned with the accuracy of the various estimation techniques. Compared to the statistical approach, the economic analysis of VaR has been neglected. The wider issue of the benefits for society of VaR-based risk management and supervision has hardly been addressed.[19]

And then proceeded to their own analysis of the economic rationales:

> We suggest that the drive for VaR regulation derives from the regulatory capture by the financial industry to safeguard its power and the preference of regulators for silent action instead of overt actions like bail-outs.[20]

Pretty strong stuff, no doubt. Just like Nassim Taleb was implying in those nascent times, Danielsson and his gang seemed convinced that the self-interest of banks was the real driver behind the imposition of the VaR dictatorship. And if they were right and regulators acceded out of a desire for discretion and distaste for loud action, well we know how that backfired 10 years later, as a VaR-infected system gave rise to the mother of all public planetary bailouts.

After having fought the opening VaR battles with the backing of his team, Danielsson gave it a go at a solo effort in 2000. He came out swinging:

> For regulatory use, the VaR measure is lacking in its ability to fulfill its intended task, it gives misleading information about risk, and in some cases may actually increase both idiosyncratic (i.e., bank-specific) and systemic risks. Risk modeling is not an appropriate foundation for regulatory design.[21]

As Danielsson points out, data-based risk models can't work during market crises because at those chaotic points the statistical properties change with regard to less chaotic, calmer times. So what was predicted improbable during stability is suddenly very real. VaR breaks down during instability. A big reason for this is that in finance, unlike the case of weather forecasting, the use of prediction models can impact the prediction: While the weather won't be impacted by what meteorologists say, what financial models say will impact what financial actors do; the very presence of VaR makes probability distributions in finance nonstationary and thus very hard to tackle. VaR can change the nature of risk in a market. It can create instability just by being there. It can unleash crises out of nothing. What's more, its very destiny may be to break down, as it transforms placidity into (unpredicted) catastrophe. In Danielsson's words, "A risk model breaks down when used for its intended purpose."

Like Avinash Persaud, Danielsson saw VaR as dangerously leading to a dangerously undiversified financial industry, with every firm owning the same positions and thus increasing the risk of cascading liquidations. Mechanical model-driven trading can introduce otherwise inexistent disturbances. "*If every financial institution has its own trading strategy, no individual technique can lead to a liquidity crisis. If many of these market participants need to execute the same strategies during crisis, they will change the distributional properties of risk. As a result, the distribution of risk is different during crisis than in other periods, and risk modeling is not only useless but may exasperate the crisis,*" came the summation.

The London-based professor ended his solitary 2000 lambasting of VaR by reminding us that modeling as a regulatory tool cannot be recommended. Risk modeling is simply too unreliable and the models can be too easily manipulated. The theoretical foundations of VaR conceptually result in misleading information regarding a firm's riskiness. It is crazy to have capital requirements fluctuate with the whims of market action (a *selective and limited* sample of recent market action, to boot); the capital required to back a trade should be a much more stable figure. Financial mandarins, the Icelandic pondered, should do away with VaR and try better ways to make sure that banks are sufficiently capitalized and protected. Danielsson made two proposals: crude leverage ratios, or forcing banks to purchase insurance (he cited the example of cross-insurance in New Zealand, with banks effectively hedging each other). After all, if solid solutions are available and even tried-and-tested, why roll the dice on the very unlikely chance that mathematical models built on wildly dubious foundations would get risk right?

A few months after his lone ranger dismissal of VaR, Jon Danielsson was back to assembling a strong anti-VaR squad with which to launch a concerted all-out assault on the regulatory fortifications. Submitted in response to the Basel Committee's request for comments, the May 2001 "An Academic Response to Basel II" paper was an assemblage of professorial grandees, with no less than six campus heavyweights lending their support to the contrarian Icelander. The regulatory elite was putting the final touches to the new Basel II rulebook and as is customary were requesting feedback from industry and academic sources. It was clear from the start that Danielsson's new team was looking to pick up a fight with the status quo:

> It is our view that the Basel II proposals have failed to address many of the key deficiencies of the global financial regulatory system and even created the potential for new sources of instability. VaR can destabilize an economy and induce crashes when they would not otherwise occur. The Basel Committee has chosen poor quality measures of risk. Heavy reliance on credit rating agencies is misguided. This set of proposals will exacerbate the procyclicality of financial regulation. In so far as the purpose of regulation is to reduce the likelihood of systemic crisis, these proposals will tend to negate, not promote this useful purpose. There is considerable scope for the underestimation of financial risk.[22]

The university Cassandras went as far as to, prophet-like, warn Basel to *"Reconsider before it is too late."* Didn't I tell you that these people tried to save us?

Unfortunately, and as we know only too well, Basel did not reconsider. VaR and the other flawed metrics were not second-guessed. They were left authoritatively in place so that things like subprime CDOs could be evaluated according to their (eventually very friendly) dictates. Writing in May 2008 on the ugly consequences of regulators not having heeded his decade-long recommendations, Jon Danielsson showed that age had not vanquished the campaigner in him. "*Model-driven mispricing produced the crisis, and risk models don't perform during crisis conditions. The belief that a really complicated statistical model must be right is merely foolish sophistication,*" opined his aptly named "Blame the Models" salvo.[23] The Viking warrior could not understand how, even in the midst of a models-authored apocalypse, regulators could continue embracing bad modeling. Perhaps, as he put it, the math is a conveniently lazy way out for the rule makers. Rather than devote time to understanding the actual positions held by banks and the interactions among them (that is, rather than devote time to really understand risk), regulators settled for the comfort of numbers. But in this case, Danielsson reminds us, "*numbers do not imply understanding.*"

Amen.

■ ■ ■

In spite of having had their warnings subliminally ignored by bankers and regulators as the twentieth century gave way to the twenty-first and as the latter advanced, the insurgent trio has done quite well for themselves since those days when they tried to draw attention towards VaR's lethality. Nassim Taleb is, of course, a much better known figure now than he was then, having magnificently succeeded at becoming a world-renowned intellectual. Avinash Persaud became a hedge fund manager and built a very high international profile as financial and economic expert. And Jon Danielsson appears to have consolidated his top-flight academic career, going from lecturer to reader at the London School of Economics, as well as becoming a fixture as commentator in the specialized and general media.

However, chances are that these men, widely known and followed as they are, are (with the possible exception of the Icelandic professor) not remembered for their anti-VaR prophecies. This is most definitely so in the case of the most outspoken, and by far the most famous, of the three. Of the millions of people worldwide who read Nassim Taleb's books and articles and follow him on Facebook, it is a safe bet that very few associate him with VaR. In the many interviews that I have observed and listened to, Taleb is almost never (or plain never) asked about VaR, the model's role in the 2007 crisis, and his earlier unheeded accusations. Beyond a small coterie of risk junkies, Taleb may not be recognized at all for his role in the VaR debate. I suspect that on the many occasions that he brings VaR into the fore, most of his followers simply don't know what that three lettered term means nor are they aware of its influence. I vividly remember a postcrisis TV interview in which Taleb was frantically trying to raise the VaR issue and the interviewers looked completely at a loss, as if he had been speaking in an alien tongue. They just didn't recognize that VaR word.

In July 2010 I sent Avinash Persaud an article of mine dealing with VaR's role in the crisis and lauding his landmark work of ten years earlier. He remarked to me that he was beginning to feel that nobody remembered his old analysis. I have to take this as evidence that no one had thought of dusting off those views following a VaR–abetted cataclysm, most likely because no one remembered those views in the first place.

Just like you, I have yet to see the special TV program or newspaper report on how Taleb, Persaud, and Danielsson (and very few others) foresaw the 2007 crisis many years prior by quickly understanding the consequences to be had from having a deleteriously malfunctioning concoction be given the keys to the risk and capital kingdom. This is doubly puzzling given the reality of a media world obsessed with seers, futurists, and prognosticators, and that is so desperate to crown prophets that it readily crowns the wrong prophets. (Of all the gurus that have been regularly presented by mass media as either ex-ante golden forecasters or ex-post golden explicators of the crisis, essentially none of them has ever mentioned VaR as a factor.)

Even when the predicted event is of the highest magnitude and even when the predictions are excruciatingly on the mark, the prophesies may be utterly ignored. And so the truly important lessons are not learned. The visionary wisdom of the rebel triad may thus get irremediably lost, rather than handed down to today's and future bankers and policy makers so that they know better than to repeat the same mistakes. In the end, VaR's best line of defense may be its anonymity, how little of it is known beyond a small band of insiders and risk wonks. If such an eventful development as the 2007 crisis (perhaps one of the most thoroughly and globally covered events ever) has not been able to make VaR generally known and if neither Taleb's, nor Persaud's, or Donalsson's predictions of the model's mischief have been pointed out to the public, then VaR can rest easy. When the damage that you've caused goes unnoticed, you get to live another day.

Chapter 4

Regulatory Embracement

Basel Power ■ *They Asked for VaR* ■ *They Got VaR* ■ *They Kept VaR* ■ *They Keep VaR*

B asel can claim ownership to several noteworthy accomplishments. It apparently is the warmest and least rainy city in Switzerland, something quite appealing in a country better known for its snowfalls. It annually hosts the premier international show for modern and contemporary art. It, of course, produced Roger Federer, arguably the best tennis player ever. And, as home of the (what else?) Basel Committee on Banking Supervision, many of the world's most influential decisions are taken within its midst.

Founded in 1974, the Basel Committee is a kind of consigliere when it comes to global bank supervision and, most notably, bank capital adequacy. While it doesn't possess any formal supranational supervisory authority, and while its conclusions do not per se have legal force, the

Committee's recommendations are usually taken on board by national supervisors, at the very least when it comes to the more developed nations. The Committee formulates broad standards and guidelines in the expectation that individual authorities will eventually implement them, perhaps after having added a bit of local flavor to those general suggestions. Global convergence toward common approaches and common standards is thus a big aim. The Committee's representatives are central bankers and heads of supervisions of member countries. At last count, the following nations were part of the gang: Argentina, Australia, Belgium, Brazil, Canada, China, France, Germany, Hong Kong, India, Indonesia, Italy, Japan, Korea, Luxembourg, Mexico, the Netherlands, Russia, Saudi Arabia, Singapore, South Africa, Spain, Sweden, Switzerland, Turkey, the United Kingdom, and the United States.

Given how important banks are for an economy and a society, a body that coordinates bank regulators and supervisors worldwide and that influences the shape of that regulation and supervision was always bound to be highly influential. But important as it already was and would be, the Committee became inescapably relevant 14 years after its establishment, with the introduction in 1988 of the Capital Accord. More commonly known as Basel I, the Accord proposed a measurement system for credit risk–related bank capital requirements. At the time, credit risk was assumed to be the number one risk for banks, not surprising given how relatively timid their trading activities were back then and the huge losses incurred on regular commercial loans (mostly to Latin American borrowers) a few years earlier. Basel I introduced the concept of "risk-weighted assets," whereby credit exposures were ranked in buckets based on a predefined set of asset classes and assigned a preset risk weight (so that loans to a developed country, say, would force banks to post less capital than loans to corporate borrowers, say; risk weights were thus a way to declare that not all exposures are the same, and that some should be considered intrinsically less or more risky than others, thus giving rise to different capital charges depending on the asset class in question). A bank's total credit exposure was calculated by multiplying each credit-sensitive position (say, $100,000,000 in U.S. Treasury Bonds, $55,000,000 in loans to IBM, and $20,000,000 in mortgage securities) by its respective risk weight (say, 0 percent, 100 percent, and 20 percent) and adding up the resulting individual amounts (in this example, $100,000,0000 * 0 percent + $55,000,000 * 100 percent + $20,000,000 * 20 percent = $59,000,000). Minimum mandatory capital requirements were set at 8 percent of that final total risk-weighted amount (so, $59,000,000 * 8 percent = $4,720,000), which in many instances meant a lot less than 8 percent of total assets, given how only a few types of exposures received a risk weight of 100 percent (risk weights of just 0 percent, 20 percent, and 50 percent were common). In our example, 8 percent of total assets would have been $175,000,000 * 8 percent = $14,000,000; a decidedly larger sum. The introduction of risk weights was supposed to align regulatory capital more closely with the actual risk of a position, so that a mildly risky asset worthy of only a 20 percent weight would demand only 1.6 percent (8 percent * 20 percent) in capital. The less intrinsically risky the asset was assumed to be by the Basel mandarins, the more leverage banks were permitted on such plays.

Basel I endowed 0 percent risk weights, and thus 0 percent total capital charge, on rich country government debt and cash and gold held. Cash to be received, rich country bank debt, U.S. government-sponsored agency debt, some municipal bonds, and some mortgage-backed securities carried a 20 percent risk weight (1.6 percent total capital charge). Other types of municipal bonds suffered a 50 percent weight (4 percent total charge). The unillustrious 100 percent risk weight (uppermost 8 percent total capital levy) was reserved for corporate bonds, poor country government debt, poor country bank debt, real estate, and mortgage loans. Where did all those numbers come from? The (arbitrary, if you'd like) estimations of the Basel capital gendarmes.

So however the assemblage of elite policy makers felt about this or that banking exposure could have huge repercussions on the world economy at large. If Basel I failed and the wrong type of asset was assigned low-risk weights, banks could economically gorge on positions that may turn out to be very problematic. On the other hand, if the right type of asset was assigned high-risk weights, certain key economic factors could see the flow of credit being constrained as banks deemed such lending too taxing capital-wise.

Having the power to dictate global bank capital requirements is thus a responsibility to be handled with the utmost care. The pace of economic growth, the occurrence of financial crises, the size of public deficits, and other essential factors would be at stake. Those people assembling at the Basel Committee literally decide much of the fate of much of the planet. Clearly, the possibility of influencing their decisions can be too tempting for bankers. And some argue that not only have bankers been tempted, but they have succeeded majestically also at the influencing. According to this argument, the years following the implementation of Basel I have been marked by a rule-making process that has been only too eager to enshrine into edicts that which banks favored and to reject that which they did not favor. Of course, the main problem with this is when *bad* petitions by the banks are accommodated. Taking on board what banks suggest need not per se be unadvisable, and listening to what banks have to say should naturally be part of a bank regulator's mandate. But on occasions, the financial system is better served when financial mandarins turn a deaf ear. When it comes to capital requirements, that was most definitely the case for the past 15 years. Those über-powerful Basel mandarins should have been less accommodative.

■ ■ ■

When the Basel Committee welcomed VaR into the regulatory realm by releasing the "Amendment to the Capital Accord to Incorporate Market Risks" in January 1996, it made clear that it was doing so at the request of banks. Having years earlier decided to demand capital charges not only on credit risks per Basel I but also on market risks (i.e., exposures derived from changes in market prices), the Committee first believed that the right path along would be to apply a Basel I–type approach to market risks: preset fixed unalterable capital charges based on the particular asset family (interest rates, equity, commodities, foreign exchange). Just like Basel I, this was a building-block approach, meaning that the capital requirements of each component of market risk are calculated and then summed up, thus making no allowance for any diversification benefits to be derived from statistical correlations within or across risk categories.

This so-called *standardized method* was proposed in April 1993, and banks instantly hated it. It probably wasn't just a matter of undue inflexibility on the part of the method, but that those inflexible capital charges may have appeared disagreeably high. Commodities, for instance, were generally taxed at 15 percent of the net position in each commodity. Foreign exchange exposures were penalized to the tune of 8 percent of net positions. Interest rate and equity risks carried not just one, but two types of market-related capital charges, one for general market risk and one for so-called *specific risk*. The latter was designed to protect against an adverse movement in the price of a security owing to factors related to the individual issuer (in a way, so as to make sure that some kind of credit risk charge was imposed on positions that were treated as market risk but carried credit risk nevertheless; things like default and event risk). In the case of interest rate exposures, the size of the specific risk capital charge varied according to the type of debt security involved, with government, public sector entities, multilateral development bank securities, and investment grade-rated securities enjoying very low levies of between 0 percent and 1.6 percent, and with other types of exposures requiring an 8 percent specific capital commitment. The general risk charges for interest rate-sensitive positions were calculated according to a complicated architecture where capital taxes depended on a security's maturity. Equity risk specific capital charge was set at 8 percent, though it could be much lower for liquid and diversified positions. Equity risk general capital charge was set at 8 percent of the net position.

Two years later, a new proposal was released, this time allowing banks to choose between their own internal models and the standardized method. This version was approved by the supervisory authorities of the world's top 10 economies, committing to domestic implementation by year-end 1997 at the very latest. In the words of the Committee,

> The main feature of the April 1995 proposals was to respond to the industry's request to allow banks to use proprietary in-house models for measuring market risks as an alternative to a standardized measurement framework originally put forward in April 1993.

The Basel officials proved generously accommodative not just through their pro-models stance, but also by finding a new definition for bank capital. Basel I originally defined *capital* as, well, capital. While some allowance for debt was made, it seemed justified on account of its longer-term nature (thus in principle being able to count as short-term shock absorber in case of a losses-inducing setback). Banks could comply with regulatory capital requirements through two conduits: so-called *Tier 1* capital and *Tier 2* capital. The former was the very best quality, comprised entirely of equity and disclosed reserves, while the latter was made up of undisclosed reserves, long-term subordinated debt, perpetual debt securities, and unrealized gains on investments. In order to guarantee soundness, Tier 2 capital was not allowed to be greater than Tier 1 capital (that is, at least 50 percent of overall capital should be hard-hard-core capital). The 1996 Amendment brought with it the surprise of Tier 3 capital, made up of short-term subordinated debt (a much shakier support base; as the 2007 crisis proved, this "capital" does not really act as capital is supposed to act come turbulent times). Tier 3 capital could only be used to cover market risks charges, and was limited to 250 percent of the Tier 1 capital required to cover market risks; that is, a minimum of around 28 percent of the market risk charge needed to be composed of best-quality capital. Some could argue that this arrangement made leverage-seeking banks quite pleased: Not only would the use of VaR promise the delivery of humble capital requirements for trading games, but a lot of that capital need not even be real capital. That is, the potential for mouthwatering returns on equity just became insatiably pronounced. Thanks to VaR you may have to commit only tiny amounts of real capital to huge market positions. Thanks to the Tier 3 gift, that grand leverage could in effect become even grander in terms of hard-core (i.e., the one and only one) capital. A VaR-churned capital requirement of, say, just 0.5 percent is fantastic for your gearing aspirations, as you need only $5 to support a $1,000 position (200-to-1 leverage); even better if only 28 percent of that 0.5 percent has to be Tier 1 capital, as now your leverage on hard-core capital is a stupendous 700 to 1.

Per the 1996 Amendment to the Capital Accord, banks were required to maintain on a daily basis a market risk capital charge equal to the higher of the previous day's 10-day 99 percent VaR or the result of multiplying the average 10-day 99 percent VaR for the previous 60 days by a multiplication factor of three (which could be elevated all the way to four, should the performance of the model as risk measure prove unsatisfactory). Ten-day VaR can be obtained from 1-day VaR by scaling the latter number (typically done by multiplying 1-day VaR by the square root of 10; this mathematical trick assumes that asset returns follow a random walk statistical process). At least one year of historical market data should be used, though banks were unconstrained beyond that. Any VaR calculating methodology could be used (most banks seem to have in time been leaning toward the Historical Simulation method). Banks could recognize diversification benefits through the use of correlations within asset categories and between asset categories, a development that was sure to yield more moderate final overall portfolio VaR figures. Banks could use VaR technology to calculate specific risk charges for interest rate and equity exposures, rather than be forced to follow the script laid down by the despised standardized methodology (most banks compute and report only a global VaR combining general and specific risk factors[1]).

It's not hard to claim that in permissively going from the standardized method to VaR, regulators did banks a big favor. Rather than being shackled to inflexible, nonnegotiable, apparently taxing preset capital charges, banks could now in effect calculate their own capital requirements, with almost complete discretion. Rather than not being allowed to have a say on the capital cost of their trading activities, banks could now have the final word. If an exposure could be qualified as tradable it could be included in the trading book rather than the banking book and thus have its capital cost be subject to, possibly much cheaper, market risk regulatory treatment rather than, possibly much costlier, credit risk regulatory treatment (foreign exchange and commodity exposures would be subject to a market risk charge whether they come from the trading or banking book). Selective past histories and statistical correlations could now be alchemized into extremely unassuming capital demands. Banks could literally scour the trading assets universe until they came up with a combination that produced the desired level of economical regulatory capital price tag. When you let leverage-loving institutions freely use an easily manipulable leverage-dictating tool you shouldn't be surprised if the final result is a lot of leverage.

■ ■ ■

The Basel Committee quickly tired of Basel I. In September 1998, it announced the kick-starting of a thorough review of the 1988 rulebook, with the aim of producing a new enhanced one. These, of course, were the seeds of what came to be known as Basel II, finally released in mid-2004. Basel II rules thus ruled the banking universe all the way to the crisis of 2007–2008.

What was so wrong with Basel I that it needed a replacement? Well, it appeared too primitively blunt. Too arbitrary. Too rustic. Too much based on flaky personal judgment, too little based on rigorous technology. In sum, too easy to ridicule and put down, and thus too easy to do away with. Few tears were shed at the sight of Basel I's demise. In contrast, Basel II was welcomed as the arrival of the prodigal analytical son, the moment when regulators finally got sophisticated and in tune with an advanced outer world.

It is true that Basel I's crude risk weights could encourage weird credit decisions. For instance, lending to the corner shop was as costly capital-wise as lending to a blue-chip multinational, perhaps tempting banks to lend more to the (riskier, thus higher-yielding) former. Banks that seemed as well capitalized as before may in fact have loaded up on much more risk. Also, Basel I was accused of not properly dealing with securitization, while encouraging the practice (as banks shifted assets off balance sheet to escape the new credit-related capital charges). By the late 1990s, capital levels across the banking industry, which had risen sharply after Basel I came into effect, were beginning to decline.[2] The final result of Basel I may well have been more risk backed up by less capital.

Five years after the first set of proposals were released in June 1999, and following intense negotiations and a myriad of impact studies and industry comments, Basel II became a reality. It founded itself on the three famous pillars (minimum capital requirements, supervisory guidelines, disclosure standards). Everybody seemed happy with the new arrangement. It was widely believed and accepted that Basel II would strengthen the financial system's stability and safety.

What changed and what stayed the same with the arrival of the new capital regulatory regime? Simply stated, banking book treatment (i.e., credit risk capital requirements) changed a lot while trading book treatment (i.e., market risk capital requirements) stayed essentially the same. VaR was kept around as king of the trading book, even though this decision had by 2004 become highly suspect, for reasons that will be analyzed shortly. But the Basel Committee was not satisfied with having just the trading book be ruled by metrics; now the banking book, too, ought to be metricized. Through Basel II, models-based credit ratings became the deciding factor when appraising the risk of a credit-related asset. Banks had two choices: the Standardized Approach based on external credit assessments, and the Internal Ratings Approach based on banks' own rating systems. Whether a position received a AAA or a BBB rating (whether externally or internally) was now the key determinant of that position's capital charge. The idea was to link capital requirements more closely with an asset's "true" riskiness, built on the notion that the cutting-edge credit analysis systems used by banks and the rating agencies were to be amply trusted as providers of truth. Securitization exposures were thoroughly addressed and idiosyncratically treated, with their own risk weights tables based on the (external) credit ratings assigned to each securitized tranche. Risk weights for the most senior tranches could be as low as 7 percent (equivalent to a 0.56 percent minimum capital charge, 7 percent × 8 percent), as high as 650 percent (52 percent charge) for BB− rated tranches, and even higher for below-BB− and unrated tranches. In other words, under the new system it really paid to have a portfolio considered creditworthy.

It was easy to argue that a metrics-charged Basel II could deliver lower banking book mandatory capital. If the credit assessments happened to be very generous, capital demands could be very generous. And not just in the case of securitization. For instance, under the Standardized Approach claims on corporates rated AAA to AA− were blessed with a 20 percent risk weight, significantly below the 100 percent weight assigned by Basel I to corporate debt across the board. Even those rated A+ to A− got a saving, with a 50 percent risk weight. Only those corporate loans or bonds rated BBB+ or less faced the undignified pre-Basel II 100 percent damnation. Claims secured by residential property obtained a 35 percent risk weight, certainly better than 100 percent. So although it's true that risk weights stayed the same for some assets and could even increase in other cases if the credit rating was really bad, Basel II could represent tasty capital savings on credit exposures (and the savings could be even more drastic when using the Internal Models Approach; this will be discussed shortly).

Some have accused Basel II of favoring the big banking guy over the little banking guy. Since only the former can really invest in the technology and human power needed to keep the advanced models humming, only the former can take full advantage of model-based capital regulation. That is, for those firms without the capacity to employ the kind of analytics able to pass the regulatory veto, there would be no option but to abide by the standardized approaches to calculate their capital taxes, both in the banking and trading books. No chance to be able to determine your own capital requirements via your own models. Rather you are kept a slave to what *others* have to say about the riskiness of your assets. And, the thinking goes, the assessments of others can be way less friendly than your own assessments. So if you are a relatively smallish and unsophisticated bank you may be condemned to suffering higher capital requirements than your larger and more sophisticated brethren. A potential source of competitive disadvantage, courtesy of the Basel folks. Studies seem to have confirmed this. For instance, in 2003 the U.S. Federal Deposit Insurance Corporation found that average capital levels in American banks adopting the most advanced approach would fall by 18 percent to 29 percent. In 2006, a quantitative impacts study conducted by the Basel Committee showed that banks employing the Internal Ratings Approach would experience a capital reduction of 7 percent to 27 percent, while those being reduced to the Standardized Approach would experience a 2 percent increase in capital demands.[3] This may sound a tad puzzling, given that one of the Basel Committee's main stated aims is to guarantee a level playing field for all and that one of Basel II's main stated goals was to enhance competitive equality. Also puzzling is the fact that the above figures obviously signal an overall decline of capital levels in the banking industry (given how it is the models-employing largest banks that hold a larger share of the market), in direct contradiction to Basel II's original primary objective.

If banks had been accommodated in 1996 when it came to market risk capital rules, they were accommodated again in 2004 when it came to credit risk capital rules. It's not so much that reliance on credit ratings would automatically and under all scenarios produce humbler requirements (though as we just saw, the new metric system made leverage a whole lot easier), but that banks (some, at least) were once more given the power to calculate their own capital charges. This outsourcing regulatory process was finally completed with the arrival of Basel II. Models engineered by banks and by those on good terms with banks were now in full command. Both credit-related and trading-related leverage ratios would be almost entirely determined by the banking industry and its rating agencies acolytes. A shiny new era of analytical dominance was fully imposed. But, what if those metrics proved exaggeratedly wrong? Through Basel II, the fate of the world (already exposed since 1996 to whether the statistical market risk forecast was right) was placed on whether AAA really means AAA.

■ ■ ■

VaR moved swiftly from the market risk amendment of Basel I to Basel II. None of the turbulence that afflicted the banking book was visited on the trading book, where things remained calmly stable. VaR was king and VaR remained king.

This was quite paradoxical. It is one thing to place trust on a model when the device is full of promise and it hasn't underperformed yet, as was the case in 1995. It is another to continue to rely on the construct after market realities have demonstrably shown it to be gravely malfunctioning and deleteriously problematic, as had been the case since late 1997. We may be charitably willing to give regulators a free pass for not having grasped VaR's conceptual defects (though this forces us to be extra charitable; after all, is it that hard to understand that a model built on historical data and suspect probability assumptions, and that can be conveniently manipulated, will by its very nature tend to behave erroneously and naughtily?), but it seems inexcusable to hold on to VaR once real-life developments openly unveil its voluminous shortcomings. How could VaR have been passed into Basel II unquestionably?

By the time Basel II began to be assembled, VaR had a negative rap sheet. The 1997 Asian Crisis and the 1998 Russia-LTCM Crisis had outed the model. VaR not only failed at signaling the emergence of severe market tribulations, it may actually have helped cause the tremors.

VaR encouraged the group thinking that led to the accumulation of similar portfolios across the industry. For the same reason, VaR later ordered the massive en masse liquidation of positions, leading to snowballing losses. Banks, possibly for the first time ever, registered VaR exceptions, with actual daily trading losses overtaking VaR's predictions. The lessons from those nasty episodes were crystal clear: Markets are not Normal, past evidence may have nothing to say about tomorrow's performance, past statistical correlations and volatilities may be turned on their heads tomorrow, liquidity is not perfect and may dry up completely, and when a lot of players abide by the same mechanical mechanism troublesome copycatting and cross-ownership can arise. If just one of those things were true, VaR would already be highly suspect. Given that they are all true, how could VaR continue to be risk Caesar?

While VaR-abiding Wall Street legends suffered during the 1997–1998 terror (in defiance of the model's precrisis dictates), perhaps the most illustrative example of VaR's failings came from a nonbanking (though more legendary back then) institution. Illustrative not only due to how the model let its users down, but mostly because of the particular nature of those particular users. Über-famous hedge fund Long Term Capital Management (LTCM) was piloted by top finance theoreticians. Of the fund's ten most important people, six or seven were former or current academics endowed with prestigious PhDs, and the other three or four were firm believers in the value that their professorial colleagues could provide. Two of those academics boasted a Nobel in Economics for their theoretical work. That is, this was the best or close to the best that the discipline of mathematical finance could offer. These analytical elite trusted quantitative risk models to guide their trading decisions. The result? A multibillion blowup that almost took the entire banking industry down. The "best finance faculty in the world" (as LTCM's honchos were dubbed) could do no better than a complete blowup, a devastating collapse. The models-supported genius-steered fund could do no better than producing returns of −45 percent in its last month of existence. The trading strategies that LTCM had nurtured, and that had worked well for a while, were vouched for by VaR. Risk control at LTCM relied on a VaR model.[4] And the model said that the fund faced little danger from its market escapades.

In April 1998, less than six months before the blowup and with the fund's capital at slightly less than $5 billion, LTCM's one-day 99 percent VaR was a tiny $105 million.[5] This meant a $480 million monthly 99 percent VaR. That figure seemed comfortable enough: 99 out of 100 months, losses were predicted to be inferior to 10 percent of the fund's capital. Some argue that this complacency-building numbers helped convince LTCM the previous December to cut back its capital base by 40 percent; after all, if your VaR deems you safe, why not get rid of bothersome capital so that your returns look even more fantastic? Of course, that leverage-enhancing decision proved to be fatally fateful as LTCM would eventually die from a lack of capital with which to cover a sudden rampage of losses and margin calls (the fund's positions could eventually have been profitable, had it survived the storm). The following month, LTCM for the first time lost serious money, with returns of −6.5 percent (a loss of more than $300 million). June was even worse, at −10.15 percent (–$460 million). In August 1998, LTCM lost $1.85 billion, an event deemed absolutely impossible by the mathematics of VaR. Three weeks later, with all but $800 million of the capital pot having been consumed by losses, the fund had to be rescued by a consortium of banks so as to avoid a systemic meltdown. Just five months after VaR had proclaimed LTCM's strategies disaster-proof, the fund had lost $4 billion and said farewell to 80 percent of its capital.

What about the banks? How did they become victims of VaR? By late 1997, let alone late 1998, the financial industry had unapologetically converted to the VaR faith. Everybody was using VaR as internal risk beacon, and as we know their trading-related leverage was already too determined by VaR. So being caught off guard by not just one but two megamarket meltdowns would in itself be sufficient indictment against the model. The glorified risk radar missed one huge international crisis and then a year later it missed an even huger one. How's that for statistical accuracy?

As was said earlier, those historical episodes witnessed what most likely were the first exceptions ever experienced by VaR, in the words of a renowned expert, "*Clear evidence that the models were flawed.*"[6] A study of U.S. commercial banks with large trading arms found that during the August to October 1998 period, at least four entities experienced two or more exceptions on their daily 99 percent VaRs, with one firm experiencing as many as five and two firms experiencing three; 99 percent VaR is supposed to be breached only two-and-a-half days a year. Not only that, the breaches were of a sizable magnitude, eight standard deviations ("sigmas") in one case, and three in another. Keep in mind that according to the Normal probability distribution a move two sigmas beyond the 99 percentile is essentially assumed to be flat-out impossible (so as to be more precise, the probability of a one-sigma move beyond the 99 percentile is 0.04 percent). A lot of things that were not supposed to happen happened. VaR, in sum, lied. For the first time, the world came to realize what a naughty liar the erstwhile unpolluted model can be.

But the worst part is that VaR caused VaR to lie. All those numerous and voluptuous violations of the statistical dogma were the result of market tremors fueled by the statistical dogma. When Russia defaulted on its debt and devalued its currency on August 17, 1998, many banks and hedge funds began to bleed losses (Russia had been a darling of the markets just a few months prior and many had accumulated substantial positions in Russian assets). This nastiness filtered through to VaR numbers all over the world. VaRs in New York, London, Paris, and Zurich began to rise rapidly. As the best source on this development put it:

> The effect was to cause many trading desks to breach their VaR limits. According to the Basel Committee rules, once such a breach took place so many times, more capital would have to be allocated or positions have to be cut. Capital is a precious commodity for banks. Cutting positions was the route taken. So risk managers would phone head traders and tell them to cut back, not just in Russia but everywhere. Even when the positions are profitable?, asked the traders. Rules are rules, replied the risk managers.[7]

Recall that the multiplication factor part of the formula for calculating regulatory capital can go from three all the way to four if VaR misbehaves, so it may make more sense to simply reduce your balance sheet, get rid of the nasty stuff, bring your VaR back under control, and start anew with a clean slate. In any case, in a culture where what the risk model says is taken on faith, a rising VaR would have been seen as an unacceptable increase in risk and thus a call for drastic risk-reducing action in the shape of asset dumping, across the board.

However such course of action, while perhaps reasonable for an individual firm, becomes self-defeating when undertaken by a group. Why? Because liquidity can dry up when everybody (or almost everybody) is frenetically cutting down on risk: Buyers may simply disappear, and it's hard to sell something in the absence of buyers. The entire idea behind VaR is that you can de-riskify your portfolio when your limits are breached. Otherwise, what's the point of establishing limits in the first place? But if a lot of big boys are abiding by the same mechanical rule and see their limits violated concurrently, rather than a healthy reduction in exposures what we have is a holocaust of risk that feeds on itself. As liquidating some part of your portfolio becomes challenging, you try liquidating another slice, and so on until everything (or almost everything) is being fire-sold. Meanwhile the volcano of volatility that has been unleashed is keeping VaR at high levels, even if the overall position may now be smaller. You may end up not having achieved your goal of humbling VaR and with a fresh new out-of-nowhere mega-disaster. Much better if portfolio management is not automatically made the slave of a statistical device that is too easily impressionable by the slightest of setbacks. This is how the VaR-spread disease was aptly described.

> VaR is a warning system that can be used to control risks. If you breach that limit too often, you cut back in a controlled way until you return to the safety zone again. That is the theory. But during August 1998, everybody tried to do this at once. The result is inevitable. The opportunists who take advantage of short-term price drops disappear. Market makers widen the spread between buy prices and sell prices, and finally there are huge jumps downwards in price. Like the proverbial fire in a movie theatre, everybody rushed for the exits.[8]

Interestingly, the Basel Committee didn't seem to think that the 1998 episode shamed or scarred VaR forever. In fact, the Committee's analysis of the model's performance during such delicate time emanates a message closer to "VaR actually did quite well. The crisis solidified VaR's reputation as solid risk estimator" than to "The crisis proved that VaR is flawed. The model did quite badly." We obviously already suspected that the 1998 meltdown did not transform Basel into VaR agnostics, given how VaR was firmly kept as part of the rules (it would be particularly creepy had regulators become convinced of VaR's dangerous deficiencies yet nonetheless had not relented in their public support for the concoction), but it's illustrative to see what the mandarins had to say. Surveying more than 40 banks in nine countries, the Committee proudly declared that, "*The market risk capital charge provided an adequate buffer against trading losses over this period. None of the institutions surveyed reported trading losses over any ten-day consecutive period that exceeded the capital requirement in force at the start of the period.*"[9] Okay, but what if LTCM had not been rescued and its positions had thus been liquidated at once? It's a safe bet that bank losses would have been big enough to surpass regulatory VaR. The president of the New York Fed (the one figure that did most to strong-arm the banks into saving the fund, and themselves) believed that big banks stood to lose $3 to $5 billion apiece if LTCM was liquidated.[10] So a VaR-abetted crisis may not have technically resulted in undercapitalized banks, but that's probably only because the game was rigged. The system cheated into not letting market forces work themselves out and led to the kind of banking setbacks that would have rendered the VaR-calculated capital charges degradingly insufficient. Basel did admit that some VaR exceptions took place, though here it too feels that the damage seemed not troublesome enough to ignite a rethinking of the status quo among the status quo-ers. "*Despite the increased volatility of the second half of 1998, almost half of the institutions reported no cases where one-day losses exceeded the daily VaR estimate. For those banks that reported exceptions, the one-day loss generally did not exceed the one-day VaR estimate by more than two times.*" And thus, VaR was accorded the punishment reserved for otherwise delightful children that unexpectedly act slightly naughtily rather than the one deserved by unrepentant malfeasants: a very mild recrimination, followed by an enthusiastic invitation to remain in the premises and continue playing. Sweet risk child.

■ ■ ■

2004 was a golden year for VaR not just because of its undoubted and untarnished passing into Basel II, but also of course due to its embracement by the U.S. Securities and Exchange Commission, the last remaining big regulator that had yet to succumb to the model's seductiveness. Before the SEC became a newborn VaRista, Wall Street broker-dealers were subjected to the Net Capital Rule, a system quite similar to Basel I and quite similar to the way the Basel Committee tried to address market risk capital rules before the banking lobby requested a prominent place for VaR at the table. Just like the dreadful standardized approach proposed by Basel in 1993, the SEC's Net Capital Rule was a building block approach based on preset nonappealable capital requirements (*haircuts*, in the lingo) that varied according to the security in question. A bank started from a given level of gross capital and then deducted from that the size of each position's haircut, yielding a net capital figure. Regulatory limits on leverage and minimum capital requirements were imposed based on that net capital number (for instance, Wall Streeters could have their indebtedness constrained to 1,500 percent of their net capital, essentially capping their gearing ratios; capital requirements were also set at a dollar figure that net capital should not dive below). So the more onerous the haircuts for a given position the less volume one could do in that position, for a given level of gross capital. Similarly, the more onerous the haircuts the less you can use borrowed funds to finance the position, for a given level of gross capital. In brief, if you want to accumulate a lot of stuff in a leveraged way, a demanding haircut architecture can derail your plans.

So what where those capital deductions like? Very short-term government securities enjoyed a 0 percent haircut, which progressively became larger as maturities grew older (1 percent to 2 percent for the 1-year to 3-year range, 6 percent for 25 years or more). Municipal securities too started at 0 percent and then went up with the maturity ladder (7 percent deduction for 20 or more years). High-grade debt started at 2 percent for the shortest maturities and ended at 9 percent for maturities of 25 years and above. Equity was priced at 10 percent. Other securities could have a haircut of 15 percent or 40 percent, depending on their liquidity. And, and this is very important, so-called *nonmarketable* or *no ready market* securities were penalized with a 100 percent haircut (that is, leverage here was constrained to 1 to 1, making it quite expensive capital-wise to hold on to those babies, and quite impossible to finance them via debt).

In April 2004, as we know, the SEC gave Wall Street the choice of switching from haircut-land into VaR-land. In exchange for letting the parent holding companies be more closely scrutinized and policed, and provided that a lower-bound limit of $500 million in net capital was respected at all times and that a $5 billion net capital alarm bell was put in place (should such lower barrier be breached, the SEC was to be notified and it then would consider whether remedial actions should be taken), the large U.S. investment banks could from then on have their capital requirements calculated by VaR, along the lines previously set out by Basel (99 percent confidence interval, 10-day holding period, multiplication factor of three that could go up to four if the model misbehaves, minimum of one year of historical data, allowance for correlations within asset families and across asset families). As the SEC itself conceded, such a switch was very likely going to result in much lower capital deductions (i.e., the same gross capital could now finance much more action). Quite possibly this was a big factor behind Wall Street's aggressive pleading for VaR in years prior.

Not content with flooding Wall Street's regulation with the VaR waters, the SEC, perhaps extra eager to please those under its watch, placed additional adornments in the capital gift bag. First, the adopted policy no longer included a planned 18-month phase-in period for the adoption of VaR, at the request of "commenters" to the original draft (with almost total certainty, industry representatives impatient to use their VaR models to calculate deductions for market risk capital without further delay). Second, and most crucial, the original SEC plan would have prohibited the use of VaR models to compute deductions for positions with no ready market and any derivative instrument based on them; that is, those positions would have been subject to a 100 percent deduction. Commenters replied that, while positions with no ready market may lack historical data, their models could nonetheless be up to the job. The SEC agreed and, therefore, the final ruling did not limit a broker-dealer's use of VaR models to securities that have a ready market. Now the most weird stuff could be traded in as leveraged a fashion as VaR may allow, rather than with no leverage at all.

And third, deductions for specific risk could be calculated through VaR; if the models that a broker–dealer uses incorporate specific risk, there is no additional deduction for that. All these adornments must have pleased many a Wall Streeter.

How did the SEC's dance with VaR end? Not well, given that only four years later all the Wall Street giants had been destroyed by a torrent of trading-related losses that unveiled them as heavily undercapitalized firms owning a lot of positions with much more market risk than what the models had predicted. Many at the SEC, and elsewhere, would later say that U.S. investment banks were well capitalized going into the crisis, by regulatory standards. By mid-2007, the storyline goes, all the big boys on Wall Street had enough net capital to satisfy the conditions imposed for the adoption of VaR. Thus, they say, capital regulation can't be blamed because capital regulation delivered well-capitalized banks. Well, not really. The main issue is not so much how much minimum capital a bank is mandated to have at any point, but rather what kind of stuff and in what quantities that capital is permitted to buy. Five billion dollars in net capital may be a lot, or it may be nothing if, thanks to statistical measures of risk, it has been possible for a bank to accumulate many billions in toxic securities. Once the value of those plays inevitably tumbles, the $5 billion cushion is reduced to ashes. By switching from prudential commonsensical policies that forced toxic punts to be matched by an equal amount of capital to models that can sanction almost unlimited leverage on the same lethal punts, the SEC effectively made any amount of net capital potentially insufficient. The SEC may have thought that $5 billion was a symbol of prowess, but VaR can render it ridiculously dwarfish (other regulators had to admit postcrisis that being "well capitalized" under policy standards may have nothing to do with truly being well capitalized when those policies are based on deeply flawed mechanisms, like VaR and credit ratings-based risk weights, with an inbred tendency to yield unrealistically timid capital requirements; for instance, the Swiss regulators claimed puzzlement at the losses afflicted on wildly leveraged UBS and Credit Suisse, given how obligingly those banks had respected the mandatory Basel capital requirements; an 8 percent charge on risk-weighted assets may have been categorized as prudently robust by the mandarins, but the prudency appears diminished once we realize that those weighted assets may stand for just a tiny fraction of total assets).

As we've said, VaR appears to have been a bargaining chip to get the holding companies of Wall Street broker-dealers to submit to regulatory policing. The Europeans provided the initial jolt for this. While the brokering-dealing arms of Goldman Sachs, Merrill Lynch, Lehman Brothers, Morgan Stanley, and Bear Stearns had, of course, been under the SEC watch for many decades, the parent company had trotted along essentially unwatched. But in 2002 the European Union demanded the presence of a "consolidated" supervisor by 2004, lest the New York giants may be exempted from doing business in the Old World.[11] The Federal Reserve did that job for U.S. commercial banks (JP Morgan, Citigroup, Bank of America), now the pure investment banks would have to find their own big regulatory sugar daddy. And they expressed their wish to be looked after by the SEC. The only problem was that the SEC had never done this kind of supervision (concerned mostly with the safety and soundness of a firm), investor protection having been its traditional mandate. In fact, the SEC did not have authority to force investment banks into consolidated supervision, so it had no option but to propose it as a voluntary exercise: Wall Streeters could or could not choose to abide. How to entice the investment banks to comply? Perhaps by dangling a carrot in front of them. What had Wall Street firms loudly clamored for all those years? The adoption of VaR for capital purposes. Okay, let's then dangle the VaR carrot and get those firms to accede to the new era of consolidated supervision.

It worked. The investment banks were dying to be afforded the same treatment as their commercial banking brethrens. They had missed the 1996 Basel boat, and as noncommercial banks Basel II was not really meant for them. They had been jealously eying how the Citigroups and JP Morgans of this world could decide their market-related capital charges for themselves, through their powerful VaR engines. In contrast, the Wall Street behemoths remained prisoners of the archaic Net Capital Rule. They had very little discretion to determine their leverage levels, and they badly wanted the total discretion that a models-based system could afford (it could indeed be considered paradoxical that Goldman et al. would be subjected to purportedly more retarded risk capital calculations, given how they had and have been considered much more glamorous and advanced entities than the commercial banks). So it's not surprising that the five legendary investment banks trampled over each other to volunteer for the new "Consolidated Supervised Entity" (CSE) program, initially put forth by the SEC in November 2003. The dangled VaR carrot proved to be intoxicatingly enticing.

So in April 2004, perhaps one of the most important meetings in the history of finance took place in Washington, DC. It may be no exaggeration to dub the gathering as "The Meeting That Changed the World." SEC commissioners voted to formally adopt the CSE program and the new capital calculations that went with it. The Wall Street elite had been employing VaR for internal risk management for years, so applying the model to a capital role was a piece of cake; the technology and the know-how were already at hand. All those commissioners knew that the new VaR reign would unleash a new era of enhanced leverage and that positions previously uneconomical (i.e., very high-risk positions) could now be economical for investment banks. Did any of them raise any concerns? Did any of them see any problem with those ramifications? Yes, one did. *"If anything goes wrong it's going to be an awfully big mess. Do we feel secure if these drops in capital and other things occur we really will have investor protection?"* presciently blurted out Harvey Goldschmid (SEC commissioner during 2003–2005) at the historic meeting. However, it seems that Goldschmid's concerns were brushed aside by his colleagues, and he was told that everything was going to work out fine.

The CSE program turned out to be a big failure, and not just because the new capital regime led to Wall Street's destruction (it has been rightly argued that while leverage did go up after the 2004 decision, the investment banks had experienced greater leverage some years back, so the CSE program was not an exclusive conduit toward excessive undercapitalization. But the key point, again, is not so much the level of capital or of leverage, rather the portfolio composition that the new rules allow: The vast amounts of garbage that can be accumulated under VaR's supervision is what eventually caused the crackdown, not so much a lowish amount of overall capital. On that point, the CSE program can be unquestionably declared guilty). Bluntly stated, the enhanced supervision stick that was supposed to compensate for the VaR carrot gift never carried any weight. The supervision never truly happened. For one, unlike traditional bank supervision, the SEC never assigned on-site examiners. The investment banks were simply subject to annual examinations, and these sometimes did not take place at all. Even when problems were detected (like the excessive accumulation of mortgage-related positions), the SEC doesn't seem to have called for corrections. Wall Street was not reined in whatsoever by the new, supposedly stringent, regulatory policies. The supposedly impressive new SEC cop did not clamp down on malfeasant practices. In a poignant episode, as Bear Stearns was terminally sinking in the second week of March 2008, the SEC was on-site conducting its first CSE appraisal since Bear's entrance exam three years earlier.[12] It was fitting, though, that regulators could witness firsthand the mess they had helped cause.

In September 2008, the CSE program was dumped into the dustbin, as Wall Street could no longer boast the presence of large independent investment banks. The remaining firms had been converted to bank holding companies or merged with bank holding companies, and as such would now be supervised by the Fed, the same Fed that they had neglected in favor of the SEC six years earlier. The new super cop was feared as a tougher one, but at least VaR would still be there, dominating the trading book just like Basel II ordered. The program that finally gave them VaR may have been terminated, but Wall Streeters nevertheless ended up comfily wrapped up in the VaR mantle. And that, in the end, is what may truly matter.

■ ■ ■

It's May 2011 as I am typing this. It's more than 15 years since international regulators endowed VaR with the power to rule the world. During that period we've witnessed four or five mega–financial crises. Markets have gone through endless spells of crazy turbulence and absent liquidity. Venerated financial firms have sunk and been exterminated. Historical data has been proven unreliable. Correlations have betrayed us over and over. Volatility estimates have fooled us over and over. Mathematical finance in general disappointed mightily and enabled chaos. Prominent voices, including top policy makers, academics, and quants have vociferously lambasted VaR. The evidence against the model as an abetter of the 2007–2008 cataclysm is mounting by the day. You would figure that no one would want to touch VaR with a 10-foot pole, nor be seen within a thousand yards of it.

You would figure wrong. It's May 2011 and VaR is still there. Still powerful, still influential, still commanding. Basel may have of late busied itself piling up add-on on top of add-on to the market risk regulatory capital formula, so as to try to make sure that trading book leverage going forward can't be as insultingly superlative as it had been allowed to be up to mid-2007, but VaR is still the main part of that ever-so-influential formula. In fact, the presence of those Stressed VaR and Incremental Risk Charge add-ons (which, recall, are presumed to help lift capital requirements by three or four times their previous levels) may tempt banks to come up with even lower main VaR numbers, so that the final result (VaR plus the add-ons) is kept as humble as possible. We know that VaR is easily manipulable into being very small. So who can guarantee that banks can't get even better at this after the crisis? Now they have a huge incentive to do so, after all. In any case, three–four times the prior capital charges is three–four times 1 percent or even 0.1 percent, not an insurmountably large number (250-to-1 leverage on trading positions may be less accommodating than 1,000-to-1 leverage, but it's not less lethal). The revised formula that is intended to abort the type of cancerous results that VaR by itself can and did deliver can still deliver cancerous results.

What explains VaR's resilience? It'd surely be nice to know.

Chapter 5

Abetting the CDO Party

VaR and Toxicity ▪ *The Swiss Connection* ▪ *Too Much Seniority* ▪ *The Marvels of the Trading Book* ▪ *Did VaR Allow CDOs to Exist?*

L et's remind ourselves once more why the 2007 crisis took place. Again, the true factor behind the global mayhem and the true reason why the episode earned a top spot in the history books was the existence-threatening (or, in some cases, existence-denying) humongous losses suffered by very large investment banks in New York and London. Those huge, and rather sudden, setbacks are the reason why the world froze in fear and despair. Without those very big bank losses, there would have been no real history-making crisis. A few U.S. mortgage lenders and brokers would have still sunk, many U.S. consumers would have still been hurt, and several pension funds and insurance companies in Norway and Korea would have still posted negative returns, but those developments per se would not have had the fuselage to ignite what has been deemed as "the worst economic recession since the 1929 Great Depression."

And why did the big banks lose so much money so fast? Because of their very pronounced leverage, much of it of the toxic kind. By mid-2007, the most influential investment banks had simply accumulated too many assets on the back of too little equity capital; many of those assets were trading-related (i.e., potentially volatile and risky) and many were nasty ones linked to subprime residential mortgages (CDOs and others). Under such circumstances all it takes is for some of those high-stakes assets to tumble in value just a bit for the bank to sink, its tiny capital base wiped out by the losses from the huge asset portfolio.

We saw in Chapter 1 how VaR enabled the overall pronounced leverage. Banks' balance sheets were dominated by trading positions, and the unrealistically and irresponsibly very low VaR figures recorded before the crisis dictated that very little capital had to be set against those. So there were 100-to-1 and even 1,000-to-1 trading book gearing levels. Such a state of affairs is by itself utterly lethal, even if the asset portfolio was comprised entirely of safe securities. A strategy consisting of owning $100 or more in government bonds backed by just $1 in capital would itself be highly dangerous. Those overall gearing levels would be enough for us to badmouth VaR as an enabler of fragility and chaos, even if we didn't know the portfolio's exact composition. That general leverage would be sufficient for us to accuse VaR of having fueled destruction.

How about the toxic part of the equation? VaR, as appointed setter of a bank's trading-related leverage, should naturally be fingered for a crisis caused by trading-related leverage. But what was its precise role when it came to the nastiest stuff? Did banks really own so many absurdly nasty assets? And did VaR really help the banks own the absurdly nasty stuff? The losses that truly mattered were those that took place in the poisonous subprime mortgage securities space, did VaR play a key role there, too?

■ ■ ■

After the "VaR led to a lot of leverage" allegation was amply proven in the first chapter, we then turn to the "Banks owned a lot of subprime junk and VaR aided and abetted them in said pursuit" imputation.

In this quest we can do worse than initially borrow from the specific experience of Swiss banking behemoth UBS, one of the biggest losers in the credit crisis, one of the most leveraged firms, and one of the most eager players in the filthy subprime CDOs sphere. In other words, UBS stands as an ideal poster child for the ravenously irresponsible behavior that investment banks felt obliged to abide by in the years prior to mid-2007. A great case to focus on if we want to thoroughly dissect that destructive behavior. A great window into how contaminated banks' trading books (VaR's domain, naturally) became.

UBS was not just overtly generous in the poisoning of its balance sheet with leverage and toxicity, it was also uncommonly generous in its explications as to how and why the poisoning took place. The bank's April 2008 report to shareholders[1] on the massive write-downs incurred in the prior nine months ought to be soberly framed and prominently displayed should a mausoleum dedicated to vast financial meltdowns ever be erected in Manhattan or the City of London. Few other sources can be better at describing in painstaking detail the rationale behind the demise of UBS and its investment banking siblings. Few other sources can be better at explaining the role of the toxic stuff. And few other sources can be better at shedding light on VaR's role in the affair.

The report begins by listing UBS's subprime losses during the fateful May 2007 to March 2008 period, when the crisis started following the bursting of the U.S. housing bubble and consolidated as the value of those securities linked to that real estate market collapsed. We will deal with these setbacks (and with the similar downfalls suffered by other banks) in later paragraphs, but suffice it to say that during that time frame the Swiss giant wrote-down almost $40 billion from its U.S. residential mortgage and related structured credit positions, fueling very substantial and headline-grabbing overall net losses for the Helvetian giant. What's more pressing now is to understand the origin of that bad news.

It turns out that a number of different people and different business lines were toying with subprime stuff inside UBS. The report names as many as five miscreants, but only three really contributed to the malaise in bulk, and of that trio only one did it in real size. Internal hedge fund Dillon Read Asset Management famously was brought down by its subprime bets just before summer 2007, and contributed 16 percent to UBS's total subprime losses for that year. Something called the Foreign Exchange/Cash Collateral Trading unit took a 10 percent share of the filthy pie (it is highly telling of the delusional state into which financiers were trapped in those precrisis years that when the FX/CCT unit had to dispose of some of its holdings of Japanese government bonds it did so by accumulating asset-backed securities, including U.S. residential mortgage-backed securities, assuming that both types of investments were interchangeable given the AAA–AA credit ratings they both then shared). But the truly big hole was caused by the Investment Banking arm's Fixed Income Division's Rates business' CDO desk, by itself responsible for 66 percent of UBS's 2007 subprime mess. And how did the CDO desk manage to pile up so much sadness? By warehousing and retaining huge amounts of subprime CDOs, in particular the "super senior" tranches of Subprime CDOs. For the purposes of this book, the CDO desk story is the one that we are more enchanted by, not just because it did the most to kill UBS (and the many other banks whose actions mirrored the Swiss') and thus to awaken a global crisis, but because it is the one most directly related to bank capital requirements and thus to VaR.

After an apparently sleepy start, UBS's CDO desk caught subprime CDO fever in 2005. Initially, the bank was a pure securitizer, in the originate-and-distribute mode: It would source the underlying residential mortgage-backed securities (RMBS, a securitization of a large pool of mortgage loans) on behalf of a CDO manager, with these positions held ("warehoused") in UBS's books prior to their being alchemized into a CDO (a pool of RMBS, in essence a resecuritization of a very large number of mortgage loans); once the warehousing process was complete, the RMBS were transferred to a special purpose vehicle and transformed (resecuritized) into CDO tranches, which were then sold to investors the globe over. Each CDO tranche was akin to a bond, offering a given return on the notional amount invested. UBS made structuring fees for its troubles, determined as a percentage of the deal's volume. As it focused on quite risky CDOs, so-called *Mezzanine CDOs* (made up of rather shaky, and thus higher-yielding, RMBS), UBS received quite hefty fees, in the neighborhood of 1.25 percent to 1.50 percent. This was better than the paltry 0.0 percent to 0.50 percent one would get from engineering sounder, high-grade CDOs made up of tentatively sounder RMBS but it also meant that UBS was more exposed during the warehousing period when all the smelly low-grade RMBS sat on its books impatiently waiting to be packaged and released onto an unsuspecting outer investment world, adorned this time with much better credit ratings (thanks to the perceived benefits of diversification, a bunch of smelly mortgage-backed securities was able to obtain AAA ratings when in CDO form; this was naturally a big reason for the creation of CDOs and its variants, CDO squared and CDO cubed, themselves further attempts to transform what was BBB into yet more AAA). There was typically a lag of a few months between the time of the initial agreement with the CDO manager to buy the RMBS and the filling up of the warehouse and release of the assets. During that time, UBS ran market risk on those positions, which generally were left unhedged. As such, warehoused RMBS were included in the bank's overall U.S. mortgage VaR limits. By the end of 2007, one quarter of the CDO desk's total losses came from securities stuck in the CDO Warehouse pipeline, unable to be disposed of once the subprime CDO market froze in earlier months following the first significant spates of mortgage defaults in the United States and of massive downgrades on subprime-linked stuff by rating agencies Moody's and Standard & Poor's.

One big reason why the CDO business came alive in 2005 was the development in June of that year of credit default swaps on RMBS, a feat that gave birth to the synthetic subprime CDO, an invention that made sure that the creation of CDOs could now proceed completely unconstrained by the actual size of the underlying subprime mortgage universe. Before, you needed fresh raw material if you wanted to create a new CDO: each CDO was referenced to a unique set of so-called *cash RMBS* (i.e., plain RMBS), so if you wanted another CDO you had to come up with another unique set of RMBS (i.e., you needed to find additional mortgage loans with which to build the new cash RBMS). Now, you didn't need new real crappy loans if you wanted to design new crappy CDOs. The credit default swap on any already existing crappy RMBS would do, and could be infinitely replicated and be part of many different CDOs at the same time. All that mattered were the cash flows that fed the CDOs and from which CDO investors received their yields: Before synthetic CDOs, cash flows came from actual loans and obviously any single individual loan can only produce one set of cash flows in the form of the interest and repayment of principal that such a loan is entitled to, so any individual mortgage could only belong to one particular CDO; with synthetic CDOs, a lot of cash flows could be created on the same individual mortgage as long as one could find several market participants willing to take the long side of a credit default swap linked to that loan and agree to make periodic payments to their swap counterparty (in a credit default swap, one party pays a regular premium to another party in exchange for a lump-sum payment later on if a given preselected bond or loan suffers from an adverse credit event; the buyer of the swap is in effect purchasing protection on the bond or loan and is willing to pay for it). While a real loan can only generate a single cash-flow stream, and thus can only be securitized into a single structure, credit default swaps on that loan can generate potentially infinite cash-flow streams, one for each swap linked to that loan that is transacted, each feeding a different new security. In theory, a single pile of RMBS could now sustain an infinite number of synthetic CDOs. There was no longer a need to find actual human beings to whom to lend subprime mortgages. After June 2005, the CDO machine could feed itself, purportedly in perpetuity.

More troubling, and fate-sealing, than the travails derived from warehousing subprime CDO's raw materials was the decision by UBS's CDO traders to keep part of the finished product. And not just the product they had themselves manufactured, but also similar product manufactured by others. Originally, and once the CDO securitization process was finalized, UBS would sell the different CDO tranches to outside investors. The "equity" tranche went to those desiring the highest yield and willing to embrace the corresponding higher risk (as equity investors would be the first to suffer losses as soon as the underlying RMBS tumbled in value; an equity investor could be completely wiped out if just a small percentage of the loan pool goes bad). The "super senior" tranche went to those agreeing to enjoy much less return but also exposing themselves to, in principle, much less danger (as super senior investors would be the last to suffer losses if the RMBS turned sour; a much higher percentage of loans had to go bad for the investor to blow up, and that is why these punts were assumed to be so solid as to warrant a "more than AAA" credit rating, even if the raw material was made up of very suspect ingredients). The "mezzanine" tranche was more problematic, given its Goldilocks feel (sitting in between equity and super senior, it looked neither too attractive yield-wise nor too secure risk-wise); the mezz portion typically was re-re-securitized into new CDOs made up of CDOs, where thanks to the assumed magic of diversification and very generous joint default correlation estimates by the agencies and the quantitative analysts what used to have a low credit rating could be transformed into a lot of AAAs (thus increasing the chances that at least a lot of the new CDO could be placed with investors eager, or forced by their internal rules, to invest in apparently ultrasafe paper).

After those initial deals, the CDO desk decided to retain the super senior part of the subprime CDOs it structured (i.e., the CDO desk decided to invest in its own creations; in effect, UBS built a huge long subprime position, exposing itself to a fast blowup should the subprime market melt), for two main reasons: One, it was viewed as a nice source of profit in its own regard; and two, retaining that tranche helped the rolling along of the very profitable CDO structuring business. Those were two very powerful arguments for the strategy. A new money machine could be created, for even as the returns on super senior were modest in gross terms they were seen as a net gain, and a small net gain on billions and billions of dollars, or Swiss Francs, of CDO notional amounts could add up to very attractive monetary windfalls. This was particularly true given UBS's very low internal cost of funding, which allowed certain units to run very profitable businesses by creating portfolios of mildly returning assets; the net margin proved attractive, as the yields from the position were higher than the cost of funding it; in the case of super senior tranches the net positive carry for UBS was about 0.20 percent, at first sight perhaps not excruciatingly enchanting but keep in mind that this was considered to be a risk-free gain as the super senior play was often internally assumed to be fully hedged and as the asset carried beyond-AAA rating. And the already designed fee-generating CDO-structuring money machine could be kept well oiled, as by retaining the super senior tranche, by far the largest share of the CDO, the traders were making sure that the CDO could be completed and transacted in the first place. Per the April 2008 report,

"*Within the CDO desk, the ability to retain these tranches was seen as a part of the overall CDO business, providing assistance to the structuring business more generally.*" Without someone hanging on to the super senior slice, the deal could not go through and all those tantalizing structuring fees may fly away. And the truth is that super senior was not easy to sell outside of the bank; it was both too sizable and too timid returns-wise, and it wasn't even the only supposedly risk-lite component of the CDO (tranches immediately below super senior and also carrying very high ratings were also available, with a better yield). So by internally amalgamating a portfolio of super seniors, UBS's CDO traders were seen as wisely helping themselves, in one fell swoop lubricating two highly lucrative endeavors. And not only that. The CDO desk fell in love with super senior so much that it also decided to purchase some of the super senior generated by other banks' CDO structuring efforts. It seems that UBS by itself could not churn out enough CDOs to satisfy its unremitting hunger for subprime seniority. CDO traders were committed to taking a huge bet on the worst segments of the U.S. residential mortgage market not going south and they were not about to let themselves be limited by their own capacity to come up with convoluted securities that bet on the worst segments of the US residential mortgage market not going south.

It is important to note that UBS did not follow just one type of super senior stratagem. It divided its super senior play into three broad categories: (1) fully hedged positions (through, say, a monoline insurer); (2) very slimly hedged positions (just 2 percent to 4 percent of the notional, based on statistical analysis of the position's riskiness that indicated that such minute cover was sufficient as losses were not expected to be greater than that); and (3) totally unhedged positions (typically, positions not yet hedged waiting to be hedged; there was a certain time lag between the retention of the super senior tranche and its hedging). When markets turned and subprime CDOs headed for the precipice, those three approaches contributed, respectively, to 10 percent, 63 percent, and 27 percent of UBS's 2007 total losses on super senior plays. As is amply known, a lot of monoline insurance turned out to be not insurance as those "insurers" went out of business flooded by the sudden massive liabilities triggered by the housing cataclysm. Also retrospectively (and, for many, also prospectively) obvious is that the statistical "forecasts" were fraudulently off the mark, irrefutably Lilliputian. And no need to dwell on the inconvenience of having unhedged subprime CDO positions.

So, the key question beckons. How much toxic stuff did the CDO desk accumulate before it was too late? As the shareholders report neatly states, UBS's super senior inventory grew from low levels in early 2006 to $50 billion by September 2007, with more than half of the latter figure either slimly hedged or totally unhedged. The possibility of synthetic and hybrid deals naturally contributed to such growth, as did the "no risk" statistical alibi (if you can get away with considering a CDO bet a fully hedged bet when you are hedging just 2 percent to 4 percent of the deal, more power to ya'). Twenty billion dollars of those $50 billion were purchased from third parties. By that date, with the market deterioration only too obvious, any exit strategy (whether sales or hedging of those long subprime positions) had become pretty much unviable due to a dry-up in liquidity and risk appetite. There was no option but to incur severe write-downs, more than $20 billion of them by mid-2008, making the super senior CDOs retained by UBS the greatest single source of loss for the bank.

Is $50 billion a lot of money to be wagering on the fate of the U.S. subprime housing market? Well, on September 28, 2007, UBS had total equity capital of around $42 billion, so yes $50 billion appears as a tad excessive (and remember that this is just the super senior stuff that was kept on the bank's books; on top of that, UBS had extra exposure to subprime through its CDO Warehouse pipeline, through the other units that punted on subprime one way or another, and through off-balance sheet activities; the Fixed Income Division's CDO desk was responsible for two-thirds of UBS's total losses, and other folks within the bank also lost a ton of dough on subprime). Any reasonably prudent person would tell you that making a "subprime will survive" punt for an amount larger than your entire core capital base would not belong to the category of prudent management. If securities entirely made up of sure-to-default loans found their natural value (i.e., zero or very close to it), the bank would be instantly insolvent.

In sum, UBS did have a lot of subprime junk on its books. The search for profit through the two conduits of CDO structuring and super senior tranche retention had condemned the bank to owning too many billions of CDO and RMBS exposure. What was the cost of this junkyard, regulatory capital-wise? We already suspect that it must have been pretty low, given that UBS's super senior position by itself was larger than its entire equity base (which, on top of the subprime cesspool, had been calculated to sustain the rest of UBS's assets, all $2 trillion of them by September 28, 2007). But, does the April 2008 report provide more detailed guidance? Yes, it does. Inside UBS, on-balance sheet CDO positions were given trading book treatment as opposed to banking book treatment, meaning that their risk and capital charge would be monitored by VaR (the report expressed its puzzlement with such arrangement, complaining that "*Super senior notes were always treated as trading book, i.e. the book for assets intended for resale in the short term, notwithstanding the fact that there does not appear to have been a liquid secondary market*"). And until Q3 2007 those VaR numbers happened to be very low. UBS used a five-year time series to obtain the super senior positions' VaR. Up to Q3 2007, subprime CDOs had experienced very little volatility as the mortgage bubble inflated unabated and, as a consequence and in the report's very words, "*even unhedged super senior positions contributed little to VaR.*" That is, the riskiness of even UBS's naked CDO punts was deemed by VaR to be small. Hedged positions, including those very scantily hedged, were deemed "VaR neutral" meaning that they were treated as if their VaR was effectively zero; so for internal risk assessment all those gazillions in super senior positions that were hedged only up to 2 percent to 4 percent of their size were judged to be 100 percent risk-free. Given that that family of the overall subprime portfolio ended up representing 63 percent of UBS's total super senior losses for 2007, it appears at the very least slightly weird to have considered them so magnificently solid. The model, certified by the Investment Banking Division's Quantitative Risk Control group, that said that by hedging just 2 percent to 4 percent of the position you could go to sleep thinking yourself unassailably protected was proven to be as creepily deleterious as the securities that it purported to analyze (CDO traders had a big incentive to believe in the model's dictums, as doing the 2 percent to 4 percent hedge was 50 percent cheaper than doing the 100 percent hedge; recall that fully covered plays contributed only 10 percent of overall 2007 super senior setbacks). The statistical assumptions were demolished by the very impressive losses that those "zero VaR" positions ended up suffering. Let's hear it from the report again, "*Investment Banking business planning relied on VaR, the key risk parameter in the process. When the market dislocation unfolded, it became apparent that this methodology had not appropriately captured the risk inherent in the businesses having subprime exposures.*"

UBS's subprime positions (the warehoused RMBS, the super senior CDO tranches) were filtered through the VaR strainer. The VaR of those positions was very low up to the crisis. This allowed the subprime stuff to enjoy very low risk estimates and capital requirements. Why did UBS decide to place its subprime holdings under VaR's tutelage? You already suspect the rationale, but the April 2008 report offers a particularly straightforward summation: "*Treatment under the banking book would have significantly changed the economics of the CDO desk business as this would have increased the required regulatory capital charges.*" In other words, VaR allowed the CDO desk (ultimately responsible for UBS's dance with death and destruction) to churn out a lot of nasty CDOs and to keep a lot of nasty CDO tranches by making it extremely economical to churn out a lot of nasty CDOs and to keep a lot of nasty CDO tranches. By late September 2007, as UBS accumulated all those super seniors and related subprime garbage, its regulatory VaR was a paltry CHF1.19 billion, just 0.35 percent of its total trading assets (or almost 300-to-1 trading book leverage); even if we assumed that that capital was supporting exclusively the CDO stuff, the leverage would still have been a very lax 40 to 1. UBS ended up owning north of $50 billion in securities backed by the most venomously polluted assets ever devised because VaR made it very cheap to do so. Had owning north of $50 billion in securities backed by the most venomously polluted assets ever devised cost the appropriate amount of capital (something like, say, $50 billion), UBS would most probably not have owned north of $50 billion in super senior tranches of subprime CDOs, or perhaps not even $1 billion. And UBS, it follows, would not have bled so dangerously profusely. And the world would have been a better place.

It is important to remind ourselves that VaR's responsibility for a financial meltdown need not depend on it having had a role in determining the leverage that banks were allowed to enjoy on their trading books. As we know there is another key, though admittedly not as decisive, conduit through which VaR can facilitate trading trouble: namely, its original and seemingly perennial role as internal market risk beacon. VaR is used inside dealing rooms the world over as the mechanism that dictates whether or not a position is put on, how much trading volume a particular desk is allowed to take on, when assets should be liquidated, and in general how comfortable and permissive senior management are with their underlings' trading forays. If VaR gives the internal okay, the asset will be purchased (and if VaR stops giving the okay, an asset will be sold). It is easier to build a case for the accumulation of an asset if VaR is low. And, as the 2008 report indicates, those low VaR numbers inside UBS allowed unfettered complacency when it came to subprime CDO games. VaR told insiders that it was okay to retain a lot of super senior trash because it was, statistically speaking, not a risky business. Any insider skeptical as to the CDO desk's activities would have been subjugated into compliance and submission by the very humble risk estimates. VaR became a powerful ally of those at UBS ready and willing to bet the bank's fate on the subprime market's future. *"In the context of the CDO structuring business and the super senior trades, Investment Banking Market Risk Control relied primarily upon VaR and stress limits and monitoring to provide risk control for the CDO desk,"* offered the report, before later on denigrating VaR by brutally bluntly stating that *"Inappropriate risk metrics had been used in strategic planning and assessment"* and that the model had been dangerously over-relied on. If you have any doubt as to the unquestionably decisive part that a tool like VaR can have in enabling a dance like the subprime CDO cha-cha-cha, recall how the biggest slice of UBS's overall super senior retention strategy got away with labeling itself fully hedged by purchasing protection on just 2 percent to 4 percent of the position's notional value, and revisit the reason why such modest-looking risk management approach was assumed to be iron-clad secure: data-driven analysis of the kind that VaR is built on. In the shareholders' report's own words, *"This level of hedging was based on statistical analyses of historical price movements that indicated that such protection was sufficient to protect UBS from any losses on the position. Much of the protection has now been exhausted, leaving UBS exposed to write-downs on losses to the extent they exceed the protection purchased."* VaR is, of course, based on statistical dissection of historical evidence. Remember that the "fully hedged" alibi permitted those massive positions to be pronounced "VaR neutral," and thus to be accumulated relentlessly (in the process, as we know, making it more comfortable for UBS's CDO desk and for other banks' CDO desks to continue manufacturing CDO garbage). And remember that those positions were in the end behind most of UBS's entire super senior setback.

VaR, together with the credit ratings and other number-crunching tricks, effectively became not just an enabler of the destructive subprime affair, but, quite conveniently, served the purpose of ex post showing "rigorous" due diligence when it came to appraising the risk of having ex ante gone subprime. Using VaR and related analytical models is great not only because their irrepressibly ridiculous risk estimates can give carte blanche to the leveraged accumulation of toxic plays, but also because after the fact, and should big loses materialize, you can always claim to have believed yourself fully hedged, according to the most glorified, accepted, and conventional methods. So VaR and similarly admired quanty tools are used not just because it aids your trading forays but also because the world will buy it when you point at the VaR alibi as excuse for your position-taking (which beats the alternative explanation of having knowingly amassed knowingly lethal assets). The "Look, those bets were riskless according to this age-old model that is embraced by regulators and taught at the world's best universities. I can't be blamed for taking irresponsibly adventurous positions. I was prudently following the model's sophisticated dictates!" line seems to have worked all too well during the last and previous financial crises. Rather puzzlingly, people keep accepting such excusing, condoning any kind of chaos-generating behavior as long as it had been sanctioned and rubberstamped by deified analytics.

Even the most illustrious of audiences submit. Take the Swiss Federal Banking Commission. In a famous investigation into UBS's subprime mess[2] (which, by the way, concurred with all the major points enshrined in UBS's own report to shareholders, including the conclusions that subprime positions were placed in the trading book, that the consequent reliance on VaR resulted in low regulatory capital requirements, that many positions were assumed to be VaR-neutral, and that VaR eventually proved to have severely underestimated danger) It concluded that everyone at UBS honestly thought of themselves as fully hedged from any subprime deterioration, this, according to the

SFBC, being particularly true in the case of the practice of retaining the super senior tranches. As far as the SFBC can tell, no one inside UBS thought that they were taking wild reckless risks, even as they accumulated north of $50 billion in assets made up entirely of the worst possible kind of debt. According to the SFBC's script,

> There is no evidence that managers at the investment bank or group level consciously incurred incalculable risks for the sole purpose of obtaining a higher bonus. Nor is there any evidence that the persons responsible for the risk control function recognized the risks UBS had taken on and deliberately turned a blind eye. On the contrary, the persons responsible for building up the problematic positions relied on the presumed robustness of UBS's risk management and risk control and that when the market deterioration commenced they believed UBS was sufficiently protected. The sense of relative security shared by those responsible for these businesses is further demonstrated by the build-up of additional super senior CDOs retained on the bank's books in the second quarter of 2007.[3]

The "presumed robustness" of UBS's risk management was predicated on VaR numbers. VaR could be employed as an alibi later on because it looked so robust. A low VaR can later act as a get-out-of-jail free card to categorize any financial action as prudent and robust, no matter how devastating the consequences of those acts. The SFBC's testimony is an incredibly powerful testament as to how readily outsiders come to comply and to believe in the "the model said no risk, thus I wasn't consciously taking any risks" excuse (such line of thinking is the most potent incentive for the preservation and build-up of models with a natural tendency to underestimate true risk, and thus for the fragilization of the system).

What the SFBC is saying is that no one inside UBS saw any problem with gorging on subprime bets until the volume of those bets dwarfed even the bank's entire equity capital support. That everyone at UBS religiously abided by the ridiculously deflated VaRs and by the ridiculously inflated AAAs. That no one inside UBS ever doubted for a moment the wisdom of considering a secure institution betting the farm on the performance of loans given under false pretenses and for unrepayable amounts to jobless, income-less, possessions-less, faceless individuals living an ocean away from Zurich. In other words, what the SFBC is saying is that UBS employees were brain-dead. What is most probable? That the UBS bankers, traders, and risk managers (many of them extremely qualified and IQ-unchallenged professionals educated in the world's finest schools) would categorize as riskless a portfolio of billions of unhedged or extremely slimly hedged or hedged-through-dubious-means subprime stuff, just because certain statistical methodologies said so? Or that at the very least many of those bankers, traders, and risk managers were entirely aware of the unreliability and uselessness of tools that had the cheek to proclaim a subprime RMBS or CDO as nonproblematic, yet found it more in their interest to play along with the "riskless" charade?

■ ■ ■

As mentioned, UBS's dance with subprime is a very good case study of the investment banking industry's overall dance with subprime, and the lessons from the Alpine giant serve us well to understand why banks failed so abruptly and deeply. They (many of them at least; there were some notable exceptions) had too much subprime securities inventory on their books. They had large warehouses of the nasty stuff waiting to be repackaged into RMBS and CDOs. They kept large quantities of super senior CDO tranches. They placed a lot of that stuff as trading assets, in the land where VaR dictates regulatory capital charges. VaR was the beacon through which the plays' riskiness was assessed. The nasty stuff was considered prudently under control. Risk estimates and capital requirements were very low, breeding untold complacency and allowing banks to play the subprime game unencumbered.

In early December 2007, a report by JP Morgan estimated that banks held around $216 billion in super senior tranches of subprime CDOs issued in 2006 and 2007. As of June 29, 2007, Merrill Lynch's net super senior retention exposure was more than $32 billion; to this we must add almost $2 billion in CDO warehousing exposure, plus several billion more in whole loans to get a grip on some of Merrill's subprime risks[4] (notice that by "net" exposure we mean total long subprime exposures minus protection purchased on those long bets, if those hedges end up not working properly then the true net exposure becomes much greater). Barely a few days before the subprime market unraveled for good, Merrill's toxic portfolio was greater than its entire just-above-$30 billion equity capital base. By September 30, 2007, Citigroup had net super senior exposure of $43 billion ($53 billion gross exposure; $25 billion came from the consolidation of off-balance sheet CDO positions), plus $2.7 billion in CDO warehousing risk, plus several billion more of subprime inventory (whole loans, etc.), for a total net subprime exposure of almost $55 billion.[5] As of August 31, 2007, Morgan Stanley's net super senior exposure exceeded $11 billion; it had an extra $9 billion gross long subprime play in the form of warehoused assets and whole loans, but a slightly net short position there given large amounts of hedging, taking the bank's overall net on-balance sheet subprime exposure to just above $10 billion.[6]

These gargantuan super senior holdings owed their existence to several main factors. Just like in UBS's case, retaining the super senior slice of a subprime CDO made sense, temporarily at least, as a revenue-generating money machine (the smallish gross returns were perceived as very tasty net income on billions of notional size; two-thirds or more of a CDO was super senior, and average size for a CDO could be $1 billion; given how very economical it was to "hedge" these very senior positions, banks could boast of generating tons of "riskless" income; plus super senior tranches could be better propositions than similarly rated alternatives, as they tended to yield a few basis points more) and as a fee-generating money machine (being willing to park the stuff on your balance sheet aided the completion of CDO transactions). Also, some banks had provided guarantees and "liquidity puts" to the off-balance sheet special investment vehicles that issued notes to investors backed by the performance of super senior subprime tranches; as those shadow banking entities got in trouble following the decline in value of subprime assets, the real banks had to made good on their precommitments and swallow the exposures into their books.

Banks got caught in a self-feeding, self-defeating spiral: The greed for upfront CDO structuring fees (especially, recall from UBS, when it came to the CDOs made up of low-grade RMBS) turned several banks into out-of-control CDO underwriters, forcing them in turn to digest ever larger chunks of super senior positions. Recall that it wasn't easy to find outsiders willing to take on the super senior tranche, given its relatively low yield and its abundant size. Sometimes the outsiders that had complied stopped doing so, most famously insurance giant AIG, which had in the market's early days been willing to insure huge amounts of banks' super senior bets at a very paltry cost. When AIG quit the field in 2005 worried about the vast amount of liabilities it had undertaken, banks became in effect the "dumb money," their CDO position now fully mirroring that of Norwegian town councils, German insurance companies, and other typical CDO investors: If the value of subprime assets fell, they would be nakedly facing large losses.

Let's dwell a bit more on why banks felt the need to engage in a steamy, sordid, titillating, scandalous love affair with the super senior tranches of subprime CDOs. After all, that romance was the main source of losses for Wall Street and London, and, therefore, the main culprit behind the maliciously brutal 2007–2008 crisis. Plus, more egotistically, the accumulation of super senior bets is a pretty big indictment on VaR, and thus its analysis should place prominently in a book such as this one. This was UBS's literal explanation as to why it chose to embrace super seniority as a profitable investment: *"The funded positions yielded a positive carry (i.e., return) above the internal UBS funding and the unfunded position generated a positive spread."* Funded positions are those where the investor actually purchases a bond, and unfunded positions are those where the investor can make essentially the same bet but without having to make any principal investment. For example, a fully funded cash CDO uses the proceeds from the sale of its bonds to investors to buy the underlying bonds or loans whose cash flows are the main source of funds for repaying the CDO's own bonds (that is, the yields on the CDO's tranches). On the other hand, a synthetic CDO with an unfunded super senior tranche pays super senior investors from the cash flows collected from those buying protection (and thus paying a regular swap spread) on the CDO's underlying credit default swaps. Those slices of the synthetic CDO that are funded would invest the principal amounts received from tranche investors in risk-free assets, which together with the swap spreads received from protection buyers would form the cash flows pot to which those investors are entitled. Access to cheap financing was essential to make the net return on funded positions reasonably interesting, given how modest the gross yield on the super senior tranche was. UBS wasn't adamant to admit that much,

> Several of the Super Senior positions (either retained from UBS securitizations or purchased from third parties) had a thin positive carry of approximately 20 basis points, i.e. the costs of funding the positions were lower than the (expected) yield on those positions. More demanding internal transfer pricing requirements could have made several cash positions unattractive due to negative carry, which may have resulted in closer scrutiny of the overall carry strategy.

In other words, if UBS had not lent money so cheaply to its CDO desk, its CDO desk would have had a much harder time building its fatal super senior portfolio.

The April 2008 report in fact intones a big mea culpa when it comes to the issue of internal funding, flagellating the bank for having passed through its cheap market borrowing costs to its business units without regard for the riskiness and illiquidity of a particular unit's assets. Why did UBS act that way? The report has an answer in hand, sharing that, "*A more stringent funding model was seen by Investment Banking senior management as potentially impacting their growth plans.*" Such ambitions, coupled with a prolonged period of very cheap financing fueled by a very easy official monetary policy regime (and by the then-fashionable perception that investment banks were unassailably robust and successful), made it certain that the net positive carry CDO cash machine would roll along unperturbed, in the process building up a ticking bomb of hidden risk inside the Swiss confines.

The economics for other banks appear to have been the same. In a conference on September 2008, Eric Kolchinsky from Moody's showed a slide where the numbers behind the so-called *Negative Basis Trade* were neatly presented: The super senior tranche would pay Libor plus 20 basis points; the funding cost would be Libor minus 10 basis points; and the cost of hedging the play (through, say, a credit default swap on the CDO) would be 10 basis points. The final result was a sweet 20 basis points net annual return on a fully hedged more-than-AAA asset; or, as almost everyone called it back then, free money. Banks had seemingly found a golden goose from where large profits and huge returns on equity could be milked, requiring not too much effort or ingenuity from them in return. As long as more subprime borrowers and/or people willing to take the long side of the credit default swaps on RMBS could be found, the alchemy would last.

Profitable as the carry trade was in itself, its full gloriousness lay in its ability to lead banks to yet another CDO field of gold, an ocean of CDO securitization fees. Even if the carry trade had delivered no gains (say, because banks' funding costs went up), it may still have made sense for banks to gorge on it, given the tasty rewards from underwriting and selling CDOs (recall that UBS was making 1.25 percent to 1,50 percent in structuring fees; other banks fared similarly well; for instance Citigroup earned 1 percent of the total deal[7]). As third party investors shied away from seniority, it was up to the CDO structurers to fill the void. The small gross yield on super seniors that would have sufficed for banks to build a money machine may not have been nearly enough compensation for other financial players. Especially given that a CDO offered other, higher-yielding, opportunities for AAA–AA investing, thus crowding out super seniors (as an illustrative example, a AAA+ super senior tranche that only suffers losses if more than 15 percent of the CDO's underlying assets go underwater could have below it a AAA tranche sheltered from up to 10 percent of portfolio setbacks and a AA tranche with a 7 percent subordination; too much internal top-rated competition for super senior). The super senior's pick up over other super creditworthy external competitors, such as Treasury bonds, would have been too limited to entice investors into a play that, at the end of the day, was linked to the default capabilities of NINJA (no income–no jobs–no assets) mortgage borrowers rather than to those of Uncle Sam. That return premia has been estimated to have been around 10 basis points.[8] The JP Morgan study mentioned above openly stated that, "*The banks ended up holding so many super-senior classes of CDOs partly because they were forced to retain about two thirds of the securities when underwriting deals in 2006 and 2007 because of weak demand from other investors.*"

Naturally, one may naively wonder why were banks so happy-go-lucky about retaining massive amounts of securities that other investors were shunning. After concurring that banks agreed to hold on to the super seniors so as to safeguard the great deal of fees generated from selling the more junior tranches, one elite regulator put it like this: "*In an originate and distribute securitization model you are not supposed to hold on to large positions, and if the market forces you to that position perhaps it's sending a signal about risk that very much needs to be heeded.*"[9] But this assumes that banks cared at all about the risks of their CDO positions. After all, weren't those AAA+? What's the problem? It's free money, right?

Super senior tranches may have been condemned to being unattractive to outside investors from the get-go. In their eagerness to create and sell CDOs, banks may have been forced to engineering the things so that the high-risk bottom tranches enjoyed really tasty returns, thus guaranteeing investor demand (after all, the junior slices were competing for investor attention with other similarly rated securities). The entire purpose of the CDO was to endow trashy securities with better credit ratings, so that people who always wanted to buy trashy assets but were pushed back by the fact that the trashy character of the punt was so openly obvious could now get their hands on the trash but under a conveniently deceitful disguise. The BBB-rated tranche of the RMBS that banks engineered was never a hit with outside investors, so banks had no alternative but to create the investor: the CDOs. As a mortgage banker told attendees at a securitization forum in early 2002, "*We told you that these BBB securities were a great deal, and priced at great spreads, but nobody stepped up. So we created the investor.*"[10] By 2005, CDOs were buying virtually all BBB RMBS tranches and turning the vast majority of them into AAA paper; in essence, through the CDO machine all the stinky garbage left out in the mortgage market was laundered into lavender-scenting delicacies.

But just because the trash is no longer deemed so doesn't mean that you have to settle for untrashy-like yields. You still demand very appealing returns. So the lower tranches had to be adorned with decent yields, but in making the riskiest tranches attractive to purchasers they were priced attractively relative to expected cash flows (don't forget that it was essential that the junior tranches were sold for the senior tranches to have very high-credit ratings; the only reason why a pool of lowly rated mortgage securities can produce AAA tranches is that enough investors are willing to purchase the subordinated tranches and thus agree to absorb first losses on the underlying loans, and thus contribute to the illusion that the senior stuff is riskless because losses won't reach that high; so if you want to alchemize trash into a lot of AAA seniority you better find someone ready to take the first hits to the CDO, and chances are you would have to compensate them nicely for that). And since the overall cash flows from the underlying bonds or credit default swaps are fixed, the outcome from skewing their distribution toward the lower tranches was that super seniors would be relatively starved of cash flow and thus yield, and more difficult to sell.[11] If you need to concentrate payments on the other tranches you probably can't make those tranches too big, implying that the remaining top tranche will be very big and very slimly yielding. If you or somebody else is going to be stuck with that investment it might as well be categorized as more than super safe (otherwise, what's the point?), and this is where risk measuring tools that assigned negligible danger to that investment helped a lot; the models that assigned very little odds to extreme events and that assumed very small correlation among the underlying subprime loans also helped in another key respect: They helped make the junior CDO tranches smaller and thus easier to place by calculating that only a bit of subordination would be needed for senior tranches to feel safe, in the process naturally helping make the top tranches very large, a boon for banks involved in the super senior carry trade.

Another rationale for the low returns on super seniors might have been a desire not to charge too much spread to those willing to buy protection and feed the credit default swaps on RMBS sustaining synthetic CDOs: Without those cash flows there's no CDO to arrange and intermediate so you better not ask those protection buyers for prohibitive sums of money, lest they fly away in disgust. A necessarily constrained cash flow pile necessarily means limited cash flow for super seniors, as more junior investors must, again, be properly spoiled.

As the subprime crisis unfolded many observers were shocked by the sight of so many super senior losses inside so many banks. Up to that point few of the few people aware of the very existence of such a thing as a CDO super senior tranche even mildly suspected that the firms designing the CDOs were also the ones exposed to super senior. It had been assumed that the purportedly super safe, ultraconservative paper had ended up in the hands of those who habitually buy super safe, ultraconservative paper. The stuff just seemed tailor-made for the tastes of staid, boring investors happy to earn low yields on surprise-free solid plays. Super senior just looked too unsexy and unadventurous a punt for high-flying investment banks to be making. Even those nonbankers who had most avidly followed the brave new world of structured finance were baffled. Take Gillian Tett, the *Financial Times* senior U.S. editor and former capital markets editor who most likely became the first major journalist to start covering subprime CDOs, and who was public in her shock when the real truth behind the super senior story was unveiled in late 2007. Tett was forced to confess once reality hit:

> When I first heard about this asset class a couple of years ago I initially assumed this stuff might appeal to risk-averse institutions such as pension funds. But nothing could be further from the truth. As banks have pumped out CDOs, they have been selling the other tranches of debt to outside investors—while retaining the super-senior piece on their books. Sometimes they did this simply to keep the CDO machine running. But there was another, far more important, incentive. Banks such as UBS and Merrill have been cramming their books with tens of billions of super-senior debt—and then booking the spread as a seemingly never-ending source of easy profit. So there you have it: in the last resort, a key reason for these record-beating losses is not a failure of ultra-complex financial strategies or esoteric models; instead it arose from a humongous, misplaced bet on a carry trade that was so simple that even a first-year economics student (or *Financial Times* journalist) could understand it. So the moral, in a sense, is also a simple one: if someone offers you seemingly free money, in seemingly infinite quantities, with a soothing new name, you really ought to smell a rat.[12]

Many didn't even understand why such an invention as super senior tranches needed to exist in the first place. Too little yield pickup for too much (real) risk. Outsiders didn't bother and couldn't banks have done the famous carry trade on more subordinated tranches of the CDO, thus generating even more income? A big reason why a big slice of something deemed more-than-AAA was a glorious thing to create may have been the urgent need by the financial industry for more-than-AAA assets. You see, really highly rated stuff is hard to come by in finance. Up to the arrival of CDOs, a very limited number of asset families (some government bonds, some corporate bonds) were considered ultrasafe. Ultrasafe assets play a key role as guarantors in financing, trading, and regulatory activities, so if you can't find them in size you might need to manufacture new ones through the alchemy of securitization. Without those sound guarantees you may not be able to borrow, trade, and comply with regulations as much as you'd like. In the words of an academic involved in the CDO business:

> A problem with the new banking system is that it depends on collateral to guarantee the safety of the deposits. But, there are many demands for such collateral. Foreign governments and investors have significant demands for U.S. Treasury bonds, U.S. agency bonds, and corporate bonds. Treasury and agency bonds are also needed to collateralize derivatives positions. Further, they are needed to use as collateral for clearing and settlement of financial transactions. There are few AAA corporate bonds. Roughly speaking, the total amount of possible collateral in U.S. bond markets, minus the amount held by foreigners is about $16 trillion. The amount used to collateralize derivatives positions is about $4 trillion. It is not known how much is needed for clearing and settlement. Repo needs, say, $12 trillion. The demand for collateral has been largely met by securitization, a 30-year old innovation that allows for efficient financing of loans.[13]

It turns out that on top of earning good fees and returns for banks, CDOs delivered a third miracle: a machine that churned out unlimited amounts of AAA assets to quench the insatiable and unmeetable thirst for the iron-clad collateral that oils financial activity. Between 2003 and 2007, as the U.S. housing sector boomed, banks issued $700 billion in mortgage-linked CDOs;[14] if we assume that 80 percent of a CDO was AAA (super senior plus the immediately subordinated tranche) then around $560 billion of new AAA securities were created just like that, through the perceived magic of asset diversification and the humble statistical loss estimates. So there was a very good reason why the "originate-and-distribute" model that presumably lied behind the securitization business in fact transformed into something more like "originate-and-distribute-a-bit-and-retain a lot." The triple AAA label must have also been of help internally for CDO traders justifying to their superiors their amalgamation of super senior positions; if a division head or bank board member peppered them with bothersome questioning the CDO folks could always counter that all they were doing was amassing the most highly rated paper and producing outstanding returns in the process; UBS's 2008 shareholders report points in that direction:

> Whilst attempts were made by Group Senior Management to understand the risks in the subprime segment before July 2007, Risk Control and business management described substantial notional exposures in AAA-rated securities, limited exposures to lower rated instruments and low stress loss on the portfolio. Group Senior Management relied on those assurances rather than obtaining all the facts and analytically reviewing the situation.

Some argue that this reality flies in the face of one of the most prevalent myths of the 2007–2008 crisis: that the creation of subprime securities was fundamentally motivated by insatiable investor demand. The CDOs and RMBS that went so bad and that wreaked so much havoc, the argument would go, had to be created to satisfy the interests of real investors the globe over, all looking for mortgage-related yield in an era of very low official interest rates and rock-solid housing markets (perhaps the biggest boom in financial history). According to this take, the banks behind the bad securities were just doing their jobs, putting their engineering and marketing skills at the service of their clients. There was nothing sinister behind the subprime structured finance business. Yes, banks made good profits out of it, but in the process lots of nonbankers enjoyed innovative products and were able to own a home. Should those who enabled such benefits be demonized?

But now that we know that up to 70 percent (or more) of a subprime CDO's size was typically held by banks on their balance sheet (or off-balance sheet but with guarantees to claim it back if things went sour), the "insatiable investor demand" story may sound less appealingly convincing. Once we look at the numbers, we may forgive ourselves for concluding that the truly insatiable demand came from the inside and not from the outside. Perhaps no one on the outside ever really cared too much for this innovation. The churning of CDOs, then, may be explained not so much as the response by dedicated bankers to their clients' requests, but rather as the oil that greased an internal artificial money machine from which only bankers benefited. Nothing wrong with financiers fabricating ways to make dough, only that this storyline would not sound as commendable and innocent as the other one. Someone who very strongly doubts the investor interest argument shattered the conventional wisdom with very strong words:

> Bankers continue to insist that they were meeting the insatiable demand of investors when they created more CDOs. Various industry apologists continue to perpetuate the myth of the exuberant buyer of CDOs, mortgage backed securities and sub-prime mortgage loans. In truth, by 2006, there were virtually no natural buyers for CDOs. This "demand" was a complete farce and if the demand for the CDOs was a farce, then the demand for risky RMBS and the mortgage loans was a farce too. The entire mortgage related CDO business was a sham. However, it had a tremendously damaging impact on the economy by grossly distorting the mortgage market. In many ways, the CDO business came to resemble a Ponzi scheme— new bonds were made to satisfy the "demand" of the CDS short sellers and the CDO salesmen at the banks who had found the ultimate suckers to dump the bonds on—their own bank and, eventually, the taxpayers.[15]

■ ■ ■

A bank's "trading book," just like VaR or CDOs, is one of those things that the general public is not supposed to be acquainted with. And just like VaR and CDOs, a bank's trading book is one of those things that one needs to be acquainted with in order to understand the

2007–2008 credit crisis. Not only that, without being familiar with the notion of the trading book it is quite hard (if not impossible) to comprehend how the modern banking industry operates.

For the purposes of regulatory capital, banks divide their assets into two main buckets: the banking book and the trading book. The former is supposed to deal with medium- and long-term portfolios that are relatively hard to liquidate fast and are subject to credit risk capital requirements (the typical example would be a loan given to a corporation; the capital charge cushions the possibility of a default). The latter is supposed to deal with short-termish positions that can be liquidated right away and are subject to market risk capital requirements (typical examples are financial instruments, derivatives; the capital charge mitigates drops in market value). As we know, the original set of bank capital rules concerned itself only with the banking book (i.e., only with credit risk). But soon it became obvious that this was a limited arrangement in the brave new world of massive trading and unlimited product innovation. Market risk began to be not just enormous in itself but in fact quickly overtook credit risk as banks' number one reason to lose sleep at night. Whether the traded value of a bond or a currency swap fluctuated mattered more for the bottom line than whether a corporate or government debtor reneged on their obligations. In other words, for the all-important purposes of regulatory capital, the trading book began not just to matter a lot but to matter most. Thus the mid-1990s amendment to Basel I to include a market risk capital levy, and thus the true beginning of VaR's imperial dominance in financeland (according to sources, prior to VaR trading activities represented just a minor proportion of commercial banks activities at less than 10 percent in terms of assets; by 2007, with VaR having reigned as capital king for a decade, in the most sophisticated universal banks trading accounted for a large part of the balance sheet, in some cases even most of the balance sheet[16]). Whatever fell under trading book jurisdiction had its capital costs determined by VaR, and this became a strong argument for banks when deciding whether to place an asset in the trading or the banking book.

For although there is firm policy guidance delimiting the definition of trading or banking asset, banks in practice have a lot of discretion in the matter. It's not too difficult to make the trading book an asset's home. All that's really required is that the bank in question declares that the asset is held either with trading intent or to hedge other elements in the trading book; the asset must either be free of any restrictive covenants on their tradability or be able to be hedged completely; in addition, positions should be frequently and accurately valued, and actively managed.

The conclusion is that if a bank wants to put something in its trading book, chances are that it may be able to do so, even if the asset had originally been parked in the banking book (while trading book positions are sometimes redesigned as banking book, it is much more usual to see this process in reverse). In fact, if the 2007 crisis shows something it's how true that is. Assets that looked more banking-type than trading-type were secluded in the trading book. The key difference boils down to having the capital cost of your activities be calculated by VaR or by banking book standards (preset fixed risk weights bucketed by asset category, credit ratings). Not a small caveat, as going one route over the other could signify costlier operations, and thus lower returns on equity, perhaps even making certain positions entirely unaffordable. It is a safe bet that if a bank chose the trading book over its banking counterpart as the destination for an asset it's because it believed that a VaR-based system can yield lower capital requirements (strictly speaking, once an asset is inside the trading book there are two possible capital-calculating methodologies available: VaR and the so-called *standardized method*, which follows a nonmathematical risk bucketing approach; so banks here would have a second choice, and VaR may in the end not be the chosen tool; nonetheless, major banks have traditionally opted for VaR, a model that, let's not forget, they invented and lobbied hard for).

Generally speaking, the trading book has traditionally been assumed to result in a lower capital number than the banking book, for a given asset portfolio. Recall, for instance, how, on granting Wall Street broker-dealers permission to use VaR for market risk capital purposes, the SEC expressed its belief that the new regime was likely to sanction more leverage than was the case under the old one based on risk bucketing. Of course, this is a tacit admission that VaR is a tool destined to produce meager numbers and a subtle way of saying that a VaR-dominated trading book creates large incentives for banks to park assets in their trading books. Or to engage in what is known as *regulatory arbitrage*, whereby banks behave like mercenary capital shoppers, shuffling their assets between the two books depending on which one happens to offer the best rate. To many observers, it may sound entirely counterintuitive that the same portfolio could have two entirely differing capital levies contingent on whether a bank uses some strange thing called a *trading book*. After all, the riskiness of an asset (and thus the prudent amount of capital needed to back it up) should not change simply because it is internally placed by a bank inside one or other parcel. The same bond or the same swap should not be viewed differently risk-and-capital wise. Nothing about the fundamental characteristics of the asset has changed one bit, so it seems only commonsensical that the leverage allowed on the play should stay the same, notwithstanding whether the bank elects to put it in the trading or banking drawer.

From the regulators' point of view, banks haven't enjoyed a free lunch by being entitled to park assets where they please. The trading book comes with strings attached, or so it has conventionally seemed. The biggest drawback typically associated with going with the trading book is that the accounting treatment of the assets would be potentially unfriendly, as positions must be marked-to-market on a continuous basis, with sudden drops in value hitting a bank's profit-and-loss statement right away. So the higher the proportion of assets that are parked in its trading book, the more a bank's net income would be affected by the vagaries of market sentiment and human spirits, possibly leading to a very volatile ride. In contrast, banking book positions, that are subjected to old-fashioned staid accrual accounting (at historical cost, less some reserves for potential credit losses; only if sold or impaired would the assets impact earnings), are much less prone to enabling an unwelcomed P&L roller coaster. Of course, the accounting earnings chute-the-chute that mark-to-market may produce would be most desirable to many when asset valuations do nothing but rise, so the perceived main drawback of the trading book may in fact turn out to be a godsend for banks that ride the wave of a market bubble, delivering a glorious duo of benign capital charges plus daily increasing asset values; the end result: lots of reported income on top of a humble capital base (i.e., fabulous returns on equity, for a while at least). Actually, the benefits of mark-to-market accounting for those bankers seeking the fast windfalls derived from leveraged plays can be self-reinforcing when in a bubbly state, as the consolidation of gains in value would translate into a track record of negligible setbacks and thus into the kind of humble VaR figures that excuse very high gearing on trading games.

There is indeed some evidence of banks openly professing their preference for trading book treatment. For instance, a few years before the 2007 crisis a so-called "Ad Hoc Working Group of Investment Banks" comprised by representatives from Bear Stearns, Merrill Lynch, Goldman Sachs, and Morgan Stanley sent a letter to the Board of Governors of the Federal Reserve in which they essentially lobbied for the continued easement of the practice of placing assets in the trading book. The Wall Street giants noted that there can be substantial divergence between the capital requirements generated for similar asset classes depending on whether a trading or banking book methodology is used (meaning that the banking approach is more expensive), and that it would be very nice if the Fed, as the natural implementer of international capital rules in the United States, didn't make it hard for them to catalog a position as trading book. To back its stance, the group complained that using a banking book approach would require considerable expense in systems and data. The document contains the shocking affirmation that three of the four firms did not even have a banking book at all, solely utilizing trading book approaches. And the lone exception placed stuff in the trading book when it pleased it anyway. It seems clear that there's something about the trading book that the most influential financial firms in the world have traditionally found very appealing. We have seen repeatedly how VaR can make the trading book a marvelous thing to embrace for those eager to lower the capital costs of their market forays (and perhaps hide tons of lethal risk in the process). To that conceptual and intuitive reasoning we can also add the highly revealing literal words of the ad hoc foursome.

Or the unabashed lobbying efforts of the Securities Industry Association, basically the ad hoc party plus the at-the-time other large Wall Street investment bank (Lehman Brothers), which in August 2003 also wrote to the Federal Reserve Board expressing its concerns for what the U.S. adoption of Basel II might do to their fortunes. This missive also emanates an unmistakable declaration of affection towards trading book treatment: Investment banks, the SIA pronounced,

[T]ypically value risky assets, including loans, on a mark-to-market basis, and estimate risk to that market value using various tools, including VaR models, which may be used to measure the risk of activities that are considered under Basel II as part of a banking book (investment banks place virtually all their financial instruments in the trading book). Our analysis suggests that an internal-models approach to calculating risk capital is more effective for many credit sensitive assets than the weightings-based approach for banking book assets under Basel II. To the extent that an institution can produce reliable mark-to-market values and robust VaR-based risk estimates we recommend that a trading book approach is permitted in lieu of a banking book approach.[17]

Any doubts as to Wall Street's strong preference for the trading treatment?

Banks had a clear incentive to place subprime CDOs and subprime RMBS in the trading book, especially the most senior and loss-proof tranches. VaR could be relied on to categorize them as riskless and unworrisome, given that the very puerile subprime CDOs market had yet to register negative news (especially the most senior slices). And the marked-to-market value of such illiquid esoteric securities may be easily propped up by the minuscule handful of traders active in that sphere. Trading book treatment offered an irresistibly tempting carrot: the possibility to build massive leverage on assets that were proving profitable through several conduits (carry trades, structuring fees, artificial mass-production of AAAs, mark-to-market bubbles). The alternative of parking the stuff in the banking book would have looked much less appealing, even though under the Basel II guideline issued in mid-2004 AAA-rated securitization exposures could carry a capital charge of only 1.6 percent of total assets or even as low as 0.56 percent of total assets; if banks still found such requirements taxing relative to what VaR offered, we can appreciate how little capital the trading book demanded (of course, it is not clear the extent to which banks had been adopting Basel II in the years prior to the crisis or rather were still abiding by Basel I rules, so the banking book treatment of CDOs and RMBS may have been more taxing than the percentages shown above).

Financial risk über-guru and über-practitioner Ricardo Rebonato explains the choice that banks made under the inebriating influence of the trading book siren song:

> There is a choice for most securities whether to place it in the banking book or in the trading book and there are plusses and minuses to both. Typically, the trading book attracts less capital but it forces you to be disciplined over daily mark-to-market so perhaps people had been placing into the trading book when the sky was blue, liquidity was high and you could find prices almost for everything. You have choices that you can make and the choices that were made by preference in the years up to 2007 was to place instruments in the trading book partially obviously because it attracted less capital and partly because the liquidity was so abundant that you could find prices for almost anything and therefore it was well justifiable in those blue sky days to put those assets there.[18]

One could justify placing securitized mortgage exposures in the trading book because there was a bull market in mortgage securitizations, making it feasible to claim that a CDO was indeed a wonderfully liquid security that could be smoothly disposed of at any point. In fact, securitization in general becomes the bridge that allows an asset class to move from banking to trading status. Securitization transforms hitherto nonsellable stuff (e.g., bank loans, mortgages) into tradable paper (e.g., mortgage-backed securities). Securitization, thus, made VaR ever more influential as the range of products and the volume of notional amounts that fell under its grip grew exponentially.

In fact, more and more credit-related assets may have been placed in the trading book. For instance, the proportion of credit derivatives activity by large French banks (world leaders in derivatives expertise and transacting, including elite firms like Société Générale and BNP Paribas) that was parked in the trading book went from around 35 percent in late 2000 to more than 95 percent in late 2004, and this shift coincided with an explosion in credit derivatives usage and credit derivatives innovation. So as they began to deal in ever larger sizes and with ever more complex products, the French chose to park almost all their credit derivatives plays under the trading umbrella.[19] Some think that Basel II, which imposed banking book capital requirements above the previous cap of 8 percent of notional value for a wide range of debt instruments, prompted, and may continue to prompt, many banks to transfer many of those instruments to the trading book, in desperate search of less unfriendly treatment (keep in mind that under Basel II those securitization exposures whose credit ratings get downgraded can begin to suffer truly accentuated capital charges; while top-rated tranches benefited from friendly treatment, the friendliness quickly ends if ratings drop toward junk status, a reason some say was behind the decisions by banks to stop retaining CDO equity tranches;[20] in contrast to VaR's numbers had no direct link to credit ratings, at least prior to the crisis). A similar effect is expected from moves to align the accounting treatment of trading and banking assets, with both books abiding by fair value (mark-to-market) rules, and thus eliminating the supposed advantage that the banking book held over its trading cousin. The inescapable conclusion is that the trading book's composition has been bastardized almost beyond recognition, welcoming in positions, like subprime CDOs that deviate enormously from the original aim of building a shelter for highly liquid, quickly disposable items. By being willing to accommodate the banks' desires for trading book dominance (with the enhanced leveraged punting that that would entail), regulators betrayed and tarnished the spirit of their very own risk control policies.

This was blindly obvious following the 2007 catastrophe. Positions that had been labeled as liquid and tradable enough to escape the shackles of the banking book suddenly couldn't find a buyer for them. CDOs proved to be neither transparently priced nor liquid (it has been said that if banks could have sold CDOs within 10 days at the onset of the credit crisis, the fallout would have been much less severe; instead they had to hold on to exposures, or even increase them by buying back assets sold to off-balance sheet conduits to protect investors' money and their own reputation[21]). In the end, securitization did not alchemize the illiquid into the tradable. A postcrisis report by the Economic Affairs Committee of the British Parliament lamented that:

> Trading book assets have lower capital requirements because it is assumed that they can easily be sold by a troubled bank.

More recently, the trading book has included instruments such as CDO tranches created by packaging illiquid instruments. CDO tranches trade infrequently and they are often valued using model-derived prices, rather than by reference to an active marketplace; consequently, these instruments are less obviously suited to a regime that was originally designed for liquid, traded instruments. Indeed, during the financial crisis, market participants became unwilling to price CDO tranches, so that trade in them was virtually impossible.[22]

Nick Studer, partner at consultancy Oliver Wyman, believes that many of the assets held in bank trading books were never designed to sit there. "*In this crisis most losses were in the trading books, where there were often no risk charges and a less than desirable understanding of the risks,*" argued the top consultant.[23] Some inside the banks themselves never bought that CDOs could belong in the trading universe, and felt that traditional and time-tested risk management practices were being threatened by such incomprehensible travesty. In particular, by not placing CDOs and RMBS firmly under the watchful eye of rigorous credit officers, banks guaranteed that a whole lot of poisonous default risk that otherwise may not have been internally accepted was internally accepted. This is how a real bank risk manager described the world before the advent of CDOs: "*Rigorous credit analysis was important. Loan risks were generally well understood.*"[24] But things took a turn for the worse as the newfangled structured finance monsters showed up in force, "*The gap in our risk management only opened up gradually with the growth of CDO tranches. They sat uncomfortably between market and credit risk.*" The price to be paid for such arrangement was too much leverage on assets whose obvious risks were overlooked, "*We needed little capital to support them. Since they were held in the trading book many avoided the rigorous credit process applied to banking book assets which might have identified some of the weaknesses.*"

Once the malicious consequences of having endowed VaR with the power to watch over subprime CDOs and RMBS became indelibly inescapable, banks repented. What had been previously presented as obvious (CDOs and RMBS should go in the trading book, the risks of CDOs and RMBS should be distilled through the VaR lenses) was postcarnage seen as anathema. In late 2007, UBS and Merrill Lynch announced that subprime securities were no longer part of internal management and regulatory VaR, and were therefore switched from market risk treatment to credit risk treatment. UBS even informed the world how those exposures would be assessed for regulatory capital purposes once they were relocated to the banking book: Following Basel II's Ratings Based Approach the assets' risk weights would depend on the credit ratings assigned by Moody's, Standard & Poor's, and Fitch. VaR, the banking behemoths stated rather a tad bit too late, is neither an adequate measure of the risks of such positions nor an appropriate risk control. By excluding the subprime junk from the calculations, VaR dropped like a fly. For example, Merrill's average 2007 daily VaR went from \$83 million to \$65 million, while 2007 year-end VaR sank from \$157 million to \$65 million. With enhanced volatility and damaging mark-to-market losses suddenly the norm in the subprime space, VaR was no longer the conduit toward insignificant capital charges that it had hitherto been. The recent past was no longer so accommodative, no longer so placid. Perhaps it would be better to pack and depart for the banking book. Justifying such turning should be easy, given how blatantly the CDOs had shown themselves to be illiquid and unsalable, and thus undeserving of trading book status. The key question, of course, is why they had been allowed to achieve such unseemly consideration in the first place.

Banks were supposed to be under close supervision as to the allocation of items between the banking book and the trading book, with especially intense scrutiny given to the classification of liquidity-challenged assets as trading book assets,[25] but supervisors seem to have been asleep at the wheel in the early years of the twenty-first century. An asset is assigned to the banking book unless it can qualify for the trading book, but as the CDO story shows it doesn't look as if the qualification process (essentially, declaring the asset to be tradable, a documented trading strategy for the position approved by senior management, and having in place clearly defined policies and procedures for the active management and monitoring of the position) was too prohibitive. Even top supervisors are willing to admit that supervisors didn't supervise wisely: "*Certain CDOs and other structured finance products are often held in the trading book and fair-valued despite the fact that there is, apparently, little trading in some of these products. The extensive use of the trading book for these illiquid, non-transparent securities is another unintended consequence of current regulatory policy,"* so blurted out Sheila Bair, chairperson of the almighty U.S. Federal Deposit Insurance Corporation (one of the world's leading financial regulators), to an audience full of VaR-loving risk managers.[26] And it seems that even when policy makers mustered the courage to suggest some controls on trading book usage, they were taken aback and neutralized by bankers' no-nos. As was reported in mid-2008,

> When global regulators started talking to some of the world's largest investment banks a couple of years ago about whether they should tighten the rules governing banks' trading books, they faced a hostile reaction. Back then, credit markets were booming and the banks were recording fat profits. Financiers felt confident enough to fight suggestions that policymakers should impose new controls on their trading activities. "They were quite angry," admits one senior western central banker with a chuckle.[27]

Regulators seem to have accepted that,

> The recent turmoil has shown that a set of loopholes had developed in the banking system in relation to how banks managed their trading books. This dry and technical issue went almost unnoticed—until it became clear that the loopholes were a main factor in allowing the losses that built up at large investment banks.

Interestingly, the financial mandarins may have assumed all along that trading books were relatively small at many banks (was anybody watching at all!?). It is obvious that,

> The trading books can no longer be regarded as a sideshow. On the contrary, their size had exploded, for the precise reason that the rules were so lax. Accepting that the trading book issues had been regarded as quite technical, one supervisor adds: "Now it is clear they deserve a lot of attention."[28]

As we can see, the regulatory failings in the 2007 crisis were severe on several fronts. To the mistake of entrusting VaR with the trading book we can now add the lack of vigilance when it came to policing the trading book and preventing its abuse, which was made irresistibly tempting precisely because of the earlier decision to proclaim VaR as market risk capital emperor.

The abuse by banks of their ample discretion to place assets in the trading book was so obvious leading up to the crisis that such actions helped prompt regulators to quickly show repentance and a desire for atonement. Not again should such gigantic exercise in blatant regulatory arbitrage be made so gigantically easy and convenient, is the message emanating from the repentant rule makers. How to achieve that end? By making capital requirements for market risk much more prohibitive and thus tentatively diminishing, if not entirely erasing, the comparative capital cost advantages of the trading versus the banking book. To that end, atoning revisions to the rules were introduced by the Basel Committee in early 2009. Add-ons to VaR in the form of Stressed VaR (to better capture extreme market events) and the Incremental Risk Charge (to better capture credit-related phenomena) are intended to raise trading book capital charges three- or fourfold, in an open recognition of VaR's incapacity to deliver prudently sound risk control. And in an even more direct attempt to do away with VaR's nefarious influence, securitized products held in the trading book must suffer the same capital tax as if they were in the banking book, making absolutely certain that no arbitrage can take place in that arena anymore.

But commendable as those remedial actions aspire to be, the big elephant in the room remains unaddressed. The problem with banks abusing the trading book lies not with the trading book per se. It's the way capital charges are calculated under trading jurisdiction that's the problem, not the presence and use of something called a trading book. If the trading book was commandeered by a mechanism that didn't make toxic leverage easily possible and that wasn't built on irrepressibly faulty foundations, having lots of stuff in the trading book would not be a big issue. The problem is that the trading book has for the past 15 years been commandeered by a mechanism that makes toxic leverage easily possible and that is built on irrepressibly faulty foundations.

And that mechanism has not been touched. It's still a ruler in the trading book, if perhaps no longer in a totalitarian way. VaR's saying in the final outcome may have been somewhat diluted by the postcrisis Basel amendments, but it still has a very big say. VaR's word may no longer be the final word, but continues to count a lot. And that, almost inevitably, means that lethal leverage may one day dominate the system once more.

By placing RMBS and CDOs under the tutelage of VaR, banks earned the right to play the subprime game in a highly leveraged fashion (notice again that using the banking book instead may have also delivered tons of leverage, if not quite as much as VaR sanctioned; Basel II, as we saw earlier, was extremely permissive when it came to assessing the riskiness of highly rated debt securities). How do we know that the fateful mortgage assets were required very little market risk capital? Well, for one the numbers seem to conclude so. Institutions with regulatory VaR of a few hundred million dollars had net super senior and CDO warehousing exposures of tens of billions of dollars. Even if those subprime punts had been the only inhabitants of the trading book, the market risk capital charge would have not been much above 1 percent of net assets (remember that if the hedges on the super senior positions did not perform, the volume of net assets would shoot up; so the true leverage afforded by VaR was actually even greater). In mid-2007, Merrill Lynch's regulatory VaR was around $700 million while its net CDO exposure was around $35 billion. Hypothesizing that all that was parked in Merrill's trading book, the leverage afforded to CDO punting would have been a notorious 50 to 1, implying capital requirements of barely 2 percent of assets (don't trust my horrendously off-the-cuff calculations? Fine, double the capital figure if you want; that still leaves us with 25-to-1 gearing on horrendously venomous assets). But of course Merrill's trading activities included much more that just subprime mortgage securitization stuff. Its total on-balance sheet holdings of trading assets was $260 billion, with a lot of things other than mortgages or mortgage-related. That is, of the roughly $700 million capital cushion that was calculated to support the entire $260 billion only a portion came from the presumed risk of CDOs and RMBS (unless one is willing to suggest that all the other trading assets had zero VaRs, an implacably unreasonable contention). It follows that the subprime contribution to the bank's overall VaR must have been significantly inferior to $700 million, and therefore that the gearing permitted on subprime rendez-vous must have been north of 50 to 1, possibly way north of 50 to 1. When one thinks of prudent capital buffers for toxic financial crea-tures, something beyond (perhaps way beyond) 50-to-1 leverage is not exactly what springs to mind.

While the above calculations may help clarify things, we can intu-itively understand that the super senior portfolios were in all probabil-ity endowed with unimpressive VaR numbers. These young creatures could boast a recent past devoid of bad news and turbulence, precisely the kind of attributes that will entitle you to a Lilliputian VaR. Merrill itself seemed to concur in its Q3 2007 regulatory filing: "*VaR and other risk measures significantly underestimated the magnitude of actual loss from the extreme dislocation that affected the US subprime residential mort-gage-related and CDO positions. In the past, these AAA CDO securities had never experienced a significant loss of value.*" In other words, it had been VaR paradise up to that point. So if VaR was indeed the mecha-nism utilized to appraise the capital needed to back up the CDOs, then the CDOs got away with a lot of leverage. Banks seemed to be aware that the trading book would prove friendlier, capital-wise. Just a few months following the unleashing of the subprime meltdown that would floor the global giant, a humbled Citigroup openly shared with a group of top U.S. financial supervisors:

> The original business model was to distribute all CDO risk. However, management found that it was unable to distribute the super senior tranches at favourable prices. As management felt comfortable with the credit risk of these tranches it began to retain large positions on balance sheet. The exposures were booked as traded assets rather than held-to-maturity assets. Business strategy was to buy and hold these exposures (which implied a more appropriate accrual based accounting); however, the incentive to hold in a trading/mark-to-market account was to maximize regulatory capital treatment. There were regulatory incentives for the arbitrage creation of the CDOs.[29]

Gillian Tett, that most notable CDO reporter, concurs, too:

As the markets had been calm until mid-2007, banks' value-at-risk models implied that the chance of losses on assets such as triple A CDO debt was almost negligible—meaning they barely needed to make any reserve provisions for these at all.[30]

Referring specifically to UBS's malaise, Tett pointed that,

UBS had quietly stockpiled tens of billions of dollars of super-senior tranches on its trading book. The bank made little provision against the chance of these instruments turning sour, because the models implied a negligible risk of losses. When the price of these super-senior tranches collapsed, this created more billions of dollars worth of trading book losses for which the bank had set nothing aside.[31]

Those tiny capital charges on the huge subprime portfolios contributed mightily to record returns on equity for investment banks of 200 basis points on average higher than the last cycle.[32] Although the net gains from the super senior CDO carry trade were, as we saw, modest in absolute terms, the very low capital that the game demanded would have made them extremely attractive since even a modest gain can look wonderful when measured against a negligible capital commitment. As one commentator summarized it,

Pre-crisis banks were holding super senior and AAA tranches of securitized assets in the trading book as they showed very little VaR and thus required very little capital allocation there. Notionally these assets were being held for trading/sale in order to justify their inclusion in the trading book, but in practice large inventories were accumulated and not shifted because even at low spreads, with very low capital requirements the return on capital was large. Leverage on these positions was thus extremely high.[33]

With the benefit of hindsight, everyone now understands how lowly VaR's capital recommendations can be. Of course, VaR's potential for smallness was always there, it's an ingrained, in-built, DNA-like aspect of the model. But it was kept more or less hidden from public view, comprehended only by a handful of insiders. However, after a systemic crisis involving trillion-dollar losses emanating from positions that were under VaR's watch, it becomes a tad more difficult to sweep the model's inconveniences under the carpet. Quite the opposite has happened, in fact. Something of a run for the exits has taken place among regulators and policy makers, each one seemingly trying to outmaneuver the others when it comes to publicly badmouthing and even disowning the erstwhile adored tool. None other than Nout Wellink, president of Holland's Central Bank and (more to the point) chairman of the Basel Committee, was one of the first financial mandarins on the VaR-bashing platform:

> I want to emphasize the importance of strong capital supporting trading book exposures. For the largest global banks, balance sheet assets have more than doubled between 2000 and 2006. Much of this growth relates to trading assets. Indeed the vast majority of bank losses have been on retained trading exposures, particularly highly rated CDOs and leveraged lending. We need to make sure that the capital underpinning the trading book is commensurate with the risks that firms face. We are therefore supplementing the current VaR-based framework with additional charges in the trading book. To address the shortcomings of VaR, it is critical that banks conduct additional analysis that translates into prudent risk taking and strong capital.[34]

Translation: VaR allowed things like CDOs to roam around banks' balance sheets in an undercapitalized fashion and that caused a big mess and we need to make sure that banks have more capital than what dangerously flawed VaR would dictate. This is almost like the Pope saying that God doesn't exist. VaR would have never been very influential without the unfettered support of the Basel Committee. For years, the saintly virtues of VaR were zealously preached by the Basel missionaries, regaling the world with spirit-lifting stories about how VaR would heal the wounded and aid the sick. VaR, we were constantly sermonized, would save the planet from the evils of market risk. But now, the tormented Basel High Clerics appeared engulfed in a storm of religious doubt. We can almost imagine the world's central bankers sheltered in their Switzerland enclave in late 2007 or early 2008, contemplating in horror the financial and economic inferno around them, fixing their eyes on the heavens and tremblingly proclaiming "Oh VaR Lord, Where Art Thou?"

■ ■ ■

So, in the end, how much did the banks lose on their subprime adventures? Quite a lot, actually. Let's retake things were we left them. On Q3 2007, UBS announced net losses on U.S. residential subprime mortgage positions of $4.4 billion (gross losses of $5.6 billion offset by gains on hedges of $1.2 billion). This was bad, but nothing compared to what was coming as the deterioration in all things subprime fully manifested itself. For Q4 2007, the losses stood at a total of $9.64 billion, sliced in the following manner: $7.78 billion on super senior subprime CDO tranches (plus $.2 billion in monoline hedges that were deemed ineffective and added to exposures), losses of $733 million on subprime RMBS (of which UBS owned more than $17 billion net), losses of $1.12 billion on the subprime CDO warehouse. On top of all that a hit of $683 million on adjustments due to the deteriorating credit quality of those entities that had hedged UBS's subprime exposures. Besides the subprime deleteriousness, UBS incurred losses of $2 billion on U.S. residential Alt-A mortgage RMBS and CDO positions; Alt-A could best be categorized as *almost subprime*. Things went on in a sour way, and for Q1 2008 total subprime losses reached $7.25 billion (losses of $5.32 billion on super senior subprime CDO tranches, losses of $2.1 billion on subprime RMBS, gains of $180 million on the subprime CDO warehouse). Plus more bad news on the almost-subprime front, with losses of $6 billion on U.S. residential Alt-A mortgage RMBS and CDO positions. Q2 2008 was in the red, too, with $848 million in total subprime setbacks (losses of $756 million on super senior subprime CDO tranches, losses of $13 million on subprime RMBS, losses of $79 million on the subprime CDO warehouse). And losses of $630 million on U.S. residential Alt-A mortgage RMBS and CDO positions.[35]

What about Merrill Lynch? Pretty ugly, too. For Q3 2007, total subprime losses of around $7.5 billion (losses of $5.75 billion on super senior subprime CDO tranches, $1.1 billion on the subprime CDO warehouse, $544 million on subprime RMBS). For Q4 2007, losses of $8.85 billion on super senior subprime CDO tranches, and $1 billion on the subprime CDO warehouse. For the entire 2007 exercise subprime losses (including CDOs, whole loans, residuals, RMBS) stood at around $20 billion. Q1 2008 saw losses of $1.78 billion on super senior subprime CDO tranches, while the corresponding figure for Q2 2008 was a $3.45 billion in the red.

And Citigroup? Not rosy either. Q3 2007: Losses of $1.8 billion, net of hedges, on subprime mortgages warehoused for future CDO securitizations, CDO positions, and warehoused leveraged loans. Q4 2007: Losses of $17.4 billion on subprime exposures ($14.5 billion on super seniors, $2.9 on CDO warehouse and lending). Year 2008: Losses of $15 billion on subprime exposures ($13.1 super senior, $1.8 CDO warehouse plus lending), on top of that $5.7 billion hit on credit adjustment on hedge counterparty exposures. Losses of $3.8 billion on Alt-A securities.

Many other banks suffered significant nightmares. As of year-end 2008 the total bill for the subprime mayhem (total write-downs and credit losses since January 2007) stood at $1 trillion. Losses on CDOs alone were several hundred billion dollars. By early 2009 it was reported that half of all subprime CDOs had defaulted[36] (it is important to note that initially, when the crisis first caught fire, losses on CDOs were of a mark-to-market nature; as many banks were at pains to point out back then, few if any actual defaults had taken place, so CDO investors kept receiving their coupons even as the CDO market was being destroyed; but eventually, the defaults inevitable appeared, too). As was reported back then:

> Almost half of all the complex credit products built out of slices of other securitized bonds have now defaulted, and the proportion rises to more than two-thirds among deals created at the peak of the cycle. The defaults have affected more than $300bn worth of these collateralised debt obligations. The first three years of the market saw less than 100 deals sold per year

and less than 10 per cent of those have defaulted. The number of deals done rose to 133 in 2005, less than 20 per cent of which defaulted, and 89 in just the first half of 2006, about one-third of which have defaulted. However, the real peak of the market saw 147 deals done in the second half of 2006 and 172 done in the first half of 2007—of which 68 per cent and 76.2 per cent, respectively, have now defaulted.[37]

In sum, it is clear that what the risk models and the rating agencies tagged as "unworrisome" turned out to be very problematic. Needless to say, banks' capital cushions were not even in the vicinity of enough when it came to absorbing the setbacks. New private capital infusions, bank mergers, and public bailouts were needed to prevent the industry from being swallowed whole by the subprime tsunami.

VaR was at the center of it all. The low-loss forecasts internally approved the playing of the CDO game inside the banks. The favorable trading book treatment provided the external okay. In fact, it almost reads like a well-thought-out plan, naughtily devised many years before: You invent a new scientific-looking methodology for gauging market risk, you lobby hard for its adoption within financial circles, once dominance inside dealing rooms is assured you lobby hard for its adoption by regulators, and then you patiently wait for the emergence of the right kind of toxic asset whose riskiness can be deemed negligible by the methodology, which also sanctions untold leverage on the play. VaR helped banks make a fortune on CDOs (and other geared trading activities) while quietly hiding and building up the monstrous exposures that would finally cause the most severe of setbacks. VaR is great for those looking to make a quick buck and to then fly-by-night with the booty. If you want to cause a crisis under the disguise of placidity and moderation, VaR will be there for you.

The super senior story reflects this subliminally. Something like super senior had never existed in finance before. Super senior was supposed to be less problematic and more wholesome than even Treasury Bonds or World Bank paper. The idea of super senior losses was deemed as improbable as baseball ever becoming England's top sport or cricket crowning itself as America's favorite pastime. Nothing had ever been considered as rock-solid, as iron-clad as super senior. And

VaR couldn't wait to concur. Yes, the glorified risk radar nodded, this is super safe stuff indeed. And yet, that which the statistical analysis had enthusiastically lauded as fortress-like, ended up unleashing a trillion-dollar global meltdown. Talk about hiding risk.

By mid-2007, VaR was at the height of its powers. More regulators than ever had embraced it and were busy proclaiming its virtues. The endless quantification of risk management and financial research lent undisputed preeminence to anything that looked analytical. Prior historical market episodes that had tarnished VaR's name had long been forgotten. The very few public criticisms of the tool had gone conspicuously unheard. For a very prolonged period, VaR had behaved fabulously (forecasting market placidity and seeing nothing but market placidity around it), apparently proving its backers right and its critics wrong. Just like in those years the reputation of top central bankers speaking of a brave new era of moderation and nonvolatile markets was unassailably unquestioned, the standing of the mathematical model which numerical outputs offered staunch support to those complacent claims was equally undoubted.

Who could question the wisdom of entrusting VaR with the system's care? The weapon that would in due course help blow up the banking industry became impossible to argue against. The model said "no risk" and the system looked nothing if not risk-proof. The model said "stability" and the landscape could not appear more stable. The model said "go ahead, freely leverage yourself up" and the need for capital could not seem more redundant. The model said "gorge on subprime stuff" and the wisdom of going subprime could not feel mightier. All the prognostications emanating from the model were not only proving themselves correct, but also sustained and reinforced the conclusions and activities favored by many of the globe's leading entities and individuals. VaR was, in essence, flaunting a tale that very influential people wanted to hear.

And thus no one saw anything wrong with vastly inflated trading books, where all kind of suspect assets that never belonged there were dumped. After all, isn't that VaR's domain? If so, won't things be properly taken care of by the undisputable theoretical tool? Any internal and external opposition would have been vanquished via the waving of the VaR wand.

But a seemingly well-functioning VaR can be indicative of a buildup of nastiness, rather than an indicator of robustness. As a bubble is created and sustained, VaR sees no losses or turbulence, granting permission to the further strengthening of the bubble, and so on until the inevitable end result is a lethal mania. So beware low VaR numbers for they may be hiding and enabling a storm of uncontrolled toxic risk. Isn't that exactly what happened up to mid-2007? Weren't the CDOs and RMBS assumed to be unproblematic on account of the lowly statistical risk estimates? VaR is, in effect, the perfect antidote against common sense. Decisions that would have never been sanctioned otherwise, get approvingly sanctioned once VaR is around. And that may be the main reason why VaR was adopted and brought into the fold of finance. With VaR, you can achieve the impossible. With VaR, the sky is the limit. Let's hear it from a renowned academic:

> Why did VAR become so popular? Using VAR brought con-
> crete benefits to specific actors in the banking world by help-
> ing them rationalize bad bets. If common sense would lead
> a risk manager to crack down on a trader taking large, risky
> bets, then the trader is better off if the risk manager uses VAR
> instead. Not only that, but imagine the situation of the chief
> risk manager of a bank in, say, 2004. If he tried to reduce his
> bank's exposure to CDOs, he would be out of a job; VAR gave
> him a handy tool to rationalize a situation that defied common
> sense but that made his bosses only too happy. And at the top
> levels, chief executives and directors were biased in its favor
> because it told them a story they wanted to hear. In other
> words, VAR was just what they needed during the boom.[38]

By mid-2007, the financial realm had become entirely dominated by metrics. It is no exaggeration to say that we put our future in the hands of metrics. The metrics didn't merely say that certain financial assets were golden, they said that they were more golden than gold. Reality later showed those things to be not just merely silver, or plain copper, but utter worthless trash. What to make of metrics that hide worthless trash under the guise of more-golden-than-gold? Aren't we allowed to feel conned? Isn't it obvious now that VaR can be the Trojan horse that dupes us into welcoming as a charming gift that which only possible destiny is to murderously ransack our village?

A while after the giant crisis wave had began to recede and everyone who had been swimming naked was revealed, Gillian Tett provided a neat summary of the truly essential point: "*What blew the really big holes in the balance sheet of banks in 2007 and 2008 was the fact that they had all taken huge quantities of so-called super-senior CDOs on to their trading books.*"[39] It is a safe bet that this sentence would have never been uttered had VaR not ruled the trading book. VaR made the trading book a paradise of very low capital requirements, notwithstanding the inescapable fundamental nature of the securities. The capacity of VaR to enable destruction can't be denied.

Consider a VaR-less world. A world where undue precision is not sought through hopeless metrics. Would the accumulation of subprime positions in excess of a bank's entire capital base have been condoned, let alone deemed worry-free? Would trading floor rules and regulatory rules have supported and encouraged UBS to own north of $50 billion in subprime garbage? The answer is most likely a resounding no (unless, that is, UBS and its peers were willing and able to post a whole lot more of equity capital, itself a very unlikely scenario). A VaR-less world is a world where the 2007 crisis can't happen.

Keep firmly in mind that the indictment against VaR may go beyond the "VaR allowed Bank A or Bank B to put vast amounts of subprime stuff on their books in a very geared fashion." If the very existence of the CDO business demanded that sponsoring banks retain the super senior tranche (by far the CDO's most voluminous slice), for otherwise the CDO would not be successfully placed and distributed, then VaR (by making it possible for banks to afford retaining those huge super senior slices) would have effectively permitted the entire CDO circus to go on, at least on a grand scale. So a tool that delivers excruciatingly low risk estimates for subprime super seniors may have been an unavoidable prerequisite for CDOs to become sizable enough to pose a threat to global stability. No wonder, then, that many would elect to have their CDO punts appraised by VaR. They must have known that the artifact has an in-bred capacity to underestimate the maliciousness of even the most troublesome of punts. They must have known how easy it is for VaR to tell big lies, and how conveniently it can be used to launder financial detritus into respectable fare. The CDO business (that hurt not just the big financial conglomerates but also a lot of unsuspecting innocent third parties) may have needed the assistance of a big liar before it took off. A laundry machine that could transform the unwashed into financial caviar might have been required. And when it comes to market risk, there's no bigger liar than VaR.

Chapter 6

VaR Goes to Washington

Backlash ■ *Media Cover Up* ■ *Capitol Hill Truths* ■
Empty Rooms ■ *It's Still There*

O n June 30, 2009, top U.S. politicians, for the first (and so far, only) time, took an interest in me. That Tuesday morning, a publicity assistant from my publisher forwarded me the following e-mail:

The subcommittee I work for is looking into the role of financial risk modeling in the recent economic crisis, and we are extremely interested in speaking with Mr. Triana about his views on Value at Risk and other, related matters. If you could send me his contact information or otherwise put us in touch with him, we would be grateful.

I can be reached by email reply or on my direct office line. Many thanks, and best wishes, Ken

Ken was Ken Jacobson of the U.S. House Committee on Science and Technology's Subcommittee on Investigations and Oversight. I was certainly intrigued by his message. It wasn't just that after doing some online searching I found that the Committee was chaired by a powerful congressman and that it dealt with funky high-tech issues, or that they had apparently mentioned to Wiley's publicity assistant the possibility of me testifying in Washington, DC (a wonderful excuse to return, even if briefly, to one of my favorite cities). What really piqued my interest was the fact that senior policy makers from the world's leading nation had shown the insight and daring to identify VaR as a key driving force behind the financial cataclysm of 2007–2008 and that they wanted to dig deeper into the matter. As far as I could tell, no national parliament had before called a mathematical model to task for economic troubles. In planning to indict VaR, the Committee was not only trying to contribute to the understanding of what had been happening for the past couple of years, but was also doing something quite revolutionary in itself.

I instantly got back to Ken Jacobson and offered him my unlimited assistance. He emphasized the Committee's desire to meet me in person soon (as they were originally planning to have a formal hearing on VaR by the following July), flatteringly telling me that, "We're not sure we've seen anyone pin the meltdown on VaR as unequivocally as you do." We exchanged several e-mails during the rest of the summer, with me providing some of the analysis that I had conducted on VaR's role in the credit crisis, and with Ken showing increasing amounts of shock at what he was reading.

In trying to shed light on VaR's nefarious performance before and during the crisis, the Committee on Science and Technology was not alone. Others had by June 2009, and many others would continue to do so afterward, pointing fingers at and badmouthing VaR for enabling the destruction. This backlash came from political as well as nonpolitical sources. The barrage of criticisms was truly outstanding and, one presumes, exasperating for VaR-lovers. While the model had been lambasted before, never on such a scale and never from so many different angles and *never* from regulatory corners. Quite telling, the first to draw attention to VaR's utter failings were the very banks suffering from the VaR-induced market cataclysm, and the very banks that had spent more than 15 years building and promoting the model. You just have to scour regulatory filings from Q3 2007 to be inundated with disclaimers and apologizing, an endless flood of "VaR failed" and "VaR is an inappropriate measure" arguments (while that looks like the central message buried underneath of that disclaiming, banks have not gone so far as to literally saying "We screwed up with VaR. Sorry").

Soon, outsiders eagerly joined the VaR-bashing dance. While, as we shall see, the media has (with some notable exceptions) mostly shied away from reporting on VaR and its role in the unleashing of the crisis, one of the first external sources of VaR denunciation came from a news outlet. In a January 2008 article unapologetically titled "Death of VaR Evoked," *Bloomberg* reporter Christine Harper went to town on VaR from the very initial sentence:

> The risk-taking model that emboldened Wall Street to trade with impunity is broken and everyone is coming to the realization that no algorithm can substitute for old-fashioned due diligence. VaR failed to detect the scope of the US subprime mortgage market's collapse. The past six months have exposed the flaws of a financial measure based on historical prices.[1]

The following April, the Swiss Federal Banking Commission (Switzerland's regulator) engaged in public atonement, intoning a somewhat delayed mea culpa: *"As supervisors we can also not deny that we, like the banks, had a little too much faith in models; otherwise we could not have approved the VaR models to calculate the regulatory capital adequacy requirements for market risks. We were all aware of the limits of such models."*[2] Now, I believe in the power of forgiveness and in the healing benefits of sincere atoning, but the Alpine repentance is more alarming than soothing. Here we have senior policy makers, grown and experienced wise men, the town's elders, sheepishly recognizing how they let themselves be hypnotized by concoctions they knew to be handicapped. What did I tell you about the analytical alibi? If you want to sell something in finance, adorn it with rigorous-looking statistical fanfare. Even the otherwise austere and sober Swiss will buy it. Later that year two top international risk gurus wasted no time expressing their displeasure with VaR. Financial mathematician-turned-skeptic and entrepreneur Paul Wilmott (quite possibly the world's best known and most successful trainer of quantitative finance professionals) minced no words as part of his "Name and Shame" postcrisis campaign. On VaR:

VaR is used to justify taking risks. Classic unintended consequences territory here. Yeah, right! Funny how "unintended
consequences" are always rather obvious, even before the fact,
but they are always brushed under the rug. "Don't rock the
boat, dear boy," cigar in one hand, Napoleon brandy in the
other. Risk managers say there's no risk according to naive VaR
so management is free to trade in bigger, and bigger, and bigger amounts. Oops . . . it seems that VaR didn't quite capture
all the risks . . . who'd have considered increasing mortgage
defaults? Everyone, except those who had a vested interest in
hiding the risks.[3]

On RiskMetrics:

Guilty of making VaR accessible to the masses. Why not give
away handguns while you're at it.[4]

A couple of weeks later, Steve Allen, former head of risk at a
large bank and a leading financial engineering academic, offered that,
"Market risk capital requirements should no longer be based on VaR."[5]
Even the United Nations got involved, leaving itself no alternative
but to point out the obvious: The 2007 crisis has outed VaR as less
than sublime and as a consequence bank regulators have had no option
but to take away some of its influence. Here's how UN folk expressed
it in 2009:

From the point of view of risk management generally, special
interest attaches to the questioning of the effectiveness of
VaR that is implicit in the Basel Committee's acknowledge-
ment that the revisions to the market risk capital framework is
intended to address VaR's shortcomings. Since the early 1990s,
VaR has been one of the principal jewels in the crown of
quantitative financial risk management. Its downgrading in the
Committee's new guidelines may point towards further reas-
sessment of ways of managing and supervising market risk.[6]

In other words, VaR is highly suspect and if even its Basel backers
are willing to belittle and doubt it, perhaps we all should.

The really harsh badmouthing from the regulatory camp began in earnest on March 2009, with the arrival of the highly extroverted Turner Review put together by the U.K.'s Financial Services Authority. The report went hard at VaR and the destructive leverage it allowed. The scent emanating from the British regulators was indelible: VaR messed up big time. And bank capital rules should be seriously overhauled. Lord Turner went for the jugular from the get-go:

> From about 2003 onwards, there were significant increases in on-balance sheet leverage of many banks, driven by dramatic increases in positions. This was despite the fact that "risk adjusted" measures of leverage (i.e., VaR relative to equity) showed no such rise. This divergence reflected the fact the capital requirements against trading books, where asset growth was concentrated, were extremely light compared with those for banking books and that VaR measures suggested that risk relative to gross market positions had declined. It is clear in retrospect that VaR measures of risk were faulty and that trading book capital was inadequate.[7]

The very reliance on VaR for rule making should be reconsidered, stated the U.K. rule maker, adding that a fundamental review of how risks are assessed in the trading book should be urgently conducted. Suddenly, VaR's deficiencies are presented ex ante as only too obvious and knowable (why, then, was the tool so rabidly promoted from policy circles for such a long time?). Turner cites the usual suspects: VaR fails to capture low probability high-impact tail events, VaR leads to procyclical behavior, VaR can suggest that banks are facing low risks just as system-level risks are at their most extreme. These concerns, the report argues, mattered lately more than ever because of the way the trading book had been abused, *"Increasingly over the years trading books were swollen by large holdings of illiquid complex structured credit products, which would have attracted higher capital charges if booked in the banking books. When the crisis broke VaR proved highly misleading as market liquidity dried up."* In other words, VaR was always bad as it is, don't make it worse by mixing it with things that have little to do with market risk. Lord Turner appeared to have no hesitations: The combination of VaR and toxic securities will equal financial apocalypse.

By late 2010, the market risk capital regime overhaul that the Turner Review demanded and wished for had taken place. This in itself was a serious indictment of VaR. The model that killed us has not been exactly killed by regulators, but, as the United Nations analysts put it, it has nonetheless been savagely downgraded. The revisions to trading book treatment aim at taking minimum required bank capital much higher than where VaR by itself had taken and would take them. The revisions are the regulators' way of saying that VaR leads to very humble risk estimates and can thus enable too much leverage. That VaR is not to be trusted. That VaR abetted the 2007–2008 nightmare. More than 18 months after the release of Lord Turner's VaR-bashing, global financial mandarins were still in the mood for publicly crucifying the model. *"Two areas the crisis has revealed as needing enhanced risk coverage are the trading book and securitizations. Here capital charges fell short of risk exposures. The major losses during the 2007–09 financial crisis came from the trading book, especially the complex securitization exposures such as CDOs. The capital requirements for trading assets were extremely low,"*[8] blurted no less a figure than the Bank for International Settlements' (BIS) second in command. So as to back up his arguments with tangible, in-your-face evidence, the top regulator produced a table numerically disclosing how negligible, in fact, the trading book contributions were to banks' overall capital requirements. At year-end 2006, trading assets represented 21 percent of Citigroup's total assets yet its market risk capital charges-to-total capital charges ratio stood at just 4 percent. The corresponding figures for Credit Agricole were 31 percent and 6 percent. Deutsche Bank's were no better, at 32 percent and 4 percent. Societe Generale's trading book leverage was even more pronounced, contributing only 4 percent when the bank's asset portfolio was 35 percent of a trading nature. Credit Suisse's numbers were very similar, at 36 percent and 5 percent. VaR gave rise to a lot of trading-related leverage, no doubt. Banks' trading games on the way to the crisis were extremely cheap capital-wise. The BIS number two repeated an oft-repeated message:

> It is now clear that quantitative finance and risk modeling techniques based on the Normality assumptions and historical statistical relationships have failed to capture the extreme events which occur in periods of systemic stress. The backward-looking assumptions

about correlations, volatility, and market liquidity embedded in banks' risk models did not hold in times of stress. Historical relationships do not necessarily constitute a good basis for forecasting the development of future risks.[9]

We get it. VaR is rotten to the core and its ubiquitous and regal presence in financeland led to wild and disproportionate trading book leverage (and not just any type of trading book, but one conquered by very nasty stuff). But, if we may ask again, why did you endorse such a deleterious machination for so long?

It is fitting that financial mandarins should feel obliged to show contrition and atonement. For the 2007 crisis was, at its core, a regulatory crisis. Either because of enforcing of conceptually flawed rules (the reliance on VaR and credit metrics) or neglectful policing of rules (giving a free pass to the abuse of the trading book), bank regulators made it possible for the big banks to toxify their balance sheets with bad leverage. Some have erroneously blamed the crisis on "deregulation." If only financiers had been more closely controlled, the argument goes, the massacre would not have occurred. While this may rightly apply to some key segments involved in the episode, most notably the underlying mortgage loans industry, it couldn't be further from the mark when it comes to the financial giants whose losses triggered the mayhem. By leveraging themselves according to the VaR and AAA gospels they were doing nothing if not precisely abiding by very precise official capital rules. By parking CDOs and RMBS in their trading books, they were making use of a regulatory allowance to choose where to place an asset and to enjoy a differing capital charge based on that decision; while categorizing those assets as "tradable" would have been a stretching of the letter of the law, it seems hard to argue that something unlawful or fraudulent took place (the abuse here doesn't seem exactly comparable to lying about borrowers' incomes as part of a subprime mortgage application or granting a $1 million loan to an illegal immigrant making $15,000 a year). The most impacting actions leading to the crisis were all rooted on strict official policies. The presence of rules, not the lack of them, fueled the inferno.

Some supervisors have argued that without supervision the banks would have taken even greater risks and would have had an even thinner capital base.[10] Maybe so. But VaR and other preexisting rulings may have delivered all the risks and undercapitalization that banks could have wished for. And, wonderfully conveniently, under the cover of strict regulation.

■ ■ ■

In the end, I did not make it to Washington, DC. The Committee never took the final step of actually treating me to a plane ticket and, as much as I wished to be there for the occasion, I thought that running the expense on my own would be a tad excessive. But, what's much more relevant, the VaR hearing did in fact occur. Eventually postponed from the tentative July date to after the House's August recess, the historic event finally took place on September 10, and with a list of expert witnesses that included several people way more qualified (if perhaps less vocal as to what VaR had just contributed to) than my humble self. Slightly disappointed though I was by not being able to physically share my wisdom with U.S. politicians, I nonetheless woke up that September day very eager to follow the proceedings via the live webcast that Ken Jacobson had instructed me would be available through the Committee's web site. I naively believed that the event was going to become the catalyst that would make everyone realize how dangerous and malfunctioning VaR can be and how urgently financial risk management and bank capital regulation needed a drastic overhaul, away from flawed and deleterious analytical models and back into the arms of equations-free reasoning. I had little doubt that upon the broadcast and completion of the hearings, severe reform would take place and that VaR's powers would be greatly diminished. VaR's shortcomings had been well known by financial insiders and connoisseurs for years, but the general public and most in the political class were not privy to such specialist intelligence. By providing the debate with a very public platform, the Committee's hearings, I assumed, would inevitably spread the message to the masses, thanks in large part to the obvious interest that the financial and general media (now loudly alerted as to the matter) were going to show in VaR and the consequences of having it around. While I would have certainly been doubly enthralled had I finally been able to be there in person, I was sure that the revolutionary happenstance about to occur in Washington had the potential to change the world. So much so that I posted a blog entry on the very popular Huffington Post encouraging President Obama to attend the proceedings. Perhaps unbeknownst to him, the theme under discussion was as relevant to our economic welfare and social stability as almost any other thing.

But the VaR hearing went puzzlingly largely unnoticed. All my expectations were dashed away. I don't think a single major (or minor) newspaper, magazine, or TV program even mentioned the affair, let alone build on it to launch comprehensive coverage of VaR's role in the crisis. No *Financial Times* or *Wall Street Journal* op-ed. No *BusinessWeek* investigative piece (even though they had just run an article of mine on VaR a few weeks earlier). No CNN or Fox News special report. The silence was truly deafening. A few online comments did surface, but quickly faded, utterly failing at generating any kind of sustained momentum. VaR simply went back to being the greatest story never told. Ken Jacobson and I consoled each other via e-mail, with the Science and Technology Committee's staff apparently describing the lack of coverage as "maddening."

How could this be? Why the insultingly obscene neglect? I mean, no other theme was more important and more present on anybody's mind by September 2009 than the financial and economic meltdown that had afflicted all the major countries for the past 24 months. How could there be no interest in a hearing by a U.S. Congressional Committee on one of the possible main causes for the meltdown? Especially when the targeted cause had hitherto been essentially uncovered and ignored, in principle generating even more external curiosity for the event? Really, where were all those journalists and pundits who seemed to do nothing but converse and muse about the crisis around the clock? To make matters worse, among the proceedings' expert witnesses was a globally renowned best-selling author that at the time was (just like he continues to be today) a red-hot international guru and thinker, someone whose words and public appearances are and were regularly and hurriedly scrutinized and commented on by dozens of influential traditional media outlets and hundreds of widely followed hip online sources. If such personality simply went to the bathroom, some commentator was bound to mention it. And yet, when it came time to cover what was likely his most important public performance ever, the media blackout could not have been more conspicuous. Why this oddity?

Bluntly stated, you can't talk about the 2007–2008 crisis without talking about VaR. If you want to be properly informed and, most crucially, properly inform others about this crisis you can't hide when it comes to debating VaR, you can't ignore it. Can you imagine a reporter covering the fraudulent accounting crisis that afflicted the United States a decade ago and not attending the Enron hearings on Capitol Hill? Or a reporter covering the OJ Simpson case and not attending Mark Furhman's testimony? Or a reporter covering WWII and not attending the Nuremberg trials?

I don't need to tell you that the crisis involved financial fraud, murder, and annihilation of the worst kind. Shouldn't media people want to dig in and truly get what happened? Some may say, come on, be fair, journalists should not be expected to be aware of the existence of abstruse models like VaR, let alone comprehend them. Really? VaR has for the past 20 years been the risk radar of choice for Wall Street, religiously detailed under regulatory filings and annual reports. And, certainly, VaR has been for the past 15 years the tool of choice when it came to determining the capital charges to impose on banks' trading activities. You are telling me that those covering the economic and business landscapes should not know this? Should not be aware of VaR? You must be kidding.

Many of the main forces behind the chaos were of a decidedly technical nature. CDOs, CDSs, SIVs, Gaussian Copula, VaR. Even those journalists who understand those things may want to shy away from reporting on them, fearing that their quick fix–seeking audience may hopelessly be at a loss and change the channel, log out of the site, or put down the paper. To the vast majority of folks out there all that continues to matter when it comes to the crisis are lax mortgage lending, Alan Greenspan's too-easy monetary policies, and Wall Street's remuneration structure. All of the above did, of course, contribute to igniting the fuse, and it is only normal that they be talked about in spades. But that should be no excuse to neglect other, perhaps less straightforward, factors that played an even more clearly direct role. By not covering the September 2009 VaR hearing and keeping their audience in the dark as to such an impacting and eye-opening development, the mediatocracy made sure that the truth was not unveiled, going a long way toward contributing to a repeat of the cataclysm down the road.

■ ■ ■

Nassim Taleb (naturally, the above-mentioned widely covered global celebrity who was ignored by the media only during the VaR hearings) was the most famous of the financial risk experts assembled to give testimony on VaR and that's probably why the House Committee on Science and Technology chose to begin the momentous event with the Lebanese-American's deposition. Following a cheeky introduction by the hearing's chairman (which included the assertions that "economists have not been known in the past for mathematical precision," "the supposedly immutable quant models did not work out, did not prove to be true, and turned out to have hidden risks rather than protect against them; all at a terrible cost," "the risks concealed and even encouraged by the models have led to hundreds of millions of losses to investors and taxpayers," "the decision by regulators to adopt VaR opened the door to banks' overleveraging problems"), and the mandatory oath-taking to assure the politicians that the truth and nothing but the truth was about to be disclosed, Taleb came out swinging. Wearing a white shirt and a dark suit and tie, a combination that lent him an austere and stern air, the former options trader wasted no time in going hard at his old mathematical nemesis (I was later glad to see that Taleb had in his testimony's written statement gracefully acknowledged his conversations with me regarding VaR and the crisis). He affirmed:

Thirteen years ago, I warned that VaR encourages misdirected people to take risks with shareholders', and ultimately taxpayers' money. I have been since begging for the suspension of these measurements of tail risks, which don't understand tail events. A lot of people say "Let's measure risks." My idea is very different: Let's find which risks we can measure and these are the risks that we should be taking instead of doing it the opposite way, we take a lot of risks and then we find some scientist who confirms that those risks can be measured and that the methods are sound. The banking system has lost so far $4.3 trillion, according to the International Monetary Fund, directly as a result of faulty risk management. Most of the losses will be directly borne by taxpayers.

Most poignantly, Taleb stated that, "*These problems were obvious all along. These should not have happened. We knew about the defects of VaR when it was first introduced. A lot of traders, a lot of my friends, I am not the only one ranting against VaR, a lot of people did it too. Nobody heard us, regulators did not listen.*

"*VaR is ineffective and has side effects,*" continued the best-selling author, "*It is not neutral. If you give someone a number, he will act on that number even if you tell them that the number is random. We humans cannot be trusted with numbers. You don't give someone a map of the Alps if he is on Mount Ararat because he is going to act on that map, if you give him nothing it's better.*" The conclusion of having VaR around was obvious: "*VaR-style quantitative risk management was behind leverage. We increased risks in society as we thought we could measure risks. If the model makes you overconfident you are going to borrow more. And debt bubbles can be vicious.*" What should we do?

Regulators should not encourage model error. Build a society that is resistant to expert mistakes. Regulators (Basel II) increased our dependence on expert mistakes, not just with VaR but also with reliance on credit ratings. The role of regulators should be to lower the impact of model error. This is reminiscent of medicine: The Food and Drug Administration does not let you bring any medicine without showing the side-effects. We should be doing the same in economic life.

As Nassim Taleb finalized his take-no-prisoners VaR-did-it opening statement, the next expert witness took to the stage. Dressed rather more colorfully (blue shirt plus yellow-and-reddish tie), veteran Wall Street risk manager and fellow author Richard Bookstaber was much less willing to indict VaR, rather toeing the line embraced by many quantitative finance professionals of belittling the model for its amply known structural deficiencies and limitations while at the same time not blaming it for any troubles and advocating for its continued use in financeland. "*VaR's assumptions are often violated, leading VaR estimates to be misleading,*" clarifyingly opened Bookstaber. "*If the future does not resemble the past, VaR will not be a good measure of risk. Which is to say, VaR is a good measure of risk except when it really matters,*" the disclaiming went on. Once the belittling of VaR had been taken care of, Bookstaber proceeded to acquit the model from the charge of having fueled the 2007–2008 catastrophe:

> Whatever the limitations of VaR models, they were not the key culprits in the billionaire writedowns central to the crisis. One has to look beyond VaR to sheer stupidity and collective management failures. VaR was not central, focus would be better focused on failures in risk governance than failures in risk models, whatever the flaws of VaR.

"*In summary,*" Bookstaber shared, "*VaR does have value. If one was forced to pick a single number for the risk of a portfolio in the future, VaR would be a good choice. Add other risk methods that are better at illuminating the areas VaR does not reach.*" In other words, even though VaR is seriously dysfunctional and even though we need to complement it with other stuff and perennially issue disclaimers as to its shortcomings, we should by no means get rid of the model. While Taleb's unequivocal main message to the Washington mandarins was that we should bid VaR farewell (protecting ourselves in the process), Bookstaber's communiqué essentially pleaded for VaR's preservation.

The initial introductory statements out of the way, it was then time for the customary Q&A session, with the politicians inquisitively grilling the two financial wizards. After pointing out that VaR supporters propose a do-over, fixing the model so that fat-tails unlikely events can be predicted, the hearing's Chairman asked whether the failure is not just in the particular case of VaR but generally in the idea that economic events can be predicted with precision. "*Do you think that it is inherently flawed to think that we can develop models that will be unfailingly reliable?*" on-pointedly queried the Chairman before giving the floor to Taleb.

"This is my life story," came the prompt reply. "I've looked at 20 million pieces of data, every economic variable I could find, and I see if there was any regularity in the data so as to be able to predict outside the sample. Unfortunately, it's impossible. The more remote the event, the less we can predict it. We know which variables are more unpredictable than others so it's very easy to protect against that. When we model in complex systems we have nonlinearities, even if I gave you all the data and you missed something by a million dollars your probabilities will change markedly."

How about you, Mr. Bookstaber? "*I don't advocate trying to fix VaR by fattening the tails. VaR is what it is, it does what it does, and the best thing to do is recognize the limitations of VaR and use it for what is good for but not oversell it. Any attempts to make it more sophisticated is going to obfuscate even more. So you take VaR as one tool for risk management and then extend out from there.*" Again, this argument has been amply heard before (in fact, for years before the 2007–2008 crisis) and continues to this day being repeated; given how resilient such "VaR is very limited but don't kill it" ideology seems to be, it is likely that it will survive any other future VaR-aided cataclysms. To more neutral observers, it may seem odd to stubbornly keep around a tool that has to be disclaimed about and excused for over and over again. It's quite likely that many of the politicians facing Bookstaber that September morning were thinking along those lines as they listened to the risk guru's explications.

■ ■ ■

Perhaps as a counterweight to the predictable VaR-bashing from Nassim Taleb, the Committee had also invited a bona fide member of the pro-VaR family. Gregg Berman of famed financial risk software analytics firm RiskMetrics was certainly not expected to bad-mouth VaR too much. As a senior representative of the company that, in fact, invented and then proceeded to fanatically peddle VaR (born in the mid-1990s, RiskMetrics was a spinoff of the original VaR group at VaR-inventing JP Morgan), Berman clearly was there to present the sunny side of VaR, so as to guarantee a two-sided discussion. "*VaR,*" the quantitative risk specialist opened his statement, "*has enjoyed tremendous success, ranging from revealing the hidden risks of complex strategies to communicating with investors in a consistent and transparent fashion.*" The model, Berman offered, had often been used inappropriately by policy makers:

> Though current VaR methodologies are designed to estimate short-term market movements under normal conditions, regulators nevertheless tried to recast these models in order to measure the probability of long-term losses under extended market dislocations. We propose that it is not the model that needs to be recast but that regulators need to recast the question itself. VaR is about making dynamic decisions, constructing portfolios, sizing bets, and communicating risks. On the contrary, banking capital is designed to protect against worst-case events and their consequences. Instead of having banks report probabilities of short-term losses, they should estimate the losses they would be expected to shoulder under a set of adverse conditions (a 50 percent default rate, a 40 percent unemployment rate) chosen by regulators.

What Berman appears to be saying is that VaR should continue to be in use for in-house risk management and trading decisions, but not for capital regulation purposes. Wait, he actually said it when closing his argument:

> In summary, VaR is an excellent risk framework for banks and other financial institutions and the development of VaR models should continue unabated, but banking capital serves a different purpose and should be driven by policy instead of by probability analysis.

This sounds like quite sound advice. Yes, Mr. Berman very publicly wants VaR to go on alive and kicking, but at least he doesn't want it where it can do the most harm. As has been stated in this book, adult institutions can manage their internal market risks any way they like (or anyway their shareholders may allow them to get away with, and provided that taxpayers don't foot the bill if things go sour), but hugely influential mandatory public policies should never be founded on deeply flawed, potentially very problematic methods. I, for one, was (positively) surprised by Berman's candor in this respect, while not being able to refrain myself from thinking that the more militant VaRistas out there must have been crying "Treason!" as they listened to or read the RiskMetrics representative's assertions.

The next, and final, three panelists (which included an academic economist) steered the debate back to a decisively anti-VaR path, voicing dictums that would make Nassim Taleb proud. Posited James Rickards (among other things, LTCM's former general counsel):

> The world is two years into the worst financial crisis since the Great Depression. The list of culprits is long including mortgage brokers, investment bankers, and rating agencies. The story sadly is by now well known. What is less well known is that behind these actors were quantitative risk models that said that all was well even as the bus was driving off a cliff. Unfortunately, we've been here before. In 1998 capital markets came to the brink of collapse due to the failure of hedge fund LTCM. What is striking to me is how nothing has changed and no lessons were learned. The lessons should have been obvious: LTCM used fatally flawed VaR models and too much leverage, and the solutions should have been clear. Risk models needed to be changed or abandoned, leverage needed to be reduced. Amazingly, the US government did the opposite.

Rickards concluded, "*None of this would have happened without the assurance and comfort provided to regulators and Wall Street bankers by VaR models. The key assumptions behind the model (efficient markets, random walk, Normal distribution) are wrong. Investors are not rational, prices do not move randomly, risk is not Normally distributed. Let's abandon VaR once and for all.*" He then passed the baton to Christopher Whalen of Institutional Risk Analytics, a provider of banks risk ratings. Whalen began:

> When you use assumptions in models, you've already stepped off the deep edge of the pool, and there's no water in the pool. You essentially are in the world of speculation and you've left the world of investing. If we used the same assumptions that go into the design of VaR models to design airplanes and dams all

of these physical structures would fail because they violate the basic rules of scientific method. If we trust assumptions rather than hard data then we are in big trouble. My firm has entirely shunned quantitative work. We don't guess, we don't speculate. A big problem is that we allowed the Economics profession to escape from the world of social science and enter into an unholy union with dealers in the securities markets.

Any hard-core financial economist or financial theoretician tuning in to the hearing's webcast might by that point fainted under the weight of such amalgamation of anti-models testimony. Even the RiskMetrics guy (in principle, the theoreticians' kinda guy) wanted to erase the math from bank regulation! But perhaps there was still hope for those rooting for the quant side. After all, the final speaker was a tenured Economics professor. Academic economics having become such an abstract equations-driven discipline, surely the prof could be counted on to enthusiastically fly the theory flag on Capitol Hill, right?

Wrong. Middlebury College's David Colander wasted no time in concurring with his panel colleagues.

We academics live in the world of suppositions because that's where our incentives are. We write articles. VaR is part of a larger problem in terms of how economists operate. A warning label should be placed on models: They should not be relied on heavily. We need a commonsense check on models. Current academic research is based on incestuous mutual reinforcement of researchers' views with no commonsense filter on those views. We must include physicists, mathematicians, statisticians, and even businessmen and government representatives as part of the reviewing process for social sciences research grants. We must fund research on the usefulness of models, going a long way towards placing the appropriate warning labels.

An academic economist asking for commonsensical checks and model warnings? By this time, any financial quant would have logged out of the Committee's site in utter despair. It is one thing to hear Taleb once more repeat his anti-models rants, it's quite another to have to hear Taleb and then a bunch of people who sound just like Taleb.

Perhaps never before had so many badmouthed quantitative financial modeling so much at the same time and in such a public forum.

Possibly animated by that bluntness, the inquiring politicians proceeded to ask the really key question, one that should have been asked much more often, much earlier, much louder by public servants not just in Washington, DC but all across major developed financial centers.

"Should we use mathematical models at all?" went the inquiry. RiskMetrics' Berman replied first: *"Models will always be useful."* James Rickards was slightly more skeptical:

> From 200 BC to 1500 AD the model of the universe was geocentric, with the sun revolving around the Earth. This was not just a religious belief, it was actually a scientific belief. Many brilliant mathematicians worked for centuries to write the equations, and when people observed data through telescopes that did not conform to the model they said well we just need to tweak the model a little bit, and they kept going down that path. But the paradigm was completely wrong. The understanding of how the world worked was wrong, the sun did not revolve around the Earth, but the other way around. That's my view of VaR today: You can tweak it, you can improve it, but they are all wrong because the paradigm is wrong in the first place. If a non-systematically important hedge fund wants to use these models that's fine, they can use voodoo as far as I am concerned. But if you are talking about a bank or a regulated financial institution they should be prohibited because they don't work.

Christopher Whalen's final testimonial in the eventful gathering neatly summarized the impact of flawed financial models on society:

> We are still paying for the (1980s) S&L crisis, there's still debt out there that we are paying interest on. We are going to be paying for this crisis for 100 years, that's how big the numbers are. So think of that as a load on the economy. That's kind of the cost of modeling run amok. I am serious about this, consumers, investors, and banks we are going to be paying for this for a long time.

■ ■ ■

It's a real pity that none of the rest of the hearing really filtered outside of the hallowed walls of 2318 Rayburn House Office Building in Washington's Capitol Hill neighborhood. The media blackout made sure of that. Few outside that room ever knew what had gone on. For the organizers and the panelists, it must have been disheartening to confront the fact that their extremely important debate was essentially ignored outside those walls. It's not just a matter of personal ego. Just like I naively expected the event to educate perceptions as to what had truly caused the credit crisis and to provoke drastic changes in risk management and capital regulation practices, so too must Nassim Taleb and the others have expected. To have to contemplate how the entire affair came to nothing must have been quite a burden. No one likes to be ignored, especially when you are disclosing a socially relevant message.

In fact, it is likely that the participants shared a profound sense of abandonment already while the proceedings went on. It was indeed creepy to observe that as some of the truly crucial factors behind the 2007–2008 crash were being so openly and boldly analyzed, the rows of chairs behind the large table around which the debating panelists were assembled stood almost completely empty. Barely any individual seemed to have bothered to attend the latter part of the historic VaR hearing. Perhaps the absence of Taleb and Bookstaber, described by the hearing's Chairman as "rock stars" when opening the event earlier in the morning, and the relative anonymity of the last four expert witnesses explained the lackluster attendance (not that Taleb and Bookstaber testified to a packed audience either), or perhaps as in the case of the media the role of mathematical models in the crisis was not on people's radar. Whatever the actual reason, it was sad to contemplate how some of the most pressing issues pertaining global financial activity were being dissected amidst a ghostly deserted room. Just as sad as not making the front page (or any other page) of any major newspaper the following day (or any other day). In spite of having made it to Washington, VaR did not become universally famous and the world at large remained ignorant as to the mysterious force that shaped and continues to shape our lives.

■ ■ ■

Given the unwillingness of regulators to completely do away with VaR and of journalists to draw attention to the model's responsibility for the 2007 crisis (coupled with bankers reluctance to depart from VaR), it is only logical that the model would continue in our midst, more than $1 trillion in bank losses later. Actually it is almost shocking how the "Market Risk" sections of regulatory filings haven't changed one bit. The VaR tables are still prominently displayed (still giving the impression to anyone poking their noses that VaR is in fact the golden risk radar and that those numbers *do* accurately represent the firm's exposures), and the VaR disclaimers are also to be conspicuously found ("This is how we measure our risks and our capital requirements but the methodology is quite disappointing . . ."). Have we not learned anything?

As I am writing this I am looking at Goldman Sachs 2010 annual report, page 79. The neat table at the bottom tells me that Goldman's average daily VaR for 2010 was $134 million, down from $218 million in 2009. There were only two exceptions to the firm's 95 percent VaR in 2010, and none in 2009. I switch from Wall Street to Old Europe to fixate my eyes on UBS 2010 Annual Report's page 135. The average 2010 daily VaR stood at CHF57 million, essentially unchanged from 2009's CHF55 million. UBS's 99 percent VaR saw just one exception in 2010 (four in 2009). I return to New York City and look at Morgan Stanley's 2010 10-K form, which tells me (page 101) that the American giant's average one-day Trading VaR for 2010 was $139 million, identical to 2009's figure. Morgan Stanley's 99 percent VaR was never breached in 2010.

This information worries me. It's not so much that VaR is still kept around in a pretty luxurious form, but that VaR is again working "too well." Calmer markets and healthier portfolios have given rise to scarce VaR breaches. Statistically speaking, VaR seems to be behaving well once again. Pro-VaR folks can boast of the model's on-target loss estimates, once more. VaR is back to looking right. The legitimacy of any anti-VaR voices may seem reduced. In sum, it all worryingly feels so pre-mid-2007.

Chapter 7

The Common Sense That Should Rule the World

A Call for Counterrevolution ▪ *Imperfect Basel I Was So Much Better* ▪ *Let's Ban the Unacceptable* ▪ *Einhorn versus Brown* ▪ *But, Will We Suffer?*

Would VaR have been enthusiastically adopted by financiers and politicians if it weren't wrapped up in sophisticated-looking mathematical symbols and analytics? I have my doubts. I quite strongly believe that VaR's quantitative cred, which as we know was particularly acute in the early days of the model, decisively contributed to its embracement as the risk guide that would solve all problems. The math helped convince many people that the new methodology was imbued with unlimited rigor, a wise conduit to financial precision, an end to bothersome uncertainty. In some cases, those conclusions would have been reached after thorough examination of the technical documents. In others, I suspect, the conclusions would have been arrived at rather unconditionally, the total acquiescence with the model not demanding an actual investigation of its analytical insides: VaR's high-tech outer appearance would be more than enough credential, no further introspection required. This speaks of the powerful status that quantitative concoctions have reached in financeland in the modern age; not only those who truthfully abide by the symbols are brought on board, but also those (a vast number perhaps) whose mathematical knowledge of the model is limited to the fact that the model is mathematical. If you want a device to infiltrate the markets, it surely helps if it is analytically clothed.

The reasons for this are probably varied, including a general human infatuation with scientific-seeming accomplishments, a reluctance to challenge apparent sophistication, or a lack of trust in the "softer" sapience of personal intuition. Whatever the actual factors behind the imposition of a financial model, it seems clear that on way too many occasions common sense is forced to take a back seat, if at all, when it comes to some of the most consequential financial decisions. The crowning of the model as supreme ruler implicates, almost by definition, the excreting of human intuition, which many proponents of the analytical way consider not just a competitor but the enemy. VaR is the most relevant example of this phenomenon, but certainly not the only one. Complaisance toward equations-adorned gadgets has convinced people to put their arms around plenty of silly notions, such that it is possible to know a priori the future risks and returns of a security, markets are perfectly liquid and continuous, crashes and bubbles don't take place, or it is possible to measure a priori the future correlation between defaults on mortgage loans. None of these assertions, I believe, would have ever become accepted wisdom had the source not been quantitative. Had a, say, innumerate cab driver, not an MIT professor or a JP Morgan quant, uttered such notions we would have immediately dismissed him as a hopeless crank. And yet, once the very same dictums emanate not from a smelly taxi, but from the hallowed ivory tower or the imposing bank we puzzlingly nod in agreement, endow the authors with the genius label, and shower Nobel prizes on them. Whether a financial tenet is dressed up mathematically or not can be the difference between ignominious rejection and getting a medal from the King of Sweden.

This is not a good state of affairs. Bad theories should be as quickly discarded as bad cabdriver advice. No amount of technical wizardry can justify the embracement of beliefs that would be deemed absurd absent the theorems. If the math becomes the Kool-Aid that makes us accept silly principles, then the math becomes a dangerous thing. If the math forces us to betray our most pure intuitions, then the math must be resisted.

Cab drivers would not have entrusted market risk management and bank capital regulation to VaR. But they, on the other hand, would not have found themselves in total disagreement with what was going on before VaR. Basel I would have seemed quite reasonable, quite acceptable, at the very least a decently sound starting point. Measuring risks to the third decimal through the use of suspect statistical trickeries and unreliable past data would appear to our no-nonsense taxi-driving friends much more unreasonable, unacceptable, and unsound than ranking financial assets by their obviously intrinsic nature (even if crudely done). Even a financially ignorant individual can see the wisdom of, first, doing no harm: Make sure that the nasty stuff is treated accordingly. Many financial mathematicians and theoreticians may want to convince us that a subprime CDO should be given the chance to appear less risky than a Treasury Bond, but that does not negate the utter silliness of the idea. The concept would not pass the cabby's test, and thus should be rejected. If the common man thinks it nuts, so should regulators and bankers. Stop flawed models from shoving insultingly unacceptable results down our throats. We can die from it.

■ ■ ■

It is paradoxical that an attempt to imbue rigorousness and sophistication into something may end up delivering outcomes that deviate from truthfulness even more dramatically than the supposedly plebeian system that had been replaced by the new high-tech ways. The pioneer Basel I international regulatory standards have been ruthlessly lambasted for their perceived lack of attunement to real-world realities. True risk, the critiques posited, is not captured by such rustic architecture, we need something much more accurate and fancy. Third-generation mathematical models that drink from actual market signals will get risk right, the thinking went (and still goes in many quarters). Such erroneous mode of thinking, it turned out, was founded on the idea that financial risk can be implied in some magic way from past behavior and statistical hypothesis. Rather, financial risk can at best be guessed and ranked. We can't imply the future riskiness of a trade, but we can try to discriminate between different trades, and rank them in buckets. This, the Basel I regime got absolutely correct. Free from the analytical shackles (the no-holds-barred quantification of finance had not yet conquered completely in the mid- to late-1980s), financial mandarins arrived at a commonsensical solution. The real value of a Basel I-type exercise is not so much that the risk buckets will be perfectly designed or organized (in fact, they were far from perfectly designed or organized), but that the discriminatory approach based on asset fundamentals is bound to guarantee that the most naturally risky stuff will be placed in the worst buckets (i.e., those demanding more regulatory capital and careful steering).

Rather than trying to measure risk, particularly through very inappropriate means, we should focus on making the worst kinds of risk unacceptable. While VaR and other metrics subliminally fail at that, something like the much derided and denigrated Basel I showed the right path to follow (of course, Basel I dealt with credit, not market, risk but what's being proposed here is that Basel I–style intuitional bucketing of risk categories be applied to both trading book and banking book assets). Thus, we should engage in counterrevolution: restore into power the old quant-less monarchy and, Napoléon-like, exile the defeated models to a faraway location. The 2007 crisis was VaR's Waterloo; we should find a remote St. Helena where the dethroned emperor can spend the rest of its life, terminally incapacitated to incite any more mayhem.

But restoring the old ways would not be enough. A healthy dose of reformation would be in order, not just to procure a more robust regime but also to limit the potential for a second quant revolt down the road. The Basel I monarchs must understand that while their system was superior at what truly matters, it can be greatly improved on.

Basel I was accused of three major sins. First, it can easily lead to higher risk by naively dumping together in the same buckets assets of widely different nature, making it for instance as costly capital-wise to lend to IBM or to the corner shop (and thus, in principle, encouraging more lending to the corner shop than to IBM, as a higher interest can be charged on the former; more interest measured against the same capital charge generates better returns on equity). Second, it could result in unnecessarily taxing capital levies by not taking into account the risk-reducing diversification benefits of owning a portfolio of purportedly uncorrelated assets. Finally, it didn't cover market exposures, focusing only on a bank's banking book. Only the third complaint carries real merit. It's not that the other two charges would be completely off-the-mark, because the old rules could indeed favor lending to weaker credits and since diversification can certainly result in offsetting positions. But the remedies to both shortcomings made things much worse, potentially and indeed in practice: VaR and credit ratings can provide much more dysfunctional risk signals than Basel I's less-than-perfect bucketing, encouraging punting on extremely dubious assets if the latter happen, possibly for sheer coincidence or reflecting a bubble, to have enjoyed a recent calm market period (much worse than making it relatively economical to lend to the corner shop is to make it almost free to lend to someone who doesn't have a job or savings or income, let alone own a shop); and allowing more leverage on account of the supposed benefits of diversification can boomerang on you, especially when the diversifying factor is estimated via the statistical concept of correlation (the system can be gamed by scouring the historical data universe for assets that happened to have been uncorrelated of late, yielding very low capital charges for a portfolio of assets that, when things turn sour, can very well tank down in value all together at the same time, rapidly eating away at the diminished equity cushion; that which was assumed to lower risks becomes a dramatic risk enhancer). Relying on correlation, just like relying on volatility, can lead to bigger and bigger portfolios backed by smaller and smaller amounts of capital.

It turns out that Basel I was a superior architecture precisely because it did not incorporate those things that its critics found inexcusably missing. By not rewarding portfolio "diversification" with lower risk estimates and capital charges, and by not drinking from "market signals" implied by past data Basel I made itself into a more robust system than its later siblings Basel II and Basel III. By not confusing statistical correlation with true codependence and by not confusing risk with volatility, Basel I won the day. Is the use of correlation and volatility always a bad thing? No, of course not. Shouldn't asset diversification and actual market data be taken into account when appraising a portfolio's risk? Yes, of course they should. So, why are we praising Basel I on account of its neglect of both factors? Because drinking from those sources, while possibly useful at times, can make unacceptable answers possible and embraceable. Denying them center stage, instead ceding it entirely to experience-honed fundamentals-based decision making, makes (or ought to make) unacceptable results impossible. It is feasible that a lot of the time, not giving a starring role to the statistical counsel may reduce the accuracy of our risk analysis. But, I believe, that would be an agreeable price to pay in return for avoiding the emergence of the utterly diabolic. I'd rather settle for the exclusion of some potentially useful bit of information from the risk appraisal than for the possibility of a banking book or a trading book or both leveraged 100 to 1 or even 1,000 to 1 on lethal assets. It's healthier to potentially err on the riskiness of a conservative or semi-conservative portfolio while making it essentially not possible for a big toxic position to be built. While the financial and economic systems could put up with the former scenario, their very survival would be threatened by the latter's.

So Basel I was more wholesome than its quant successors. The "improvements" that were required upon it from analytical corners should not have been taken on board. However, and retaking the key point introducer earlier, a number of other tweaks certainly were and would be required to correct for some obvious imperfections. How should this perfected, superior regulatory structure (let's call it Basel I.5) look like?

■ ■ ■

One inescapable flaw of Basel I was that it allowed unlimited leverage on developed country government bonds–loans, by forcing a regulatory capital requirement of 0 percent on such positions (technically, on debt obligations by members of the Organization for Economic Cooperation and Development, or OECD, a Paris-based assemblage of rich and quasi-rich nations; 24 members when Basel I was put together in 1988, 34 at the time of writing). Toxic leverage is very bad, but excessive vanilla leverage should be equally avoided. Government-issued securities, even if issued by the most robust of nations, are not riskless, neither from a credit nor from a market point of view. The chance that an OECD country would default on its debt obligations is not zero, and certainly those assets can suffer from the volatile whims of global investors and tumble in value at no notice. Granted, such debacles would almost certainly never mirror those shouldered by more daring securities (while a subprime CDO can go to zero market value, an OECD bond is unlikely to sink nearly as much even under dire government financing circumstances), but they can potentially be significant nonetheless. Thus, for a bank to bet the house on government-issued securities could lead to losses significant enough to drive it out of business and to ignite widespread economic despair. Regulators, therefore, should not enable free gearing on such plays. Accumulating Italian government bonds or U.S. Treasuries should cost a little bit more than nothing.

It is often said that regulators decided to treat public sector debt so generously capital-wise as a way to guarantee that developed countries would find it easy to raise the funds they needed at any point; clearly, making that debt very economical for banks to hold is a powerful incentive for banks to lend to governments. So the OECD-originated mandarins in charge of Basel I decided to help their countries by helping global banks accumulate OECD debt very cheaply. Basel I may have placed OECD debt in the right risk bucket (in principle, that asset category should be placed among the safest) but got the risk weight wrong. Future regulatory regimes didn't exactly correct the problem, as the humble capital charges afforded by Basel II to securities with the highest credit ratings made sure that large leverage on developed nations' debt (which tend to be endowed with top ratings) continued to be affordable. That, combined with the reign of VaR on the trading side, potentially gave rise to a particularly dangerous combination of very low capital requirements for both esoteric and government assets. Making leverage on the latter very economical is especially worrisome when leverage on the former is too inexpensive, given that the financial, economic, and social mess that would be triggered by the more-than-likely blowup of the toxic plays would normally lead to shocks in public finances deriving from costly banking bailouts and stimulus policies; the end result could very well be greatly enhanced volatility and price declines in the government securities sphere, inflicting severe setbacks on those institutions that had accumulated sizeable amounts of those assets on the back of a very generous capital treatment (the banking industry, in essence, would be exposed to facing a fatal double blow: first, massive write-downs on the exotic stuff, then more massive losses on the vanilla stuff). So the urgency to correct for Basel I's lenient attitude toward OECD debt, highly advisable in itself, would be even more pressing under a system where VaR still roams around.

The meltdown that began in 2007 attested to all that. As the dust settled on the mortgage market massacre, an additional crisis was unleashed in certain corners of the sovereign securities arena, particularly in the Eurozone. By mid-2009, the headlines were no longer dominated by CDOs, massive losses on subprime loans, or rescue packages for Wall Street, but by the humongous difficulties faced by countries like Greece, Ireland, Portugal, Spain, France, Italy, or Belgium to deal with ever more unbearable fiscal deficits and levels of indebtedness. Of course, those difficulties had been accentuated by the earlier private-sector financial crisis, as governments had to rush in expensive rescue packages for banks and other firms and as tax receipts suffered from the abrupt decrease in economic activity and the abrupt increase in unemployment. The real plus the perceived risks of sovereign defaults collided to condemn those governments' bonds to a sharp decline in price, hurting anyone who had dared accumulate them in bulk. On December 31, 2010, the FTSE Global Government Bond Indices indicated the following miserly 12-month returns for some of the above mentioned sorry cases:

Greece	−20 percent
Ireland	−12.5 percent
Portugal	− 7.3 percent
Spain	− 3.9 percent
Italy	− 0.8 percent

Don't tell me that developed country–issued securities aren't risky, or that they should deserve a 0 percent regulatory capital charge.

Another obvious flaw of Basel I was that the maximum minimum capital requirements were set at a way-too-low level. The max min capital charge was capped at 8 percent of risk-weighted assets, which effectively implied a cap of 8 percent of total assets on those asset families deemed riskiest (and thus deserving of the top 100 percent risk weight). An 8 percent total capital charge, implying leverage above 10 to 1, can be too lenient if the asset is too daring. The top capital charge should be set at 100 percent, limiting gearing to a 1-to-1 ratio. This naturally implies that those assets placed in the most lethal risk bucket would be assumed capable of losing their entire value in a downturn. Such assumption may be seen by some as a tad excessive: Even highly illiquid stuff may be liquidated into something more valuable than nothing. However, slightly unseemly as they might appear, very steep top capital charges would serve us much better in our efforts to ban the unacceptable than an 8 percent max charge ever could. Again, the main goal is not to get risk metrics precisely right, or to design a risk system that is so fair and just that no asset family is ever demanded more capital than it should. Many times, the steep top charge would seem unfair and uncalled for. Too bad. What truly matters is to fence hellish trades so stringently that they can't be accumulated massively, or if they are accumulated massively never without a correspondingly massive equity shield. If a bank wants to lose $100 billion in mayhem-destined positions, it should back that wish up with a $100 billion capital commitment. That way, losses on the bad stuff won't consume equity raised to support the good stuff. Every dollar of lethality should have its own equity cushion. An eye for an eye, as they say.

The key idea here is discouragement. A 50 percent or a 100 percent capital charge may turn out to be an inappropriately untruthful characterization of some of those assets unsound enough to qualify for the worst risk buckets, but it would always be appropriately discouraging, turning banks away from those, now taxingly expensive, punts. The markets and the economy at large become more resilient, as the possibility that the banking industry may finance a toxic orgy with but a tiny capital slice is made unfeasible. In essence, regulatory capital's main role becomes the de facto banning of the obviously unacceptable; short of legally banning certain plays, the best weapon against the fragility of finance.

Quite prominent people would cast their vote for such initiative. Famed hedge fund manager David Einhorn is a case in point. Following the fall of Bear Stearns in March 2008, but before the crash of Lehman Brothers (which Einhorn famously shorted) the following September, the successful money manager saw it only natural that as a result of the malaise financial authorities would force banks to accumulate much more capital going forward. His most revolutionary recommendation? 50 percent to 100 percent charge for "no ready market," that is, dangerously illiquid plays. Einhorn had no doubt that very low regulatory capital requirements, on the back on very low VaR figures, had sunk Wall Street, and that the unavoidable remedy would be to force banks to delever and to make trading on suspect assets much more costly. Capital should also be only of the highest quality, Einhorn offered.[1] Anything other than core equity should not be allowed to call itself capital. The president of Greenlight Capital, in other words, presented himself as an indefatigable defender of down-to-earth, dogmatism-proof, common sense: Too much bad leverage is bad, and should not be condoned. The sad irony is that it took a "contrarian" (Einhorn has been portrayed as a quixotic figure, a roguish anti-system maverick recklessly betting on the end of the financial order) to point what should have seemed only natural to anyone all along. When those tagged as rebellious contrarians are the ones lonely carrying the flag of commonsensical decision making, that's when you realize how maddeningly fragile the VaR-dominated financial universe had become.

■ ■ ■

There are also prominent individuals on the other side of the debate, financial risk grandees that would find a return to something resembling Basel I impossibly allergic. To them, there's no turning back from metrics-based analysis. Give me historical data and quantitative models or give me nothing, seems to be the chant of those bent on protecting the status quo (notice that those fellows would now be firmly part of the "traditionalist" camp, given how entrenched analytical risk management has become; those proposing commonsensical, intuitional risk management would nowadays be the "revolutionaries," inexcusably daring to challenge the supreme authority of the mathematical emperor).

Some of those opposing change would be untameable reactionaries, quantitative Torquemadas for whom law is only what the dogmatic book says. Others would be much more enlightened, much more tolerant, yet still enthusiastically quant-oriented folk. People like successful real-world risk manager and guru Aaron Brown. In an exchange with David Einhorn in mid-2008, Brown defended the supremacy of "risk-sensitive" bank capital regulation, toeing the familiar analytical line that data-based statistical identities like standard deviation (volatility) and correlation provide a much better picture of a firm's exposures than fundamentals-based assessments.[2] On top of the typical reasons, he defended VaR as a great way to gather information and improve communication within a firm, stating that you could completely disregard the final number (actually, that doesn't sound like an entirely crazy proposition . . .) and still have reaped ample benefits from going through the calculation process. Like many, Brown seems to care much more about the tails (what VaR doesn't cover, the 1 percent or 5 percent) than about the measured perimeter (what VaR does cover, the 99 percent or 95 percent), essentially assuming that while the former is unknowable the latter is trustworthy. I think that's a big problem, especially when it comes to the use of VaR as capital-charge setter. Saying that VaR is right but what lies beyond VaR is a mystery may be passable for risk management purposes (as you complement your VaR with whatever fancy analysis you've built to deal with the extremes), but it's outright dangerous when it comes to capital regulation because here there is no (or at least there wasn't between 1996 and 2008) add-on mechanism that may help yield a sufficiently large figure; here, VaR alone is all that matters (mattered) so if VaR is wrong the capital requirement will be wrong. And the key idea that seems to be ignored by the pro-VaR crowd is that the 99 percent or the 95 percent or whatever percent VaR number is going to be wrong and, much worse, could easily err on the side of smallness. The 1 percent or 5 percent or whatever percent tail will certainly be a problem, but so will the larger probability chunk covered by VaR. It's not okay to say that VaR tells the truth but only up to the 99 percent or 95 percent confidence level. VaR will lie often (what we tag as 99 percent probability may actually be a 70 percent or 60 percent probability event), and some of those lies can result in very bad outcomes. It's not only what VaR doesn't capture that's a problematic issue; VaR itself is a problematic issue and as long as VaR plays an important regulatory role that issue will be highly problematic for all.

Brown compares VaR to a friendly fence protecting the financial village from the monsters lurking outside.[3] Those monsters are unknown to us (as in, "these rare events only happen 1 percent of the time, or twice a year; it's hard to know much about them"); what lies within the fence is safely certain (as in, "these normal events happen all the time; they are very familiar to us"). The only reason the monsters are deemed monsters is because they are infrequent; we have much less historical data for, say, 1 percent events than for, say, 99 percent events. But that doesn't mean that so-called 99 percent events are potentially less dangerous: Just because they behaved a certain way yesterday doesn't imply that they won't act much differently, perhaps much more unfriendly, tomorrow. We think we control and understand what's inside the fence (say, market losses never above $50 million), but in fact we don't: Just because we were able to measure it doesn't mean that the measure will be on target; and an off-target measure may show far less danger than there actually is. We took shelter within the fence only to find that the monsters lay inside, not just outside. We thought we had a 99 percent strong fence, only to realize that it was in fact only 50 percent or 60 percent strong: What was assumed to lurk only outside the fence materialized inside, slaughtering the complacent villagers. The measurers said that the tigers (market losses above $50 million), lay only outside the fence, and thus we could sleep easy. But one day we wake up to find the beasts tearing the village apart, from the inside. What was deemed impossible to happen within the walls happened. We assumed no knowledge of events outside the fence because we couldn't measure them, we assumed total certainty of events inside the fence because we could measure them. As we get eaten by the tigers, we comprehend how naive we were to rely on those measures and to organize our defenses around them. If you use wrong measurement tools, what takes place inside the village can hurt you and surprise you; it's not only in the jungle that cold uncertainty and terrible pain can await.

Those who state that capital should be risk-sensitive choose the wrong way to define risk. Mathematical estimations based on past data, probabilistic assumptions, and computational games are not risk. We shouldn't blame statistics too much: When shaky and unreliable humans shape the action, divining what's next is impossibly hard.

In his exchange with Einhorn, Aaron Brown declares himself not a big fan of making banks hold a lot of capital in general. Rather, he believes in dynamic capital management: If you get in trouble, recognize it early and humbly seek new equity infusions from outside investors. You may start with a relatively small chunk of capital, which would get augmented dynamically as you suffer setbacks. If this is done properly and if you retain a solid balance sheet, you should do fine attracting extra investors. The real reason why Bear Stearns fell, added Brown, is that it utterly failed at raising more capital once its problems became obviously public. More capital at the beginning would not have helped much plus it would have been a drag on returns and leads to waste, posited Brown. Starting with less equity support and addressing any problem early and aggressively would be a superior course of action. No wonder that Brown would not vote for the 50 percent–100 percent capital charges favored by Einhorn. Not only would they (sin of sins!) be VaR-independent, they would be much too sizeable for his taste.

While Brown's dynamic capital strategy is not devoid of seductiveness, I fear its practicality may be found lacking. Just like with the other dynamic strategies sponsored by the quant community (the Black-Scholes-Merton option pricing model, for instance) one would be making the brave assumption of unlimited liquidity at all times: New outside capital infusions will be at the ready whenever I demand them. That may always be true depending on the circumstances and the firm in question, but then again it may not be true for other circumstances and other firms. Perhaps putting all our trust on ever-perfect dynamic capitalization would be a tad courageous.

And dynamic capital replenishment may not add a thing if the original sin of toxic leverage has been previously sanctioned by "risk-sensitive" lax and permissive capital requirements. If the small initial $10 million sliver of capital is allowed to finance $1 billion in subprime CDOs, the damage is irreparably done. After I lose the first million I might find a friendly sovereign fund in Singapore or Norway ready and willing to add a few millions more to my equity coffers, but really who cares? Once the toxic stuff was allowed in such quantities, your fate is sealed. The $1 billion will soon be worth much less (maybe $1 billion less), and not even the most accommodating of overseas investors would want to keep that sinking ship afloat.

Much better to redefine the main role of capital. Neither as guarantor of an orderly liquidation of a firm, nor as dynamic corrector for possible bumps on the financial road. Rather, as a preventer of the chaos-promising unacceptable. In that light, and respectfully contradicting Brown, Bear Stearns (like any of its Wall Street siblings) was not well capitalized going into the crisis because it held too much "no ready market" stuff ($29 billion by November 2007) on top of too little equity ($10.5 billion by that same date). Official capitalization ratios may have declared Bear okay capital-wise, but that only means, of course, that the regulation was obsolete. What matters is not the amount of capital you have (whether initially or progressively) but what kind of stuff you can get away with purchasing and at what cost. If the lethal plays are not made impossibly expensive from the get-go, your capital base (irrespective of how many zeros it displays) may be condemned to melting under the abrasive heat of a toxic catastrophe. I agree with Brown that once Bear saw tens of billions of liquidity disappearing in a few days, a billion or two extra capital would not have done much. The real problem is what caused the humongous losses in the first place: too much leverage at Bear and across the Street, and too much toxic leverage at Bear and across the Street, courtesy of a financial universe dominated by VaR and other metrics.

In the healthy quest to avoid unacceptable outcomes, regulators should rediscover the joy of basing bank capital rules on fundamentals. Financial mandarins should travel back in time and get reacquainted with their younger selves. Dust off the Basel I rulebook, revise it and improve it by correcting its true flaws, and unleash it onto the modern world. Models-based regulations can, did, and will tolerate the unacceptable because they easily can, did, and will deliver unrealistically low estimates of risk and, much more poignantly, because they can be, were, and will be easily manipulated into delivering unrealistically low estimates of risk. Bring back the days when VaR and other mathematical tricks could not dictate the fate of the banking industry,

Implement Basel I.5: Both credit and market capital charges would depend on elaborate and modern risk buckets, clearly discriminating against naturally riskier asset families and imposing very hefty equity fees on unacceptably toxic punts. The risk weights on those buckets may be modified through time as the appropriate regulatory committee sees fit, based on economic realities and (why not) how assets have performed. So what carried a weight of 15 percent may be forced to carry one of 20 percent or rewarded with just a 10 percent one a year later. But the core principle should firmly remain: Make use of the risk buckets to guarantee that toxic leverage can't happen. The common sense behind Basel I may have been a tad simplistic, but that's no reason to forgo common sense. Rather, give it another try. Make it better and more attuned to modern-day financial activity. That should be amply superior to the analytical alternative that was allowed to steamroll over Basel I in the name of sophistication and that, inevitably, resulted in a deadly flood of destructive outcomes.

Some would concur. A leading academic expert on bank regulation,[4] rather than applauding the marginal changes proposed by the Basel Committee as a result of the 2007 crisis, proposes a radical overhaul of the system, moving away from risk calibration and raising capital requirements very substantially. With mathematically defined risk-based policies, it is very easy for a bank to end up ultraleveraged because the risk-weighted assets over which regulatory capital is determined may turn out to be just a fraction of total assets: *"Many institutions had equity amounting to 1–3% of their balance sheets even as they were vaunting themselves as having 10% core capital. The latter quantity is of course useless if the risk weights have not been chosen appropriately."*[5] What's more, regulators may have been privy to that fact all along:

> The regulatory community has been unable to put up stronger resistance against the industry's claims that capital regulation must be finely attuned to the actual risks that banks are taking. Dysfunctional effects of the regulation have by and large been overlooked. The regulatory community knew that risk calibration was mainly a tool to reduce capital requirements. However, they also knew that, in discussions about risk management, they were no match for the industry.[6]

Just because the financial risk professionals employed by banks may be highly educated, top-level individuals should not automatically imply that the tools that they produce should be automatically deemed infallible and worthy of embracement. Humble policy makers should not allow themselves be subjugated by purported mathematical sophistication. If a model leads to unacceptable results, it should not be condoned, no matter how superiorly smart the model's peddlers may be. Back to our academic expert witness:

> While accepting that risk modelers and risk managers in banking institutions are highly professional and very competent, we need to appreciate that a bank's private interests in managing its risks is not the same as the public interest in having banks manage their risks so as to avoid systemic damage. Therefore, the professional competence of risk controllers in banks is not a good reason to shape the regulation to the bankers' wishes. Regulators may be less competent in matters of risk management, but this is no reason to eliminate their role in giving voice to the public interest.[7]

Sometimes the (supposedly) smarter guys can be wrong. Let's not make society pay a big price for it.

■ ■ ■

Some may ask, why the need to call for counterrevolution when policy makers have already shaken things up? Isn't the common sense already introduced by the latest revisions in bank capital rules enough? Why stir the pot, when regulators have been busy doing plenty of stirring themselves? It is undoubted that, as we've amply covered in the book, capital regulations have gone through a cleansing dose of repairing following the 2007–2008 cataclysm. We've seen how capital charges on resecuritizations were bumped up. We've seen how trading book charges were inundated with add-ons to VaR. Isn't that sufficient?

Not really, as long as the elephant in the room continues unaddressed, unrevised, and unquestioned. Occasional tweaks to the rules and procedures behind the calculations rather appear as concerns-allaying decoy that allows the underlying main structure to go on unperturbed.

Whenever VaR and other regulatory metrics turn naughtily malfunctioning, the mandarins in Basel treat these deficiencies as punctual technical flaws, to be duly corrected by making some modification to the calculation formula. But the overall wisdom of having a models-based approach is not put in question. VaR's influence has been decisively downsized but neither VaR itself nor analytical risk analysis in general were expulsed from the premises. Mathematical models have not been a casualty of the crisis. They have been preserved, allowed to fight another day. Through their nonstructural tweaks regulators have preserved the analytical reign, while giving the appearance of having conducted thorough, remedial surgery. Outsiders may have been assuaged by such patching up, believing the system to be now much more robust to shocks. And yet, the original sin (the fantastical illusion that financial risks can be measured, by suspect concoctions to boot) remains.

Many say that it's okay to have mathematical models around, even if they can obviously fail, because they are complemented with other tools. Such people typically argue that warnings were erected as to the wisdom of not relying exclusively on the model, so those who eventually did so should be the ones to truly blame. With one hand this pro-models crowd tells us how important models are and how crucial it is for your organization to employ them and with the other they tell us how stupid it is to trust the models and how reckless financiers were for listening to the math. This is akin to a salesperson aggressively peddling a device only to berate the customer later on for employing the device.

These arguments have been heard when it comes to VaR, credit ratings, and other analytical constructs. Don't rely exclusively on the models, we've been repeatedly told. Complement the models with other analysis, we are instructed. But this, of course, does not solve the problem. The problem with flawed, deleterious models is not that they exist in exclusivity but that they exist at all. As long as the models are out there and can be used as alibis for certain trading and dealing actions, the bad models will continue to be abided by and the world will continue to be in danger. Just because you warn that the AAA rating should not be taken in isolation doesn't mean that people won't be able to justify financial decisions based entirely on the fact that the play got the AAA rubber-stamp. Just because you warn that the low VaR number should not be taken in isolation doesn't mean that people won't be able to alibi decisions exclusively on the premise that the risk radar said there was no risk. If you let the bad models loose, someone will pick them up and milk them to their benefit. They know that the reckless build-up of ultraleveraged positions or the irresponsible accumulation of toxic securities will be condoned and even applauded if they happen to be backed by low quantitative measures of market risk or default probability. How many traders will be scrutinized for punts that show negligible VaRs and/or imperial credit ratings? Notwithstanding how often and how loud the bad models are disclaimed and warned about, the bad models have continued and will continue to be successfully employed as justification for actions that may lead to chaos. This is just how things are. If you doubt it, consider what took place during the 2007 crisis: The globe's most influential banking firms saturated—unopposed—their balance sheets with the worst possible kind of financial crap because and only because of what VaR and the credit ratings had to say in the matter. The zero VaR and the AAA+ flags were waived in front of mesmerized bosses, regulators, and analysts who, hypnotized by the assurance, fell on their knees in total submission and eagerly cheered the traders on their glorious pursuit, refusing to ask for "complementary analysis" or for "additional tools."

The only sure way to make sure that bad models won't affect us is to stop having them around. The impact of having bad models around is not neutral, no matter how many warning labels you place on the container. If they can be used as alibis for certain actions, some smart operators will find them and use them as alibis for those actions, regardless of the mountain of advice urging not to use the models in isolation. The point is not how wrong everyone knows the models to be (and openly say so), the point is whether it is possible to nevertheless continue to get away with using the knowingly wrong constructs to back terminally harmful behavior.

■ ■ ■

Doing away completely with VaR, credit ratings, and similarly manipulable and flawed metrics-based approaches to bank regulation would go a long way toward helping prevent the emergence of unchecked leverage, in particular that of the most toxic kind. That would naturally be a good thing in itself. However, there is another side to that coin. Intuition and fundamentals-based alternatives may result in much too higher capital requirements, constraining banks so much that the economy at large suffers. Regulators have amply recognized (witness Basel III) that the analytical regime is bound to lead to intolerably undercapitalized banks, but will their reaction prove excessive? Commonsensical attitudes towards financial risk may prevent one type of cataclysm, but might give raise to a new source of bad news. Very little bank capital is obviously dangerous, but perhaps too much of it won't be healthy either Blaming one regulatory structure for the past crisis while replacing it with another that contains the seeds of future discontent may not be a good move on the part of politicians. Does that mean that perhaps we shouldn't rush too blindly into the arms of common sense? Should we maybe think twice before completely dismantling the analytical setup? Would the price of getting rid of VaR be too high?

Many financial institutions, let alone die-hard VaRistas throughout the academic and risk consultancy universes, seem to think so. It has been forcefully argued that Basel III (with its demands for more bank capital, and for far more "real" capital at that) could seriously dampen worldwide economic activity. In June 2010, for instance, the Institute for International Finance (IIF), an organization set up by a large number of global banks, concluded that Basel III would result in lower economic growth for the United States, the Euro Area, and Japan by an average of 0.6 percent annually during the 2011 to 2015 period, and by an average of 0.3 percent annually for the 2011 to 2020 period.[8] In other words, for each of the world's three biggest economic zones (the analysis was done before China's economic might overtook Japan's in early 2011), the IIF expected on average a sharp 3 percent growth decline in the decade following the formal announcement of Basel III regulatory measures. It seems logical that the impact would be more concentrated in the initial years because that's when banks would suffer the sudden hit of more taxing capital requirements.

The IIF's study found that the tougher financial policing should result in higher lending rates (by an average of above 1 percent annually in each of the G3 zones, for 2011 to 2020) as well as higher unemployment (by about 10 million people in the G3 combined). Credit to nonfinancial corporations is projected to be constrained: For any given price level (spread over government debt), less financing would be available, with small- and medium-size enterprises bearing the brunt of the cuts.

Obviously, not all countries would be affected equally. The most important differentiating factor is most likely an economy's dependence on banks. The less bank financing matters for economic activity, the less new bank regulation that (potentially) hampers such financing may matter. Also, the smaller the banking sector's slice of a national economy the less significant a (potential) shrinkage of the banking sector's size may be. As of end 2009, the Euro Area was the most bank-dependent of the G3 with banks assets equal to 350 percent of GDP, in contrast to Japan's 170 percent figure; in the United States, banks only accounted for 83 percent of GDP. America was the most diversified in terms of financial intermediation, with bank lending making up just less than 25 percent of total credit intermediation, in sharp contrast to the Euro Area's 74 percent and Japan's 53 percent. So in principle the United States appeared to be less vulnerable to the Basel III tsunami, with the Euro folks being the most exposed.

Why should Basel III have negative effects? Why should it lead to lower bank lending, lower growth, and higher unemployment? Well, "should" is perhaps a strong word, but it is not exactly impossible or unreasonable to argue that the new policies "could" indeed yield said negativity (though the exact dimension of the bad outcomes is hard to prospectively get right). The essence of Basel III is higher capital requirements, more real capital, and somewhat less permissive risk weights. That triad could result in greater demands for equity capital or reductions in asset holdings (for the same asset portfolio as before, more capital will certainly be required; for the same capital as before, the asset portfolio will have to shrink or change). When higher capital ratios are being demanded, either the ratio's numerator, that is, capital, or the ratio's denominator, that is, risk-weighted assets, must be modified so as to arrive at the required figure. So either equity capital is increased or asset positions are decreased. The need for more equity can translate to more earnings being internally retained, rather than externally distributed. The need to reduce the balance sheet can translate to less loans (i.e., less debt-related assets). At the same time, the capital structure of banks gets tentatively more costly, as equity capital is typically seen as more expensive than borrowed funds; banks may in turn pass this extra cost on to their own borrowers, in the form of higher lending spreads. These effects can generate the kind of ugly consequences that the IIF warns about. So even if some might cynically argue that the IIF (as the public megaphone of banking institutions populated by people who may be allergic to Basel III's impositions) has a vested interest in being abruptly alarmist, there are in fact conduits through which the new rules may prompt at least some unpleasing economic (and thus social) outcomes.

Prudently preemptive, the IIF asks itself the kind of queries that would be raised by those in disagreement with its less-than-rosy findings. For instance, why can't banks just absorb internally the new costs supposedly imposed by the new regulations, rather than alchemize them into higher lending rates for the rest of the populace? Or more to the point, do we really need banks in order to grow? Can't we grow even in the face of a supposedly weakened and diminished banking sector? In a commendable display of honesty, the IIF concedes that given their control over noninterest costs (such as employee compensation), banks could in principle swallow any Basel III–induced pain without having to make it harder for everyone else to finance their activities or lifestyles, and, yes, an economy could do better even if confronted with more restrictive bank lending activity (among other things because mature and semi-mature economies tend to enjoy other financing alternatives, like those creatures called bonds). Nevertheless, the IIF clarifies, it is unlikely that higher costs won't be passed on externally or that the link between banks' health and economic activity won't remain powerful.

Not everyone agrees with the IIF's rather somber assessment of the impact of Basel III. Who? Well, the Basel Committee for starters. In a December 2010 report, the international financial mandarins projected a much sunnier future. Economic growth, the conclusion went, will be affected only very modestly by the new capital regulations. Assuming that banks begin to increment their capital ratios from 2011 (rather than 2013, the official launch date for Basel III), the study assumes an eight-year transition period (as the full set of new requirements must be met by early 2019). It is estimated that during said timeframe the median (most frequent) expected macroeconomic outcome of a 1 percent point increase in required equity capital would be a reduction in total growth of 0.17 percent per country (implying a median reduction in annual growth of around 0.02 percent points per country), followed by a gradual recovery of growth afterward. Recall that per Basel III required minimum equity capital is slated to progressively go up by about 5 percent points (from 2 percent to 7 percent[9]) during 2013 to 2019, so even if banks started with the smallest amount of hard-core equity demanded by the prior rules (i.e., 2 percent of risk-weighted assets) we can appreciate how little policy makers thought their new policies will subjugate prosperity. But in truth banks embarked on the new world of Basel III with more than just that paltry 2 percent. The Basel report set the figure at, on average, 5.7 percent, based on a survey of large international banks. Thus, to achieve the 7 percent target from such starting point banks would need to raise their capital ratios by 1.3 percent points, therefore yielding an overall decline in GDP of 0.22 percent (1.3 percent * 0.17 percent), or some 0.03 percent per year up to 2019. Certainly not something capable by itself of sinking a nation, especially when compared with the benefits of making it harder for a taxing and costly bank crisis to occur.

Several others concur with the Basel Committee's Basel III-won't-kill-us analysis. In one of the earlier papers to analyze the possible impact of the new post-crisis rules,[10] Douglas Elliott of the prestigious Washington DC–based Brookings Institution matter-of-factly concluded that there would likely be only relatively small changes in loan volumes by U.S. banks as a response to higher capital requirements, and that the cost of such loans would rise only modestly (by around 0.20 percent points on average, not much to worry about if we consider for instance how modest the economic effects from a 0.25 percent point increase in official interest rates tend to be). In another contribution to the debate, top-notch academics from Harvard University not only argue that the new higher capital requirements ought to be enthusiastically embraced, but go further by opining against the long phasing-in of the new requirements. The long transition all the way to 2019 is unnecessary and potentially harmful, posited the professors.[11] Much better to demand substantial infusions of fresh new capital right away. Contrary to many bankers' assertions, more capital should not automatically lead to reduced or dearer bank lending, given that more capital makes banks safer institutions and thus their financing costs should not rise up too much (as shareholders and creditors demand lower returns than would be the case in a capital-lite environment).

Another ivory-tower study, the result of the combined brainpower of brainiacs from Harvard and the University of Chicago,[12] highlights a key drawback of insufficient bank capital: namely, the possibility of crisis-igniting asset fire-sales. If just one lightly capitalized bank gets into trouble and decides to shrink its asset holdings as a response rather than try to raise fresh capital out there, such dumping may not lead to overall troubles. That is, the problem remains at a "micro" rather than a "macro" level. But what if multiple financial firms get hit at once? What if the asset dump is generalized, rather than isolated? This could lead to a credit crunch, when the asset sale takes the form of reduced lending, or to a sudden market meltdown if the liquidation focuses on trading-related positions (which may be illiquid and thus drop even more in value). Obviously the worst scenario in this respect would be one where all banks hold little capital and own the same type of toxic assets, a scenario that as we know VaR is uniquely equipped to deliver.

Naturally, a pretty effective way to avoid the dreadful effects from such balance-sheet shrinkage would be to prevent the balance-sheet shrinkage from taking place by making banks hold lots more capital so that the desired capital ratio is maintained even if banks are hit by a decently sized shock: the capital buffer should be, in principle, sufficient to withstand the losses without having to engage in asset dumping in order to retain a given capital-to-assets ratio (say your desired, or mandatory, target ratio is 8 percent and you want to be able to withstand a loss in the value of your assets of 4 percent; then you should keep a 12 percent ratio just in case). Also, the more capitalized you are the easier it should be for you to raise extra capital should the need arise, particularly if your capital base is prominently made up of true (truly loss-absorbing, or more junior) common equity capital. Finally, banks could be required by policy makers to post up specific amounts of capital rather than abide by a mandated minimum capital-to-assets ratio; this is the approach actually favored by the Harvard-Chicago economists, forcing banks to raise capital in a tangible manner and up to the limits deemed prudent while avoiding the shortcomings associated with the capital ratio approach, such as the reliance on the fluffy concept of "risk-weighted" assets and the often fluffy criteria behind the determination of such weights (as we know, total capital could not rise or even go down as a higher capital ratio is mandated if banks decide to switch their positions into assets that happen to be endowed with lower risk weights; a badly designed system that showers negligible risk weights on certain asset families can lead to infinitesimal total capital, no matter how tough the capital rules may appear to be).

Fine, but at what cost sufficient capital? Better put, at what cost sufficient *real* equity capital? The answer from the Harvard–Chicago alliance is blunt: While increased capital requirements might be expected to have some long-run impact on the cost of loans, this impact is likely to be quite small. This, of course, flies in the face of conventional wisdom, that invariably states that equity should be quite costlier than debt for the well-rehearsed reasons (equity investment is riskier and thus should command a premium, interests on debt unlike dividends on equity are tax deductable, very cheap short-term borrowings may be amply available, the supply of equity capital may be limited). But the academic contrarians nonetheless stand their ground and stubbornly hold on to their main assertion, on two main conceptual grounds: First, the riskiness of equity investing should go down as a bank's leverage goes down (in a self-feeding process, the less debt in your capital structure the cheaper equity financing should be and thus the more equity you can afford to issue); second, the tax costs from substituting debt with equity should not be that taxing (borrowing from their example, if we assume a debt coupon of 7 percent and a 35 percent corporate tax rate, each percentage point of increased equity raises the weighted average cost of capital by 7 percent * 35 percent = 0.0245 percent; thus, even a 10 percent points increase in equity would increment capital costs by less than 25 basis points, a decidedly modest impact).

On top of the conceptual claims against the hypothesis that enhanced equity capital requirements will mechanically lead to more expensive credit for the average Joes that fuel a nation's consumption and for the average companies that produce real goods and employ real people, the Harvard–Chicago team also points at historical evidence. Banks, you see, used to be way more capitalized in the past. In the 1850s, book equity stood at 40 percent to 50 percent assets for

U.S. commercial banks. By 1900 the ratio was still at almost 20 percent. The descent into below-10 percent figures only happened in the 1940s. Surely, if the conventional storyline is to be adhered to, this phenomenon must have translated into much cheaper bank credit, right? And yet, the academics find no detectable correlation, in spite of such pronounced historical developments.

But if more equity capital should not, by itself, equate with vastly enhanced financing costs, why do banks (the larger ones in particular) have at least in more modern times shown an insatiable thirst for leverage? "*If significant increases in capital ratios have only small consequences for the rates that banks charge their customers,*" ask the researchers, "*why do banks generally feel compelled to operate in such a high-leveraged fashion, in spite of the risks it poses? And why do they deploy armies of lobbyists to fight increases in their capital requirements? After all, non-financial firms tend to operate with much less leverage and appear willing to forgo the tax (or other) benefits of debt finance altogether.*"[13] In a word, Harvard-Chicago states, competition. Due to banking's intrinsic nature, cost of funding becomes a powerful source of competitive advantage. The most important edge for a bank over its competitors may be its ability to obtain cheaper funding. This is in sharp contrast with other industries (think computer manufacturers) where relative funding costs are unlikely to be the deciding factor when determining which entities come on top and are more profitable. Although this argument seems to make sense, it is also obvious that all banks benefit from more accommodative capital regulation (i.e., they can all at the same time enjoy higher leverage) so the competition angle may not be the main reason why the aggressive lobbying has taken place. Rather, competing entities would yearn for lower capital requirements not so much as a selfish pathway toward the attainment of individual, sink-your-enemy comparative advantages but as a colluding way to collectively achieve an identical individual benefit, namely rosier returns on equity. This may not give any particular bank any extra edge over the rest, but it does guarantee that the entire group enjoys something golden: the turbo-charged reputational and monetary rewards that come with disclosing outstandingly high return–on–equity (ROE).

Further academic evidence against the "enhanced bank capital requirements will sink the world" verdict comes from yet another notorious academic institution, Stanford University. In a truly contrarian analysis, three scholars from Stanford's Graduate School of Business (together with a fourth contributor from Germany's highly-regarded Max Planck Institute)[14] ruthlessly refuse to embrace the pervasive notion that equity financing is more expensive, labeling the arguments typically made to support such sacrosanct view as "fallacious, irrelevant, or very weak." Therefore, enhanced capital demands on banks should not impact the availability and cost of credit, and should not have a deleterious social effect. Given, on the other hand, how deleterious excessive bank leverage can be, the Stanford–Max Planck foursome concludes that raising equity requirements higher (particularly *significantly* higher) should entail a huge net social benefit.

The U.S.–Germanic professorial alliance ruthlessly decapitates, one by one, the most commonly heard bromides against the wisdom of asking banks for more equity. For example, it is often argued that capital held for regulatory purposes would be wasted capital, as it sits idle in the bank's balance sheet without playing any useful role. But this confuses bank capital with bank reserves. Bank capital refers to how banks fund themselves (the debt–equity mix) and thus their activities. It is not uselessly and idly "set aside," but rather forms the funding foundation that enables banks to do, hopefully useful, stuff (like lending or accumulating trading assets). Far from being relegated to an irrelevant role, capital allows banks to actually be active.

What about the also-familiar claim that banks' funding costs would go up because equity requires a higher rate of return than debt? Nonsense, blurt out the professors. Just like their Harvard-Chicago colleagues, the Stanford–Max Planck tag team counterpunch that equity's risk premium must decline as equity gains share in the bank's capital structure, given that the bank is now in principle a more solid, less vulnerable entity (possibly also resulting in a cheaper cost of debt as a result). In their own words, "*Any argument or analysis that holds fixed the required return on equity when evaluating changes in equity capital requirements is fundamentally flawed.*"[15] The overall funding costs of a bank should remain constant even as the more expensive equity component goes up relative to the cheaper debt component, because as more equity is accumulated the cost of equity should go down.

Okay, but won't banks' ROE drop like a stone thus erasing value for shareholders? In good times ROE would go down with less leverage

(ROE would raise in bad times though; any given negative return would now be measured against a larger capital pile, meaning less bad news per unit of equity), but shareholders would be compensated by the solidity brought about by that reduction in indebtedness, so overall they shouldn't feel worse off. Also, whoever said that ROE is a good proxy of bank performance, especially in relative terms? We should rather focus more on return on assets (ROA). A highly leveraged bank with a superior ROE than a better-capitalized competitor may in fact present a much inferior ROA than its more prudent counterpart: Bank A with ROA of 6.5 percent and 10 percent capital would enjoy a better ROE than Bank B with 7 percent ROA and 20 percent capital, but would that allow us to categorize A as more productive than and superior to B?

And, won't bank lending be cut back as a result of more stringent equity demands? Not necessarily. Banks could still go on doing exactly the same things, only now those activities would be financed less via debt and more via equity. As long as a bank can raise the extra required capital, it can keep in place all the assets, including loans, it previously had. If more equity than the minimum regulatory requirement is raised, the new funding structure could actually lead to an asset expansion, including perhaps an expansion in lending. So let's not automatically assume that increasing the size of the equity cushion per se limits a bank's activity. In fact, an equity-challenged banking industry is what can really, truly lead to a crippling credit crunch: Undercapitalized banks that get in trouble because of their undue leverage are in no good position to satisfy the demand for loans from industrial companies or from individuals (witness the 2007–2008 crisis, when the mother of all leverages led, predictably, to the mother of all credit crunches). Anyway, quality may be more important than quantity. The Stanford-Max Planck professors argue that more leveraged banks make less appropriate lending decisions and are incentivized to take on more risky positions, possibly because the gains afforded by leverage make high-yielding daring plays extra enticing. It follows that better capitalized banks will engage in more appropriate lending; this may lead to reductions in the overall amounts of lending (as "bad" loans are discarded), but could still well be beneficial to the economy. In their own words:

Equity holders in a leveraged bank, and managers working on their behalf or compensated on the basis of ROE, have incentives to make excessively risky investments, especially when the debt has government guarantees. Under significantly higher capital requirements, banks would be more likely to make better, more economically appropriate, lending decisions and engage less in either too much or too little lending from a social perspective. To the extent that banks can quickly get to the point of being better capitalized, there should be no concern with any negative impact on the economy of increased equity capital requirements.[16]

If all those contrarians (the Basel Committee, the Harvard-Chicago-Stanford-Max Planck academics, the Brookings Institution) unafraid to counter conventional wisdom by bombarding the "higher bank capital demands will lead to an economic downfall" dogma are to be believed, then a regulatory system based less on mathematical gimmicks and more on commonsensical appraisements (one that, again, should in principle result in better capitalized banks) would help avoid the unpleasantness derived from excessive leverage with negligible collateral damage. Although the minus side (reduced lending, more expensive lending, asset dumping) would be expected to be of a limited dimension, the plus side would be exceedingly beneficial. Can we actually calculate the size of said benefits? Just like we earlier showed various numerical estimates of the potential negative impact of higher capital, is it possible to estimate the potential *positive* impact of more prudent capital rules? In other words, can we measure the gains to be had from not endowing VaR with regulatory powers?

Naturally, we intuitively fully perceive the boon to be had from a not-wildly-leveraged banking industry. Mountainous gearing can quickly and suddenly sink a bank. Distress in one institution can quickly spread to others. All this leads in turn to recession-depression and to taxing government rescues. If the 2007–2008 crisis showed something it's how creepily true the above statements are. Let's now try to back those intuitive conclusions with some numerical support.

We draw once more on the Basel Committee itself. In an August 2010 report, the Committee reached the conclusion that a significant positive net economic benefit would result from the enforcing of its new capital rules. Such net gain derives mainly from a reduced probability of banking crises (and the associated loss in output) thanks to higher capital standards. And this even while assuming that the potential costs from the new policies would be close to its upper bound (for instance, banks in the study are expected to pass all costs on to borrowers in their entirety and to maintain their pre-reform ROE figures). What's more, the report concluded that such large net benefits would still take place under truly stringent capital demands, such as requiring banks to hold equity capital in excess of 10 percent or even 15 percent of risk-weighted assets.

The August 2010 study makes two main calculations: one, the probability of a banking crisis; and two, the discounted economic cost of a banking crisis. The output saved by preventing a banking crisis can thus be obtained by multiplying the reduction in the probability of a meltdown times the projected cost from the meltdown. Borrowing from a bunch of academic exercises, including those that do and do not allow for the possibility of permanent effects from a crisis, it is concluded that the median cumulative economic loss from a banking catastrophe would be 63 percent of the precrisis GDP level (the figure becomes around 20 percent when working under the hypothesis that economic activity is affected only temporarily). That is, for every 1 percent point reduction in the annual probability of a crisis we would obtain an expected benefit of 0.63 percent (or 0.2 percent) of GDP per year. That is economic production that would otherwise be lost, probabilistically speaking.

So how far can more conservative capital requirements diminish the chance of a banking disaster? Although the econometric wizardry behind the analysis should be taken with a pinch of salt (like with any such analytical games in the social sciences), a consistent result across the different models relied on is a significant reduction in the likelihood of a banking crisis at higher levels of capitalization. A ratio of equity capital to risk-weighted assets of 7 percent is equated with a 4.5 percent probability of crisis, roughly what historical evidence would dictate (a nasty episode happens to take place every 20 years give or take). Going from a 7 percent to an 8 percent ratio would lower the chances of mayhem to just 3 percent. If the capital ratio reaches 11 percent, we "should" expect a systemic bank failure only once every 100 years. Want to set that probability at essentially zero? Force banks to suffer a 15 percent capital target. After that, the marginal benefits from yet higher requirements kind of plateau.

If the Basel August 2010 report's estimations are to be trusted, it seems clear from the above numbers that the gross economic benefits from less accommodating capital regulations would be tantalizing (and not just in terms of prevention of output losses; the volatility of output would also be limited by stronger capital bases that absorb losses better during bad times and that restrains lending during good times, thus smoothing the credit cycle and consumption and investments). What about the *net* benefits? Assuming, as was said before, that any higher funding costs for banks would be passed on by raising loan rates (100 percent pass-through), that the cost of equity capital should mirror its rather generous precrisis average, and that the relative costs of equity and debt financing are not affected by banks being more prudently capitalized, each percentage point increase in the capital ratio is determined to result in a median increase in lending spreads of 13 basis points; if those putative assumptions don't hold (for instance if rather than engage in 100 percent pass-through to borrowers banks retain internally some of the new regulatory capital costs) that increase would naturally be lower than 13 bps. How would such rise in the cost of financial intermediation translate in terms of economic activity? The report states that a 1 percent point increase in the capital ratio translates through that conduit into a median 0.09 percent output reduction per year. Based on this, we can now approximate the net expected long-run annual economic windfall from adopting a tougher policy stance *à la* Basel III: If the capital ratio goes from 7 percent to 8 percent the net expected benefit would be 0.90 percent of GDP; if we jump to a 10 percent ratio then the gains would net 1.70 percent output growth; if we dare to go to a 15 percent ratio then we get an economic improvement equal to 1.90 percent of GDP.

Those are quite impressive estimates. That's a lot of output that may have otherwise been lost in the face of banking setbacks caused by too much leverage. Notwithstanding the fact that those estimations are bound to be inexact, they let us put a numerical face to the economic torment that a leverage-enabling tool like VaR can fuel. And it's not a pretty picture.

■　■　■

It is obvious from our earlier analysis that many elite finance academics don't like bank leverage and consider a financial regulator's primary role to make sure that such gearing doesn't go too far. Contrarians even among contrarians, they don't even feel that the Basel III efforts to increase equity capital are in the vicinity of enough. "*While moving in the right direction,*" they say of the new rules, "*Basel III still allows banks to remain very highly leveraged. We consider this very troubling.*"

I have been positively surprised by the professors' candor and their brave contrarianism when it comes to the capital debate. And not just the academics cited above. In late 2010, for instance, a much larger group of distinguished financial economists (including some of the field's most sacred cows, and even a Nobel winner) wrote a public letter to the *Financial Times*[17] staunchly defending the position that much-needed higher equity requirements won't lead to social and economic malaise, nor will they place an insufferable cost burden on banks.

But I wonder if the finance theorists realize the implications that their arguments have in terms of the use of theoretical models in finance. Naturally, for the past 15 years capital requirements have been based on models. These models, not surprisingly given their flaws, have enabled unlimited leverage and have allowed banks to trot along equity-free. So an argument for equity should automatically imply an argument against said models. And an argument against said models should imply at the very least a very serious rethinking of the overall role of models in finance. Among other things, the models used for regulatory capital include some of the ideologies and tools held most sacrosanct by theoreticians. If those models fail (because they inexcusably sanction too little equity) then those ideologies and tools fail. If those fail, what does that say about the discipline of finance theory?

Shouldn't these valiant profs take the leap from "more equity is good net net, leverage is bad net net" into "theoretical finance has failed us much too much, let's rethink how we teach and what we publish"? I understand that for many that may be a contrarian bridge too far, but it would nonetheless be a positive development not just in the aid for truth but also from a social point of view (it is obvious to these academics that bank leverage is a horrible thing that causes untold mayhem, so fighting those tools that abet the monster should be a good deed, right?).

Some outside of hard-core academicism have made that leap several times. Nassim Taleb, that very notable and veteran critic of the mathematics behind regulatory capital models and that early predictor of the havoc that such analytics would wreak, is an obvious example. I, much more humbly, am another. Wouldn't it be nice if über-prestigious tenured ivory-towerists too chose to leap forward?

Finale

The Perils of Making the Simple Too Complex

Wh
en you think about it, financial risk is a simple discipline. Or rather, a discipline that ought to be based on fairly simple tenets: Financial risk is not measurable or forecastable, the past is not prologue, battle-scarred experience-honed intuitive wisdom should be accorded utmost notoriety, certain assets are intrinsically riskier than others, too much leverage should be avoided, and too much toxic leverage should be banned. When one examines old-age risk rulebooks, like the Net Capital Rule or Basel I, it is easy to detect all those uncomplicated principles. Imperfect as they surely were, the ancient guides did not betray the simplicity of risk. They treated risk as something fairly simple that deserved aptly simplistic treatment. Not too many complications, not too many weird assumptions. Nothing too fancy, nothing too out of the ordinary. Stuff that anyone could understand.

Imperfect as simple risk rules can be, they help avoid very bad outcomes. Just by abiding by them you should do all right, keep yourself

213

alive. It is when the simple gets improperly complicated that very bad things can happen. It can make you forget the sacred lessons detailed above. Worse, it can make you embrace their opposites as gospel. The main problem with complicating a simple field is the amount of noise that is introduced into the decision-making process, contaminating and polluting what was a purer environment. The picture gets irremediably blurred, people lose focus lost in the ocean of equations and soon no one is thinking straight. Consider the enormous amounts of papers and books on quantitative risk models circulating out there. What if all of those technical gymnastics amounted to nothing? What if (as some posit) no single sensible insight, accurate metric, or on-the-mark prediction could be distilled out of the ocean of mathematical and statistical symbols? Then the pollution of the risk process would be unacceptably exaggerated, prohibitively dangerous. Financial risk is too important to allow ourselves to be distracted by misguiding complexity that confuses us and leads to weird actions.

■ ■ ■

It shouldn't be surprising that those who most fervently abide by the complex tools may have a tendency to take bad risks and to blow up. By focusing on guidelines that are destined to prove misguiding (trying to find quantifiable precision where quantifiable precision doesn't dare to tread would be a hopeless task), those folks take their eye off the ball, their reasoning gets clouded, focusing on fantastical depictions of financial reality rather than on financial reality itself. Instead of abiding by the simple, true, disaster-proof risk principles described earlier, complex operators may well end up embracing the complete opposite: false, chaos-enabling dictums. Through complexity, a parallel universe is created, far distant from the real one where stocks and derivatives are traded. In essence, complex operators fly the markets blind (worse than that, under false pretenses; like venturing into Nepal with a map of the Sahara). That's why so many times what was seen as risk-lite via the complex lenses was risk-loaded in truth.

By respecting the simplicity of risk, you can avoid lots of trouble. If you humbly accept that numerical precision is not feasible, you won't base your decisions on models that promise numerical precision.

If you humbly accept that the past is not prologue, you won't base your decisions on models that use the past as prologue. If you humbly accept that some assets are intrinsically more daring than others, you won't trust models that deem those assets trouble-free. Simplistic people would not have bought into VaR's or the credit agencies' generous assessments of subprime CDOs. Why not then humbly abide by the conservative and reality-grounded simple principles of financial risk, instead of being distracted by complex inventions that can't work? Those distractions take you away from the righteous path, prevent you from doing the proper thing, make you dazed and confused.

The final outcome is bad: dominance of tools that are condemned to fail combined with the excreting of prudent simple approaches. Never had financial risk been more formally studied, quantified, and discussed as in the three decades before the subprime meltdown. Thousands of former scientists switched careers and became risk analysts, scores of academic courses on the subject flourished, global risk professional associations sprung up, conferences and debates took place every week, the chief risk officer figure was born and accorded ever more stardom. And yet, the final result was the worst market cataclysm ever. The impact of the complexification was not neutral; rather it shaped the outcome. All those courses, all those conferences, all that scientification mercilessly eroded the idea that risk is simple and ruthlessly redefined it as a complex endeavor. Soon, the complexity version permeated it all. An entire financial system was predicated on voodoo.

One could say that complexity had a bigger constituency, or at least a more active one. Many had much to gain from the unsimplifying of finance. For some, the glorification of complexity was an aid in the battle to have VaR crowned capital king. For others, it could justify entire professions and support entire careers. On the other hand, the benefits to be derived from a simpler path were not obvious (who exactly gains personally from a nonleveraged banking industry?). Those most negatively affected by the complexification of financial activity (pension funds that invest in toxic waste deemed riskless by the models, innocent taxpayers that shoulder the bailout and the government spending cuts) are not an organized lot and are not in the know as to the forces that shape the markets; they can't oppose and prevent complexity because they never knew it was happening in the first place.

Mary Kate Stimmler, a PhD candidate at the Hass School of Business at the University of California Berkeley, has conducted extensive research on the impact of complexification in financial decision making.[1] She concludes that the adoption of risk-based metrics by banks led to greater risk taking. Borrowing from data on all publicly traded U.S. banks from 1994 to 2008, she demonstrates that when banks employed new ways of measuring uncertainty, they became increasingly risk tolerant. Using software specifically designed for extracting risk-based metrics and other risk terminology from annual financial statements, Stimmler counts every use of risk-based metrics (such as VaR), qualitative description of risk, and discussion of risk management within annual reports. Using her bespoke model, she finds that the more a bank measures risk, the more risk-seeking it becomes and the more it increases its leverage. The conclusion is a familiar one: The organizational adoption of models alters the framing of firm-level decision making. The mere presence of VaR inside trading floors shapes the types of actions taken by traders and their executives. The same individual will act differently based on whether VaR is around or not. Complexity changes minds. Complexity determines outcomes.

Of course, we know that there is a very good explanation for Mary Kate Stimmler's findings: The metrics adopted in the period under study led to greater risks and leverage because those particular metrics happen to have an in-bred structural capacity to hide and to underestimate risk and to produce untold gearing levels. VaR was the leading risk metric in 1994–2008 and VaR leads to a lot of risk and a lot of leverage, so any such analysis would inevitably conclude that the use of risk models by banks unleashes risk and leverage. VaR yielded tons of risk and tons of leverage because that was precisely the point.

But we can go beyond the coincidental to the generalized. Having concrete numerical precision around can encourage recklessness, independent of the actual intrinsic characteristics of the models. People become more confident, more complacent, more sure of themselves. Risk models fool people into convincing themselves that they have conquered and subjugated the wild beast of risk. People feel invincible—of a superior intelligence. They are not at the mercy of events for they can visualize the future through their quantitative magic goggles. Timidity is rejected and frowned on, daringness is applauded and rewarded. Prudence is for the weak, the antiquated, the innumerate. With mathematical certainty comes bravery. Grab the modeling sword, jump onto the quantification horse and gallantly charge the market fields. Risk models incite and intoxicate those looking for glory. When you believe a game to be statistically and mathematically tamable, rather than something in which output is impossibly uncertain and unforeseeable, you naturally will tend to commit more money to it. You con yourself into believing that you can understand, that you can calculate odds, that you know the probabilities. This sounds better than resigning yourself to the fact that it's all a mystery wrapped up in an enigma. Interestingly, Stimmler points out that training in financial economics steers people into embracing alternatives that are clothed in the complexity veil. Those whose education has been more complex may have an innate tendency to choose that which looks complex, over what looks simplistic. Using laboratory experiments, she finds that finance-educated individuals take greater risks when these are explained with complex mathematical models than when they are explained with simplified models that are identical in meaning. On the other hand, individuals without an educational background in finance take the same amount of risk regardless of how the choices are framed. These studies show that the bias is unique to the culture of finance: It affects only individuals with a finance education and only when the decisions in question are related to financial investments. If it's complex it must be truer and more commendable, the indoctrinated would inevitably believe. This psychological trait is dangerous for the obvious reason: It makes it easier for bad models to filter through into practice, unopposed and unquestioned. As I've said before, a lot of the popularity of VaR is explained by its mathematical decor, especially in the key early days: many people have been taught to unquestionably kneel at the sight of elaborated quantitative finance machines.

The appearance of complexity in the form of convoluted theoretical models expanded the boundaries of what was considered predictable in finance, posits Stimmler. This had institutional ramifications. Institutional logic went from risk mitigation, where the goal is to avoid and minimize risk, to risk management, where the goal is to measure risk. Through a study of finance textbooks from 1961 to 2008, she charts the effects that this development had on the ways risk and uncertainty were taught within finance. She finds that standardized recommendations that firms set aside prescribed amounts of capital to cover risk were incrementally replaced with equations that assumed that the future likelihood of events could be accurately calculated. The quantification of finance education was a key driver in the diffusion of the new risk management logic, until it became indelibly embedded within practice.

Stimmler's psychological explanation for the embracement of complex paths in finance is perhaps even more worrying than the alternative cynical explanation. Many see naked self-interest behind the adoption and promotion of constructs like VaR: Those who embraced the models did so under no mathematical illusions (they knew the models were unsound), but had too much to gain from widespread acceptance of the models, so they kept their reservations to themselves.

But what Stimmler seems to say goes beyond that: Complexity per se can be an addiction that blinds people and contaminates decision-making processes. Folks may actually believe in the model simply because of the model being a model. The theoretical and quantitative dogmatism of the finance education schools may have produced deluded indoctrinees, not calculating cynics with an agenda. Those educated in advanced analytical finance methods may find it impossible to act in disagreement with the dogma. Even contact with the real world may prevent them from realizing how unworldly the complex tenets can be. Nassim Taleb and Gorge Martin found in 1998 that all the finance and quantitative economics professors from major universities whom they tracked down and who got involved in hedge fund trading ended up making bets against extreme market events, those deemed impossibly improbable by the standard Nobel-endowed finance theory that has ruled supreme around campus since the 1950s, and yet so obviously recurrent in reality. This wasn't random, as less than half of nonacademics took similar bets. These professors, by religiously obeying the complex theories that they had been taught before they taught them to others, exposed themselves to highly likely blowups. Taking the simple path (opening their eyes to the inescapable true behavior of real markets) may have been anathema to them. Abiding by the simple rules of risk may appear intolerably rustic. Lemmas-devoid simplistic reasoning may have been exorcised out of them a long time ago, upon solving one too many stochastic differential equations. It's as if not following the path dictated by theory would amount to unforgiveable treason, even after you've stepped out of the classroom and into the dirty real world. A misguided sense of loyalty to sacred academic lecturing may prevent you from exercising free will, from reasoning your way out of a condemned course of action. You force yourself to trek to Nepal with a mathematically designed map of the Sahara as only guide, because that's what you learned at school. If someone tried to talk you out of your confused ways and hand you a map of Nepal, you would dismiss them as backward luddites who don't believe in technological progress. While the map of Nepal has no equations on it, the map for the Sahara is full of them. And that, you'd say, is what makes it subliminally superior and that's why you are going to rely exclusively on it.

Fanatical believers in flawed financial models present more of a threat than cynical defenders of flawed financial models. For while the latter may be reined in, the former may be beyond salvation. And if too many of them spread around, the markets and the economy at large may become terminally infected.

■ ■ ■

Before VaR showed up, financial risk management was a simple affair. The rules respected the simplicity of it all, were unpretentious. They saw reality for what it was, not for what it should be. They made no claims to have been able to discover the deeper truths of finance through numerical wizardry. They were humble, not hubristic. They were robustly rigid, not fluffy and malleable. Risk was sometimes badly captured and underestimated, but not in a structural way. Some things were wrong, but the foundations were right. They didn't overtly facilitate trouble. They were like a stern, circumspect, penny-conscious parent: unexciting perhaps, but the family was unlikely to be ruined.

In contrast, VaR was more like the charming, flashy, spendthrift uncle: irresistibly glamorous, but prone to drowning under the weight of debts taken on to finance an overextended lifestyle. The ostentatious complexity, the flamboyant analytics seduced the world into abandoning the old prudent ways. The extravagant relative, not the responsible parent, was put in charge of the household. Rules were turned upside down. Lots of expensive trading toys were purchased on credit. Champagne flowed, no one saved a dime. VaR erased the simple rules, went against them, and that is why the losses eventually and inevitably experienced by the banking family weren't understated at all.

Almost 30 years since Kenneth Garbade at Bankers Trust began building VaR–type models, more than 20 years since Ray May and Michael Eindhoven had the meeting that gave birth to JP Morgan's VaR, and more than 15 years since Till Guldiman released his version of the JP Morgan VaR to the world and bewitched global regulators, what is the verdict on the model? If you have followed this book attentively, you already know my take: VaR overall has been a very negative influence, and we would be better off without it. It may have some use for risk control issues, but it can't have a predominant role and certainly not a policymaking role.

Let's weigh the evidence. VaR, its defenders typically posit, was a beneficial discovery for several key reasons: Its calculation enhances internal knowledge as to a bank's risk taking and portfolio composition; it can be applied to any asset class; it is very easy to understand; it can make comparing positions and institutions very convenient; it creates a single unified risk language for the industry; it can help detect market trends; it drinks from actual market intelligence. Even those quantitative risk managers who are willing to concede that VaR won't get risk right and that statistical analysis of market activity is bound to be hopelessly inexact (thus essentially admitting that the informational content of the VaR number won't be worth much), would point at those above side benefits as proof that the model should be kept around.

Would those positives compensate for the negatives? I don't think so, by far. A tool that can lead to 100-to-1 or even 1,000-to-1 trading book leverage, that can proclaim as worry-free the most lethal financial assets ever devised by humankind, and that can underperform so savagely as risk estimator as to experience 10 or more times mis–predictions of losses (the bad news happened 10 or more times more often than the model foresaw) shouldn't dominate any risk control toolkit, let alone any regulatory playbook. VaR not only totally missed the worst market crisis ever, it decisively helped create it. How can we keep such an instrument in our midst, in a powerful position no less? Are we for crises or against crises? Are we for robustness or for fragility? Are we for safety or for disaster? Are we for prosperity or for mass unemployment? Are we for secure banks or for imperiled banks? Are we for capitalism or for chaos? A tool born to hide and misrepresent risk and born to aid those who wake up every morning with a desire to take on the most reckless exposures no matter the social cost of such actions cannot be given credence and cannot be relied on. Placing the fate of the world in VaR's hands is among the most irresponsible decisions to have ever been taken. If our worst enemy wanted to do us harm and destabilize our lives, they would begin by installing VaR as risk radar and as capital king. When did we become our own worst enemies?

I am willing to admit that VaR may have made some sense at the beginning. Even more than that: The original creation of VaR would have been amply justified, and those who took part in it were performing work that needed to be performed. Market risk was growing massively in size and complexity in the late 1980s and early 1990s, why not try to design a universal risk model? The hours spent at that chore would have been hours well spent. Risk is so important that it should be attacked from several angles, even if you intuitively distrust the power of analytics in finance. However, that same process should at the same time have awakened people as to the potential damages to be wrought by VaR. It should have been clear from early on that the promising mathematical baby could very easily transform into a destructive out-of-control Frankenstein. The VaR effort, while initially necessary, should have been short-lived. Rather than derive into the global imperial dominance of a flawed mechanism with in-bred appetite for destruction, the original VaR adventure should have led to the conviction that modeling market risk in that fashion was bound to be wildly inaccurate and possibly wildly troublesome. The manufacturing of VaR should have led to the conclusion that VaR should be scrapped. Ray May and Sir Dennis Weatherstone tried to tackle very serious issues and embarked on a worthy cause, but the conclusions were all wrong: If VaR has shown something it is not so much that its invention was a criminal mistake, but that its ongoing adoption has been a crime. VaR needed to be invented and then it needed to be promptly discarded, once the really important questions had been asked and answered ("Can this go bad? How? Can risk be underestimated? How and by how much?"). The obscenity was not to have VaR around in 1990.

The obscenity was to still have it around in 1995. The latest mega-crisis should be the catalyst that forces financiers, academics, and policy-makers to ask themselves a very simple question prior to considering the adoption and embracement of a theoretical concoction: Can this model lead to financial, economic, and social harm? Any quantitative construct should be put to that test, and mercilessly vetoed if the answer is unsatisfactory. If there's any positive outcome from the latest disaster, let that be the one.

Guest Contributions

Why Was VaR Embraced?

A Q&A with Nassim Taleb

*I*t's July 2011. The waters from the VaR-enabled flood have receded, if only a bit. The time for alarm and shock has, somewhat, subsided. The time for reflection can thus begin. Which is why I asked veteran option trader and best-selling author Nassim Taleb to participate in a brief Q&A on the crisis and the malfunctioning risk tool he so loudly warned about so many years ago. In so doing, I wanted to close the chronological circle: In 1995 he publicly alerted the world, in vain. What is there to say 16 years later, his prescience now so obvious? How could all this destruction happen? Taleb was the loudest and most prominent VaR skeptic. His warnings, in fact, make him the true predictor of the 2007 cataclysm (he even foresaw the necessity of a public bailout). He is thus most suited to tackle this perplexing issue.

Q: Why was VaR adopted for so long, and why is VaR still in use?

NT: Principally, there is a moral hazard/agency problem. An academic is never penalized for selling you something, unlike a pharmaceutical company. Nor is a risk vendor. A software vendor can thus replace heuristics accumulated over years. When things work, it is their idea, and they sell more of the stuff, when it fails they have no downside. We need to remove people's free option at the expense of society by making them liable.

The problem we had is not just VaR, but the rise of quants in replacement of more heuristically oriented, more realistic practitioners. It is the wedge between declarative knowledge (simplistic) and more complicated class of know-how you can't transmit without experience because it is too rich.

A professor of finance can teach VaR, not experience. Hence the charlatanism.

But there is the "it gets jobs" problem. What I witnessed teaching in various programs was depressing; students in math finance wanted math, not finance, and certainly not knowledge. They were interested in learning what would get them jobs, not truth. And the faculty sold them what they needed to get jobs hence helped blow up the economy.

Q: You saw this crisis coming many years ago, by warning about VaR. Why weren't your warnings heeded?

NT: First, people individually accepted my ideas—but collectively they could not. There is the mechanism of diffusion of responsibility that you and I have discussed in the past. There is the "other people use it" effect.

Secondly, there is the problem of professional associations such as the very dangerous CFA (Certified Financial Analysts) institute or the smaller but toxic IAFA International Association of Financial Engineers. They never suspended teaching or promoting modern finance techniques such as portfolio theory and giving them the stamp of "professional toolkit"—their argument seems to be that there are no other techniques (heuristics are teachable by experience and apprenticeship, not through such method of certification). These associations do not realize that they are making people take risks they would not otherwise take.

Q: Where do you see the solution?

NT: I learned from reading the heuristics research that, in effect, complex problems require simple solutions—in a complex world complicated solutions bring more problems, hence swelling bureaucratic Soviet-style nightmares. My solution is to apply an old principle to eliminate the agency problem:
       Captain goes down with the ship, all captains all ships.

       You should be able to sue—just as (American political activist) Ralph Nader did—any institution that caused harm. This would eliminate the "other people are doing it" argument.

       A bit of background. When I finished *The Black Swan,** I heard all kind of insults, such as "give me something better, I will keep using what I have." But people don't use such fallacious argument when their own life is in danger. They would never accept to be on a plane to the Himalayas if the pilot announces that he has no map on hand, but that he will use the map of Saudi Arabia because "this is the best he has." They would prefer canceling the trip, or even walking to the destination than be on that plane. But in finance they do make such elementary mistakes. What is the reason?

       Well, the reason is that when you fly, the pilot is on the plane, something we don't have in finance. Simply the idea is to put all the pilots on the plane and make them share the downside.

---

*Random House, 2007

A Pioneer Wall Street Rocket Scientist's View

An Essay by Aaron Brown

Aaron Brown is risk manager at AQR, one of the world's leading hedge funds/asset managers, and the author of The Poker Face of Wall Street *(2006)* and Red-Blooded Risk *(2012), both published by John Wiley & Sons, and coauthor of* A World of Chance *(Cambridge University Press, 2008). Brown is one of the top quantitative risk experts on the planet, having made outstanding practical and intellectual contributions. While he has voiced some concerns about VaR in the past, if we had to choose, we'd have to place him firmly in the pro-VaR rather than the anti-VaR camp. Some may then ask, why invite him to contribute to a book that blames VaR for mayhem and misery? Well, I thought readers would benefit mightily. The book is, rightly so, full of "blame VaR" testimonies and evidence (both by me and by a lot of very prominent people), so why not further enrich the experience for readers by offering a differing view? Besides, Aaron Brown was there when the whole VaR thing started and has remained there ever since. And, unlike many diehard VaRistas, he articulates his points seriously, rigorously, respectfully, and with very fine prose. Even if Brown and I seem to disagree on VaR's responsibility and capacity for financial terror, I simply couldn't refuse the reader (and myself) the chance to hear the take of this elite risk pioneer.*

The key discovery that gave birth to Value at Risk (VaR) was not a flash of enlightenment but a slow dawning realization, which is why it is hard to credit it to any specific individual or time. The impetus for the discovery, however, can be located precisely. It was the stock market crash of October 19, 1987. To explain why that was pivotal we have to go back another quarter century to a group of disaffected quants in the 1970s. To understand their disaffection, we have to start more than three centuries farther back, to 1654.

1654 is the year that two great French mathematicians, Blaise Pascal and Pierre Fermat exchanged letters concerning a long-standing problem in mathematics: how to divide a stake in an interrupted dice contest. For example, two players each put up half a stake to be awarded to the first of them to win seven games. The contest is interrupted after one player has won six games and the other player has won five.

Fermat noted that two more games must settle the outcome. Letting W represent a win for the first player, the one with six wins, and L represent a loss, the two games could result in WW, WL, LW, or LL. In practice, in the first two cases the second game would not be played, because the contest would be over. But Fermat argued this did not matter, the stake division would be the same if the players were compelled to play both games. The first player wins in three of the four cases (all but LL), and therefore should get three-fourths of the stake.

Although Fermat was the lawyer, it was Pascal who took a legalistic approach instead. He reasoned from the principle that if the contest is tied, the stake should be split equally. If the first player wins the next game, he is entitled to the entire stake. If the first player loses the next game, the series is tied, so he is entitled to half the stake. You can consider the situation as the first player owns half the stake, because he is entitled to that whether he wins or loses the next game, and the next game is then a contest for the other half of the stake. Thus the first player is entitled to half the stake, plus half of the remaining half, for three-fourths in all.

The emotional high point of the letters is when Pascal realizes the two approaches always give the same answer. This ignited a radical change in thought. I say "ignited" because the change was too rapid to be attributed credibly to the letters themselves. A lot of people must have been thinking along these lines for some time; Fermat and Pascal provided the seed around which these ideas crystalized. Within a decade of 1654, people are poring over lists of raw data like parish birth and death records to gain insight into demographics and policy, explicitly probabilistic analysis becomes common in legal disputes and philosophic writings, statistical methods such as averaging are applied to scientific measurements, the study of probability becomes a recognized subfield of mathematics, actuarial concepts are introduced to annuity pricing and men of affairs adopt conditional reasoning—what we call today "Bayesian" logic—to practical questions.

Confusion

This change in thinking was a major part of the Enlightenment. It was not a discovery, however, it was a confusion of two concepts. Fermat made a mathematical statement about long-term frequency that would be made rigorous by Jakob Bernoulli in *Ars Conjectandi* (*The Art of Conjecturing*, written between 1684 and 1689, but not published until 1713). Pascal made an assertion about what the gamblers should accept as a fair outcome. It's easy to confuse these two things when discussing dice rolls because rational belief has to correspond to long-term frequency. But what about things that cannot be repeated, like who will win the next U.S. Presidential election? Why do we use the same word, "probability" for the long-term frequency of outcomes of repeatable experiments and our degree of belief in an uncertain one-time proposition?

The illogic of confusing these two concepts has been pointed out many times over the centuries, often by people who think they are the first to notice. The most familiar to modern readers is Frank Knight, who said we should use "risk" for the frequency concept and "uncertainty" for degree of belief. John Maynard Keynes made similar points around the same time. A century earlier, the mathematician Siméon Poisson suggested "probability" and "chance" instead. Fifty years before that, the Marquis de Condorcet wanted "facilité" (facility) and "motif de croire" (reason to believe). Rudolph Carnap came up with the über-geeky "probability$_1$" and "probability$_2$" and also "statistical" and "inductive" probability. In the early twentieth century "propensity" and "proclivity" were used, and in the early twenty-first Donald Rumsfeld highlighted the distinction again with "known unknowns" versus "unknown unknowns." Not all of these authors distinguished frequency and degree of belief in the same way, but all agreed there were two types of probability.

Mathematicians struggled to resolve this issue by pushing deeper and deeper into the theory of probability. Unfortunately, by the mid-twentieth century, we had two completely rigorous theories, one based on repeatable experiments and one based on subjective degree of belief. There was no mathematical way to reconcile the two, and no avenues for future research. The interesting work in statistics was being done in nonparametric methods and exploratory data analysis, fields that were weak in consistent theory.

I was one of a group of students with quantitative training who came of age in the 1970s and became known as "rocket scientists." The name is stupid and inaccurate, but it had a different connotation at the time than it does today. The glory of the 1969 Apollo moon landings was still fresh. We admired scientists who actually did things, and participated in adventures, and contributed to all human knowledge, not just their narrow technical field. That's what we all wanted to do.

Rocket scientists were disaffected for many reasons. We felt that most quantitative investigators used bad data and worse logic to come up with conclusions on which they wouldn't bet a nickel. Mathematics was invoked to justify all kinds of dangerous nonsense, and you could get statisticians to testify on both sides of every issue from whether cigarette smoking caused cancer to whether racial discrimination was real. Too many quants regarded their expertise as a fortress to defend rather than a tool for honest inquiry. The world seemed to be going to Hell, and quants were part of the problem, not the solution. No doubt this attitude was exaggerated by youth and inexperience, but I still consider that it was basically correct.

Types of Statisticians

"Frequentist" statisticians who base their methods on long-term probability arguments can't tell you the probability of anything happening. Instead, they can make a statement and (if their assumptions are correct) can tell you the maximum long-run frequency that the statement will be incorrect. For example, a frequentist might tell you he can reject at the 1 percent level that a certain levee will be breached in the next year. That might mean he's done an extensive, careful study. Or it might mean that he put 99 true statements into a hat plus one piece of paper saying, "The levee will not be breached next year." If he drew out the levee statement, he is entirely correct in making his statement. After all, the probability of drawing a false statement out of a hat that contains 100 statements, at least 99 of which are true, is less than or equal to 1 percent. There is nothing in frequentist statistics that requires the statistician to actually know anything about what he's talking. The reliability of a frequentist statistical claim is not determined by the significance level, but by the vigor and sincerity of the falsification effort. Yet the former is required for every academic paper while the latter is often omitted, or is pathetically weak.

The other major camp of theoretical statistics is Bayesianism. It is based on subjective belief. The brilliant Italian mathematician Bruno de Finetti codified it in the 1930s. His favorite example was the probability that there was life on Mars a billion years ago. It might seem that this probability is impossible to define, much less estimate. De Finetti claimed not only that there was a meaningful probability, but that you know what it is. Suppose an expedition will determine the answer tomorrow. There is a security that pays $10 if life indeed existed on Mars one billion years ago. You can pay the price and receive $10 if the answer is yes, or receive the price and pay $10 if the answer is yes. You have to set the price (with a gun to your head if necessary) at which you are indifferent between buying or selling. If that price is $0.10, then you believe the probability is 1 percent.

What rocket scientists realized is that the answer depends on the currency in which you are betting. For example, suppose the expedition to Mars financed itself by issuing bonds in Mars Expeditionary Currency (mecs), which will be used by the colonists. Today, one mec sells for $1. But if life is found to have existed on Mars, the value will shoot up to $10 due to the possibility of useful artifacts or discoveries plus an increased chance that Mars can be made habitable. If you would buy or sell the $10 security for $0.10, logically you have to be willing to pay 10 centimecs (worth $0.10 today) for a security that pays one mec (worth $10 if you get it) if there was life on Mars. So your subjective probability that there was life on Mars one billion years ago is 10 percent measured in mecs and 1 percent measured in dollars. Probability depends on what is at stake. This inconvenient fact is obscured by most statistics texts, which either assume a perfect numeraire that has the same value in all future states of the world, or have only a single thing at stake. Neither assumption is useful for real problems.

Rocket scientists also worried about whom you're betting against; you might quote a different price to an idiot in a bar versus a professional exobiologist versus a little green man who just landed his flying saucer in your backyard. The price you set depends not only on what you believe, but on what you think the person on the other side believes. Even who "you" are matters as your price depends on how you feel about possible future states of the world. Loosely speaking, we decided that the probability that mattered was the one that would clear the market in an open-betting forum of voluntary participants (no guns to anyone's head), set via a mechanism that did not lose money long-term. There could be multiple probabilities for the same event, set by different markets or denominated in different currencies, but the differences among them were constrained by arbitrage considerations. Probabilities always had a bid/ask spread range large enough to prevent market makers from losing money. That doesn't mean just that there is noise in *estimating* probabilities, there is inherent uncertainty in *defining* probabilities. And if you couldn't create or credibly hypothesize an active betting market for a question, its probability was undefined.

It turns out similar considerations apply to frequentist statistics as well. If a frequentist tells you 1,000 things at the 5 percent significance level, it's unlikely that many more than 50 of them are false. But what if the 950 true things are trivial or things you knew already and the 50 false things were crucial unknowns? The frequentist statement is meaningful to someone who cares only about the number of correct statements, such as someone making equal-size bets on each one. A frequentist doesn't have to specify currency and betting participants in order to define a probability, but she needs precisely those things to translate a statement about long-term frequency into a degree of belief useful for a practical decision.

The Rocket Scientist View

I won't go through all the logical twists and turns, but rocket scientists decided there was no such thing as a fully defined probability distribution. Any probability statement, whether frequentist or Bayesian, depended on what was at stake. For practical problems, multiple things will be at stake, so you need some kind of numeraire to relate them all. In simpler words, you need to price everything in some kind of currency. But money cannot buy everything, and there are circumstances in which money becomes worthless. Moreover, relative prices of the things at stake could change in different outcomes. And aside from the theoretical issue, you never really know all possible outcomes, nor exactly how you will feel about them, and you will not have enough data to make meaningful probability estimates of rare events. These are not minor technicalities that affect probability calculations on the margin, these are essential points that go to the heart of statistical theory and practice.

This may seem like an inadequate theory of probability, but it's at least as sensible as the alternatives. To a Bayesian, there's a different probability for each person and in practical applications Bayesians often have to resort to improper priors (probability distributions that do not add up to one) and distributions chosen for mathematical convenience rather than subjective belief. To a frequentist, there's one probability for every experiment and no reason to expect that the significance levels of a set of exhaustive and mutually exclusive statements will add up to one. Frequentist distributions add up to one in theory, but in practice statisticians of all camps exclude outliers from analysis. Sometimes these aberrant observations are data errors or exceptional cases of little interest to the question at hand, sometimes they evidence crucial factors more salient than the variation among normal data points, but either way it rarely makes sense to combine outliers with the rest of the data in the same statistical analysis. In effect there is a probability distribution that only covers the nonoutlying data, and therefore that does not add up to one.

Rocket scientists believed in probability distributions that were consistent with both rational subjective belief and long-term frequency, but that couldn't cover all possible outcomes. Moreover, even within the domain of the probability distribution, probability could not be defined with complete precision. There could be multiple probabilities for the same event, but differences between them were constrained. We believed in precise mathematical optimization wherever probabilities could be defined and estimated, constrained by the requirement to survive the outcomes outside that region.

This view of the world, plus other issues, sent rocket scientists away from academia, government, and business, out in search of quants who would bet on their conclusions, and, crucially, had long-term success taking on all comers. Those among us with frequentist leanings gravitated toward "advantage gambling," playing casino games with the odds in your favor—the best-known example of this is blackjack card counting. These people wanted to earn money from superior predictions of long-term frequency. People said you couldn't beat the house, but quants found we could beat the house.

Rocket scientists who felt more at home with Bayesians moved into sports betting. Quant sports bettors spend little effort worrying about the probability of one team or another winning a game. The easy money is in predicting the subjective beliefs of other bettors. For example, predicting the score in a National Basketball Association game between the Los Angeles Lakers and the Seattle Sonics from first principles is a daunting task. But if you know the game is being played in Los Angeles, a much higher betting town than Seattle, and that the Lakers are a glamorous team with a national following, unlike the Sonics, you don't need to be a genius to figure there will be extra betting pressure on the Lakers. That means the point spread will be adjusted so that it will be favorable to bet on the Sonics. This rule by itself is too simple to work (although bet against the Lakers at home was pretty good in the 1970s) but it illustrates the flavor of the analysis. Quants completely revolutionized the sports betting business.

An advantage gambler, if discovered, is ejected from the casino, or worse. A sports bettor, on the other hand, is the organization's friend. She helps it set more accurate point spreads and she supplies capital to help the organization's books balance so it takes no risk. Advantage gamblers tended to be antisocial loners. They counted on predicting long-term frequency, and feared the actions of people. Sports bettors got along with people, and often joined or started betting businesses. They counted on predicting the actions of people, and feared events like fixes that would skew the frequencies.

I did a little of both of those, but mainly thought of myself as a poker player. In those days that required some social skills. You had to get invited to good games, collect from losers and avoid getting cheated or arrested. You can't be as indifferent to other people as an advantage gambler, but you don't need the skills required to work in a successful organization. A professional poker player had to accept challenges in all kinds of games: backgammon, gin rummy, golf; or sports or proposition bets. If you won someone's money playing poker, you were expected to give him a chance to win it back in some other activity. If you refused you got treated like a hustler, someone only playing for the money, and only at games in which he had an advantage. That happened to be true in my case, but I understood pretending to be a sportsman was one of the conditions for getting invited back. For reasons I feel but cannot explain, pretending to be an unskilled poker player would have been dishonest, but acting like a sportsman was just part of the game. The first would be deliberately misleading people about a fact for profit—fraud—the second was pretending to want to do something I actually did because other people wanted me to— civility. At the table, poker requires both computations of long-term frequency and predictions of what other people will do.

Beat the Street

In the early 1980s, the rocket scientists moved to Wall Street, where there were few quants at the time. We remade finance as thoroughly as we remade gambling. I compare it to the difference between a 1980-era point-and-shoot film camera and a modern digital camera. They look similar. Both have lenses and shutter buttons and flashes. They run on batteries, in some cases the same batteries. People use them to take pictures of vacations and parties and kids. They cost about the same. But to someone building a camera, there is no similarity at all. They work on entirely different principles. Wall Street did not evolve on its own in a manner that induced it to go out and hire quants; quants showed up on Wall Street and changed it on their own.

The frequentist advantage gamblers thought of what they were doing as exploiting market inefficiencies. They thought they could find bets in which they had the edge, and if they made enough of them, long-term frequency virtually guaranteed them a profit. They studied securities, not people. They didn't care who was on the other side of a trade, only what the odds were. The only way they could lose would be if the market got even more irrational and they were forced out of their positions by investors or counterparties. Thus the market was their friend, and people were their potential enemies. As antisocial loners, they tended to form small hedge funds that did not solicit outside money.

The Bayesian sports bettors looked instead for market disequilibria. They thought they could find transactions that should take place but weren't, and that they could earn a profit intermediating them. They concentrated on the people on the other side of trades, not the securities themselves. They wanted to make money predicting the actions of people, and could lose only if the market turned against them. Bayesians went into securitization and found homes in large organizations.

As before, I did a little of both, but preferred a middle way that considered both inefficiencies and disequilibria. People like me ended up at trading desks or running businesses.

For a few years, everything went great. All of us were making lots of money and reengineering finance rapidly. Then came October 19, 1987, which wiped out most of the quants. The surprise was not that the stock market could fall more than twice as much in one day than it ever had before. We knew all about fat tails. None of us were long the stock market. The problem was a complete realignment of prices in all markets, a realignment that seemed fiendishly calculated to destroy quant strategies. Most of us held positions that would have been profitable had we been able to hold on to them, but we couldn't.

People who are not in finance often think of trading opportunities declining smoothly. If an asset is underpriced, for example, smart traders will buy it, forcing the price up to its fair value. In fact, things are messier than that. The price may not move at first, or it might even go down. Then at some point it may jump up far above fair value. It's even more complicated with hundreds of thousands of prices moving all at once. Things tend to realign suddenly and simultaneously, often in entirely unexpected ways. The one generally reliable prediction is that the realignment will hurt the smart money—or the money that is smart in between realignments anyway. The smart money is what's pushing the market, and the market pushes back.

The example I like to use is the earth. Academic studies demonstrate that the market is very efficient, but they necessarily deal with averages of large portfolios over long periods of time. Inefficiencies or disequlibria on the order of 0.1 percent would be too small to measure, yet could amount to $100 billion in a $100 trillion global economy. Similarly, if you shrank the earth to the size of a basketball it would be smoother than a billiard ball, but at a human scale roughness like mountains and oceans make a difference.

One way to exploit a disequilibrium would be to roll rocks down a mountain into the ocean in order to generate energy. As you did this, both the mountain and the ocean would shrink. You would smoothly erode the disequilibrium away. But that's not what people do. They're more likely to harness the water flowing down the mountain to drive water wheels or hydroelectric plants. This does not bring things closer to equilibrium; the water would have flowed down anyway. If anything, it slows the process because you dam up some of the water. Therefore, there's no physical law that says the exploitation cannot go on forever. Similarly, there's no reason to assume that people exploiting market inefficiencies and disequilibria are helping to make the economy more efficient, or that exploiting a market opportunity causes it to go away. Those things do happen, but their opposites can occur as well, at least on some time scale.

Imagine many people exploiting the same river, without coordination. Just as people and institutions in the market do not all have the same numeraire, or the same goal of short-term risk-adjusted profit maximization, people using the river may be generating energy, irrigating crops, protecting against floods, or other things. It's safe to predict that something will upset the best-laid plans of mice and men, but it will not be a smooth process of getting to equilibrium; it will be a disaster like a dam bursting, or river flows higher or lower than anticipated in plans, or pollution from the hydroelectric plant killing enough trees that the river becomes a swamp, or any of a million other possibilities. The disaster will likely wipe out everything built to exploit the river, not just the thing that caused the disaster or gave into it first. Similarly a financial crisis can threaten everyone exploiting inefficiencies, not just the ones that bet against the specific disaster. It's not enough to account for local conditions and plan for specific extreme events, you need to structure things with the knowledge that there will be disasters and that you need to have a strategy that involves surviving them, assessing the changed conditions and rebuilding your business.

This is the kind of fun challenge that delighted rocket scientists. The hunt was on to find quantitative methods that made a lot of money in normal markets and could survive the periodic crises. As usual, we divided into three camps.

Exploring Risk

From the perspective of a frequentist running a small hedge fund, the main issue was capital. You needed enough to get through the realignments. On the other hand, you didn't want too much, as that might require outside investors. This led to a definition of risk as the maximum drawdown you could expect with some defined probability over a period of time, usually a year. It didn't depend on your current positions so much as on your strategy. For example, you might hold a risky portfolio, but have stop losses that you were confident would keep your drawdown below some level. Frequentists compared their drawdown probabilities to bond defaults. For example, if you thought there was only one chance in 200 that your worst drawdown would be $1 million over the next year, and you felt one BBB bond in 200 defaulted every year, you said you needed $1 million of BBB capital to run the strategy. You could see the cost of BBB capital in the market, so you knew your cost of capital as well.

To poker players running trading desks and business, daily profit and loss (P&L) was the focus. We defined risk as the standard deviation, or usually some more robust statistic, of P&L. That came to be known as the "value" camp because we marked everything to market value every day. For technical reasons we actually measured the change in the value of the positions we had held at the beginning of the day and (remember we didn't believe in fully defined probability distributions) specified normal markets. The Bayesians in structured products had a deal cycle longer than daily trading but shorter than hedge fund strategies. They liked measuring risk to earnings. Earnings are designed to be a more accurate assessment of actual economic gains and losses than P&L, and can be more objective when liquid markets do not exist for all relevant assets. But earnings require many assumptions and can be manipulated.

A couple of years after the crash, memories faded and concerns shifted from extreme price movements to aggregation of risk. Institutions had gotten larger and more complicated. Even if risk was managed correctly in each business, there could be a firm-wide disaster if each business was making the same bet in different ways. Some of this was actually a misunderstanding of what happened in 1987—unrelated businesses failed not because they were all making the same bet, but because market realignments tend to destroy any system optimized for prior conditions.

As usual with top-down requests, the pressure was on for quick and simple answers. Quants looked around for the available tools. Value was the only measure that could be defined consistently across business units. Everyone computed a daily P&L, but capital and earnings meant different things in different businesses. However, no one knew how to aggregate the probability distributions from each business unit into a joint distribution for the firm. There were no useful data or models for that purpose. What we could do, however, is measure how often firm-wide trading P&L exceeded some threshold. So we grafted the capital metric, drawdown at a specified probability and horizon, to the value measure. Value at Risk was born. The name makes no sense. Value is not at risk. But the capital folks called their measure capital at risk, which does make sense, so when you replaced capital with value, VaR was inevitable.

Two Surprises

Now comes the bad surprise. VaR was very hard to compute. You have to produce a number for every strategy, trader, desk, and business plus the firm as a whole, every day, before trading begins. VaR is never restated afterward; all that matters is the number in use when decisions were made. Usually at least some data were missing, and there were always lots of errors. It took the accountants several days after trading finished to get the P&L measured right; VaR demanded a prediction before trading started. Moreover, even with the right data value proved very difficult to predict.

There are three main tests of a VaR. First, you have to have the right number of breaks (days when losses exceed the VaR) within statistical error. Second, the breaks have to be independent in time. You want the same frequency of breaks the day after a break as when there hasn't been a break for months. Third, the breaks have to be independent of the level of VaR. It's easy to pass two of these three tests, difficult to pass all three at once. More generally, no one should be able to make money betting for or against VaR breaks.

Nobody but the quants cared about this; for everyone else's benefit we could have given them any plausible number at all. But we worked hard to get things right out of pride or stubbornness rather than a belief that it was a useful exercise. We learned that the data everyone relied on were hopelessly inaccurate, and that we knew very little about our risk in the center of the distribution. Everyone worried about tail risk, but they hadn't mastered center risk yet. We pulled out techniques from advantage gambling, poker, and sports betting; and made up new stuff. We partnered with the back office and learned a lot from controllers and auditors. We adopted "trigger" algorithms that inflated risk instantly if any data were inconsistent with prior predictions, but relaxed moderately quickly when things got consistent again. It took a few years of concerted effort, but finally we learned how to produce VaRs for all businesses, on time, every day, that passed backtest.

Now comes the good surprise. When you finally get a good VaR, it turns out to be incredibly useful. Changes in the VaR and VaR breaks are far more valuable signals for risk management than anything anyone ever designed for the purpose. Before this insight hedge funds had been around for 40 years. Successful managers were moderately wealthy. Suddenly the number of hedge fund billionaires exploded and these tiny (compared to the overall economy) pools of capital became dominant forces in finance, more powerful than the largest institutions and governments. The financial sector quadrupled in profitability and went from only-noticed-when-it-screwed up to popular obsession. VaR was the lightning that ignited the quant revolution on Wall Street.

The Decline and Fall of VaR

No sooner was the value of VaR discovered when people started tearing it down. VaR was too hard for nonquants to compute, so many of them didn't bother. They put out some number based on a bad model and worse data. It might be late or revised later, no one cared, because no one used it. It never passed backtest.

We also saw an influx of quants without risk-taking backgrounds, often without any experience of living under capitalists. They called themselves "financial engineers," and many sneered at the disreputable resumes of rocket scientists. Although some of the new generation understood risk and contributed greatly to the advance of finance, too many others were wedded to the coin-flip model of probability and gave little thought to theoretical or data issues. They wanted to solve equations for big salaries, not make bets, and they'd rather have been doing physics, except that the funding for blowing up the world had disappeared.

Real VaRs caused problems for rigid institutions because they would change unexpectedly. You couldn't reverse engineer the complex algorithms that computed VaR, so you couldn't point to a specific event or position that caused the change. To a risk-taking quant, any good risk measure has to surprise you. Your only choice is to be surprised by your risk measure before trading begins, or be surprised by the market afterward. But to nonquants and risk avoiders, hard-to-explain numbers were inconvenient. Stable, reassuring, rational fiction was preferred to messy and inconvenient truth.

A related problem was that regulators and auditors like numbers produced in controlled systems through validated processes. VaRs require layered algorithms that compensate for missing or erroneous data, and they have to be maintained constantly. They must evolve to remain relevant. That conflicts with control and validation. Another related problem is that there is no easy way to control VaR. If the CEO orders VaR taken down, it can be tricky to figure out how to do that.

Next, some people decided to use VaR as a risk measure. It's not. It cannot be. For one thing, it measures only the center of the probability distribution. Risk is mainly in the tails. For another, it's not the most you can lose, it's the *least* you will lose on your worst days. And most important, a low VaR portfolio or business is not safer than a high VaR one; it just has a smaller range over which you can make reliable predictions. Reducing VaR is squeezing your center risk, which is like gripping something more tightly. In some cases that's good, but in other cases you might break what you're holding, or cause it to squirt out of your hand, or your hand might tire and cramp. Similarly reducing VaR might reduce tail risk or might increase it.

Basel II

Remember that VaR was a fusion between ideas from advantage gamblers and poker players. What about the sports-betting quants? They were Bayesians, people people. Not for them the grim frequentist hanging on to losing positions knowing that long-term frequency would eventually triumph. Sports bettors not only embraced VaR, they largely took it over. Hedge funds and trading desks have continued to use VaR and gain dramatic improvements in risk management. But in big institutions, VaR effectively has been redefined.

The sports bettors thought that risk should be measured by threats to earnings, not changes in mark-to-market valuations. So they put in rules allowing VaR to be backtested not against objective arms-length market transactions but against models and valuations done according to accounting rules (which contain a large measure of management opinion among other defects). They still called it *value* at risk, but it became more and more like opinion at risk.

Sports bettors also worked at a longer time scale than poker players; earnings were measured quarterly and annually, traders think about daily and intraday price movements. VaR was invented at a 95 percent confidence interval over one day. A good statistical rule of thumb is that it takes 30 observations to estimate one parameter reliably; 95 percent one day VaR should have 30 breaks in 600 trading days, about two and a half years, a reasonable interval over which to estimate. Sports bettors preferred 99 percent 10-day VaR, which takes 30,000 trading days or 115 years to validate (some even went as far as 99.97 percent one-year VaR, which requires data going back to the Trojan War). This removed VaR from an objective number to a matter of faith.

Advantage gamblers had also used long time periods and high confidence, but they never based capital at risk on a backtest; they thought they had good models.

The Bayesian sports bettors were not stupid. They knew their VaR was a matter of opinion, but opinion was their stock in trade. Reality didn't matter. If you had good earnings on small amounts of capital, you got good return on equity. That pushed up your stock price, which kept your bonds yields low. As long as you were in investors' good graces, you could raise plenty of capital to replenish any losses. You could also reward your revenue-producing employees handsomely, meaning you retained and attracted people who contributed to more earnings. It was all a virtuous cycle. This may sound like a Ponzi scheme and it's not my preferred way to run a business, but with the right people managing the risk, it can work. Earnings may be a matter of opinion in the short run, but honest people will eventually detect divergences between earnings and tangible cash flows and will adjust their models accordingly.

This is the form of VaR that was incorporated into the Basel II capital accord, which was based almost entirely on VaR-like concepts. Using VaR as a risk measure makes no sense in theory, but in practice there was nothing better available. Moreover, computing VaR, even with undemanding backtesting, forced improvements in information systems. The effort improved risk in many ways. People began mitigating counterparty risk through netting and collateral agreements. Clearing was improved. For all the problems we had in 2008, things would have been far, far worse without the changes implemented in the prior two decades.

There was one unfortunate aspect of this effort. VaR was very expensive to compute. In order to incent banks to make the effort, they had to be promised capital relief. This made sense; if you improve your risk systems, you should be allowed to hold less capital. However, as people began analyzing risk systematically, it became obvious that there was far more risk than anyone had imagined. The 8 percent capital levels for banks without VaR was far too low. The sensible thing would have been to raise overall capital requirements, then the VaR banks could get a discount from that. But that was a political nonstarter. So the devil's bargain was made to dilute the rules so the VaR banks would come in under 8 percent. This was done in many ways. Backtesting requirements were watered down, then all but scrapped. Stress testing, a key component in early drafts, was downplayed. Optimistic assumptions were baked into the requirements.

This effort was aided by the extraordinary decline in market volatility from 2002 to 2006, the years leading up to the planned Basel II implementation. Every time people discovered more risk, market volatility dropped so computed capital requirements could remain constant. Of course, everyone knew that volatility would increase again, sending Basel II advanced approach capital requirements far above 8 percent. The hope was that wouldn't happen until the new rules were in place. In that scenario, it just might have been politically possible to force higher capital requirements on the banks that did not compute VaR.

I have sympathy for the people who did this. Risk management was greatly improved by the Basel II effort, and capital levels were not being reduced, they just weren't being raised to the extent new information warranted. Basel II did not cause the recent financial crisis, it made it much milder than it would have been otherwise. On the other hand, I understand why most people believe the opposite and why people like the author of this book blame VaR for the problems.

The VaR discovery is causing changes beyond finance. For any problem in probability, you begin by defining a numeraire with which you will measure success (VaR uses daily mark to market P&L). You carefully delineate the circumstances in which the numeraire is meaningful ("normal markets" in the case of VaR) and also the range of outcomes for which you have meaningful data. The crucial step is that you then estimate the probability that your observation will be in the normal, meaningful range. Until you can do this accurately, so accurately that you could publish your estimate and let anyone take either side of a bet at the implied odds and not lose money, you do not have a reliable system. Once you have a reliable system, you will have plenty of data to make predictions inside your range. These will be far more solid than conventional probability analysis that neglects the VaR step. More important, changes in the level of your VaR and VaR breaks will prove to be as informative, or more informative, than your predictions within the VaR boundary.

Of course, this is much harder than just running some unexamined data through a cookbook statistical analysis program. But I know of no other way to get statistical conclusions you can safely bet on. And I have no use for statistical conclusions you cannot bet on.

Notes

Chapter 1   The Greatest Story Never Told

1. Data source: Companies Quarterly and Annual Reports.
2. Lord Turner, *The Turner Review*, UK Financial Services Authority (March 2009) 20.
3. Based on November 2007 data.
4. UBS, Q3 2007 Report.
5. Parr Schoolman, "Risk Disclosures and the Credit Crisis," *Risk Management* (September 2009).
6. Merrill Lynch 10-Q, September 28, 2007.
7. Ibid.
8. Christine Harper, "Death of VaR Evoked," *Bloomberg* (January 28, 2008).
9. Quarterly Report, Q3 2007.
10. The Basel committee is the Switzerland-based compendium of central bankers and policy wonks established 20 years earlier and the goal of which is to make recommendations on minimum, uniform, capital charges for global commercial banks, starting in 1988 (Basel I) with credit risk-related guidelines.
11. G-30 Global Derivatives Study Group—Practices and Principles.
12. Glyn Holton, "History of Value at Risk," (July 25, 2002), www.stat.wharton.upenn.edu/~steele/Courses/434/434Context/RiskManagement/VaRHistlory.pdf
13. Philip Best, *Implementing Value at Risk* (New York: John Wiley & Sons, 1998).
14. Ibid.
15. Financial Times Fund Management online debate on VaR.
16. Lord Turner, *The Turner Review,* UK Financial Services Authority (March 2009).

Chapter 2   Origins

1. http://loomlearning.com/category/tags/raymond-may (video interview).

2. Author interview with Ray May.

3. Ibid.

4. Ibid.

5. Ibid.

6. Ibid.

7. Ibid.

8. Ibid.

9. Bethany MacLean and Joe Nocera, *All the Devils Are Here* (Portfolio Penguin, 2010).

10. Ibid.

11. "Till Guldimann's Second Life," DerivativesStrategy.com, November 1995.

12. Ibid.

13. Philip Best, *Implementing Value at Risk* (New York: John Wiley & Sons, 1998).

14. Ibid.

15. Celine Lazaregue-Bazard, "Exceptions to the Rule," *Risk Magazine* (January 2010).

Chapter 3   They Tried to Save Us

1. Nassim Taleb, "The World According to Nassim Taleb," *Derivatives Strategy* (December/January 1997).

2. Ibid.

3. Ibid.

4. Philippe Jorion, "In Defense of VaR," *Derivatives Strategy* (April 1997).

5. Ibid.

6. Ibid.

7. Nassim Taleb, "Against VaR," *Derivatives Strategy* (April 1997).

8. Ibid.

9. Avinash Persaud, "Sending the Herd Off the Cliff Edge," (December 2000), personal essay.

10. Ibid.

11. Ibid.

12. Ibid.

13. Ibid.

14. Ibid.

15. Ibid.

16. Ibid.

17. Ibid.

18. Jon Danielsson et al., "The Value of VaR: Statistical, Financial, and Regulatory Considerations," *Federal Reserve Bank of New York Economic Policy Review* (October 1998).

19. Jon Danielsson et al., "On the (Ir)relevance of VaR Regulation," London School of Economics, mimeo (1998).

20. Ibid.

21. Jon Danielsson, "The Emperor Has No Clothes: Limits to Risk Modelling," (June 2000), www.ioes.hi.is/publications/wp/w0004.pdf.

22. Jon Danielsson et al., "An Academic Response to Basel II," (May 2001), personal essay.

23. Jon Danielsson, "Blame the Models," Voxeu.org (May 8, 2008).

Chapter 4   Regulatory Embracement

1. "Trading Losses at Financial Institutions Underscore Need for Greater Market Risk Capital," Standard & Poor's (April 15, 2008).

2. Ranjit Lall, "Why Basel II Failed and Why Any Basel III Is Doomed," Oxford University's Global Economic Governance Programme Working Paper (October 2009).

3. Ibid.

4. Michel Crouhy et al., *The Essentials of Risk Management* (New York: McGraw-Hill, 2005), 359.

5. Nicholas Dunbar, *Inventing Money* (New York: John Wiley & Sons, 2001), 186.

6. Ibid., 147.

7. Ibid., 203.

8. Ibid., 204.

9. "Performance of Models-Based Capital Charges for Market Risk: 1 July–31 December 1998," Basel Committee (September 1999).

10. Nicholas Dunbar, *Inventing Money*, 220.

11. "Financial Crisis Inquiry Commission Report," (2011), Chapter 8.

12. Ibid.

Chapter 5   Abetting the CDO Party

1. "Shareholder Report on UBS's Write-Downs," UBS (April 18, 2008).

2. "SFBC–UBS Subprime Report" (September 30, 2008).

3. Ibid.

4. Merrill Lynch 10–Q Q3 (2007), 76.

5. Citigroup 10–K (2007), 48.

6. Morgan Stanley, *Subprime Analysis* (October 31, 2007).

7. Financial Crisis Inquiry Commission Report (2011).

8. Gillian Tett, "Super-Senior Losses Just a Misplaced Bet on Carry Trade," *Financial Times* (April 18, 2008).

9. John C. Dugan, U.S. Comptroller of the Currency, before the Global Association of Risk Professionals, New York, February 27, 2008.

10. Financial Crisis Inquiry Commission Report (2011).

11. Erik R. Sirri, "Remarks Before the AICPA/FMD National Conference on the Securities Industry" (November 28, 2007), www.sec.gov/news/speech/2007/spch112807ers.htm.

12. Gillian Tett, "Super Senior Losses Just a Misplaced Bet on Carry Trade," *Financial Times* (April 18, 2008).

13. http://fcic.gov/hearings/pdfs/2010-0227-Gorton.pdf.

14. Financial Crisis Inquiry Commission Report (2011).

15. Tom Adams, "The Myth of 'Insatiable' Investor Demand for CDOs," NakedCapitalism.com (April 14, 2010).

16. www.amttraining.com/technical-updates/regulatory-capital-for-banks-trading-activities-set-to-increase-to-eliminate-regulatory-arbitrage-between-trading-book-and-banking-book—january-2009.html.

17. SIA's Risk Management Committee, August 5, 2003.

18. Interview with Russ Roberts, June 8, 2009.

19. Olivier Prato, Banque de France Financial Stability Review (May 2006).

20. Matheson Ormsby, "Basel II Is Having Minimal Effect So Far in the Securitization Market," Prentice Hall, 2007.

21. www.amttraining.com/technical-updates/regulatory-capital-for-banks-trading-activities-set-to-increase-to-eliminate-regulatory-arbitrage-between-trading-book-and-banking-book—january-2009.html.

22. www.publications.parliament.uk/pa/ld200809/ldselect/ldeconaf/101/10107.htm#n7.

23. Renée Schultes, "Basel II Revision Signals the End for Regulatory Arbitrage," *eFinancialNews* (August 18, 2008).

24. "Confessions of a Risk Manager," *Economist* (August 7, 2008).

25. John Deacon, "Global Securitization and CDOs," (West Sussex, UK: John Wiley & Sons, 2004), 227.

26. Sheila C. Bair, remarks to the Global Association of Risk Professionals, New York, February 25, 2008.

27. Gillian Tett, "Battered Banks Face Regulators' Harder Line on Trading Books," *Financial Times* (June 3, 2008).

28. Ibid.

29. Notes on Senior Supervisors' Meetings with Firms, Citigroup, New York, November 19, 2007.

30. Gillian Tett, "Battered Banks Face Regulators' Harder Line on Trading Books," *Financial Times* (June 3, 2008).

31. Ibid.

32. Andrew Scott and Nick Studer, Oliver Wyman Financial Services—Point of View Series, November 13, 2008.

33. James Parsons, "The Regulatory Response to Bank Capital Adequacy as a Result of the Financial Crisis," *LTP Trade Research* (January 31, 2009).

34. Nout Wellink, Remarks at the GARP 2008 Risk Management Convention, New York, February 27, 2008.

35. Company Quarterly and Annual Reports.

36. Paul J. Davies, "Half of all CDOs of ABS Failed," *Financial Times* (February 10, 2009).

37. Ibid.

38. Simon Johnson, "Seduced by a Model," Economix Blog *New York Times* (October 1, 2009).

39. Gillian Tett, "Why a Ban on Proprietary Trading Could Have a Catch," *Financial Times* (February 19, 2010).

Chapter 6   VaR Goes to Washington

1. Christine Harper, "Death of VaR Evoked," *Bloomberg News* (January 2008).

2. "Global Credit Crisis: Consequences for Banking Supervision," Swiss Federal Banking Commission (April 1, 2008).

3. Paul Wilmott, www.wilmott.com, November 12, 2008.

4. Ibid.

5. Steve Allen, "A Few Immodest Proposals," (December 4, 2008), www.garp .org/media/417012/a%20few%20immodest%20proposals_allen.pdf.

6. "The Basel II Agenda for 2009: Progress So Far," United Nations (2009).

7. *Turner Review*, UK Financial Services Authority (March 2009).

8. Herve Hannoun, "The Basel III Capital Framework: A Decisive Breakthrough," Hong Kong, November 22, 2010.

9. Ibid.

10. "Global Credit Crisis: Consequences for Banking Supervision," Swiss Federal Banking Commission, April 1, 2008.

Chapter 7 The Common Sense That Should Rule the World

1. "Private Profits and Socialized Risks," *GARP Risk Review* (June 2008).
2. Ibid.
3. Ibid.
4. Martin Hellwig, "Capital Regulation After the Crisis," Preprints of the Max Plank Institute (July 2010).
5. Ibid.
6. Ibid.
7. Ibid.
8. "Interim Report on the Cumulative Impact on the Global Economy of Proposed Changes in the Banking Regulatory Framework."
9. At the time of writing, the Basel Committee was considering asking for additional equity capital from large, systematically important banks, so the 7 percent figure may end up being something like 8 percent or 9 percent.
10. Douglas J. Elliott, "Quantifying the Effects on Lending of Increased Capital Requirements," (Brookings Institution paper, September 21, 2009).
11. David Scharfstein and Jeremy Stein, "Basel Needs a Firm Hand and Fewer Delays," *Financial Times* (September 13, 2010).
12. Samuel Hanson, Anil Kashyap, and Jeremy Stein, "A Macroprudential Approach to Financial Regulation" (2010), www.economics.harvard.edu/faculty/stein/files/JEP-macroprudential-July22-2010.pdf.
13. Ibid.
14. Anad Admati, Peter DeMarzo, Martin Hellwig, and Paul Pfleiderer, "Fallacies, Irrelevant Facts, and Myths in the Discussion of Capital Regulation: Why Bank Equity Is Not Expensive," (March 16, 2011), https://gsbapps.stanford.edu/researchpapers/library/RP2065R1&86.pdf.
15. Ibid.
16. Ibid.
17. Bill Sharpe, Eugene Fama, Stephen Ross, Hayne Leland et al., "Much More Bank Equity Is Needed and Is Not Socially Costly," *Financial Times* (November 9, 2010).

Finale The Perils of Making the Simple Too Complex

1. faculty.haas.berkeley.edu/mkstimmler.

Acknowledgments

This book owes its existence to many individuals. Pamela van Giessen at John Wiley & Sons generously said yes when I proposed this project. She quickly realized that such a book was needed. Pam has provided decisive help in my growing up as a writer, offering highly useful advice and support. Her team at John Wiley & Sons has proven as cooperative as before, and I thank Emilie Herman, Stacey Fischkelta, and Simone Black for their invaluable backing.

I thank Nassim Taleb and Aaron Brown for their collaborations. These members of the financial A-team share an intriguing make-up: They are both successful market players and successful intellectuals. For most of us it is impossibly hard to achieve just one of those two goals, but they have mastered both gloriously for decades.

I thank my parents for their never-ending support. They enjoy seeing me write because they know I like it, but they also appreciate the relevance of having one's views distributed worldwide from a prestigious platform.

I thank Professor Eloy Garcia, who at American University taught me VaR for the first time. His 1996 course changed my life by forcing me to focus on derivatives, risk management, and financial models. One of the world's most voracious readers and buyers of financial books (first thing he does when he moves to a new city is locate the top technical bookstore, where he duly becomes the number one regular customer), Professor Garcia too values the effort and importance of producing a book such as this.

Finally, I thank those bankers and those regulators bent on preserving the system that can give us so much and on protecting it from those who would rather destroy it in the search for fast easy fly-by-night profits.

About the Author

Pablo Triana is a professor at ESADE Business School. He is the author of *Lecturing Birds on Flying* (John Wiley & Sons, 2009) and *Corporate Derivatives* (Risk Books, 2006). Triana has published widely on risk management, derivatives, and banking regulation in many of the world's leading financial and business imprints. He has held various roles in the financial industry as well as at top international business schools. He is contributing editor to *Corporate Finance Review* and holds graduate degrees from NYU and American University.

Index